Life in the Spirit

Spiritual Formation in Theological Perspective

EDITED BY

Jeffrey P. Greenman and George Kalantzis

IVP Academic

An imprint of InterVarsity Press
Downers Grove, Illinois

InterVarsity Press
P.O. Box 1400, Downers Grove, IL 60515-1426
World Wide Web: www.ivpress.com
E-mail: email@ivpress.com

InterVarsity Press® is the book-publishing division of InterVarsity Christian Fellowship/USA®, a movement of
students and faculty active on campus at hundreds of universities, colleges and schools of nursing in the United States
of America, and a member movement of the International Fellowship of Evangelical Students. For information
about local and regional activities, write Public Relations Dept., InterVarsity Christian Fellowship/USA, 6400
Schroeder Rd., P.O. Box 7895, Madison, WI 53707-7895, or visit the IVCF website at <www.intervarsity.org>.

Design: Cindy Kiple
Images: Peace Be Still by He Qi

ISBN 978-0-8308-3879-0

Printed in the United States of America ∞

Library of Congress Cataloging-in-Publication Data

Life in the spirit: spiritual formation in theological perspective /
edited by Jeffrey P. Greenman and George Kalantzis.
    p. cm.
  Includes bibliographical references and index.
  ISBN 978-0-8308-3879-0 (pbk.: alk. paper)
  1. Spiritual formation—Congresses. I. Greenman, Jeffrey P. II.
Kalantzis, George.
  BV4511.L54 2010
  248.4—dc22
                                                                              2009048955

P	20	19	18	17	16	15	14	13	12	11	10	9	8	7	6	5	4	3	2	1
Y	27	26	25	24	23	22	21	20	19	18	17	16	15	14	13	12	11	10

Dedicated to Duane Litfin,

Seventh President of Wheaton College

Contents

Introduction

JEFFREY P. GREENMAN AND GEORGE KALANTZIS

The apostle Paul was supremely concerned that through the transforming power of the gospel, men and women would become "mature in Christ" (Col 1:28 NRSV). Maturity in Christ means being whole, complete and fully grown up. The goal of Paul's ministry was not that people would merely hear the gospel proclaimed, or understand it principally at an intellectual level or even become converts to a new social movement. His aim was that the proclaimed good news would be received and would enact its effective work at the deepest level of the human spirit, shaping the hearts and minds of people so that the new life of Christ, given by the Holy Spirit, would so animate their character and conduct that they would truly become "like Christ." This goal was not reserved for a small spiritual elite but was intended for everyone. It was meant to mark individual lives and communal experience. Similarly, Paul tells the Galatians that he is "in travail" (ministering with an agonized yearning and consistent striving) until Christ be "formed" in them or "until they take the shape of Christ" (see Gal 4:19). Paul is clear that becoming like Christ means being conformed to the crucified One and therefore living a "cruciform" life (see Gal 2:19-20).[1] Despite our contemporary individualism, we need to recall that

---

[1]For a splendid exposition of Paul's understanding of being conformed to the crucified Christ,

Paul is thinking primarily of the church as a corporate entity, a body, being formed into Christlikeness, not merely about individuals. This "cruciform" life is marked by the presence of the fruit of the Spirit: love, joy, peace, patience, kindness, goodness, faithfulness, gentleness and self-control (Gal 5:22-23).

The apostle is also abundantly clear in arguing that becoming like Christ in attitude, character and self-giving service is not something that results from human effort alone. Rather, he is clear that being formed in Christ necessarily involves "walking in the Spirit" and "living in the Spirit" (see Gal 5:16, 25). One astute commentator wrote: "For believers, this walking by the Spirit remains a constantly renewed mandate and a continuous exertion."[2] Thus, for Paul it is the Christian's responsibility to allow the Holy Spirit's transforming work to take full effect in our daily lives. This emphasis on formation into mature conformity to Christ through cooperation with the work of the Spirit is not exclusive to Paul; the same basic claims are found throughout the New Testament in the varied language of the four Gospels, Peter's letters and John's epistles. Christians of every age and every tradition are called to "life in the Spirit."

Arising from these core biblical teachings is the central concern of the Christian tradition for what is now customarily called "spiritual formation." Although the church's language to express this area of interest and commitment has varied over time and between different streams of Christianity, familiar phrases such as the pursuit of holiness, godly living, spiritual perfection, the deeper life and the like all point to a common core of ideas. The basic goal of spiritual formation—becoming like Christ through the Spirit—is shared across Christian confessions and has remained constant across the centuries in diverse communities.

The 2009 Wheaton Theology Conference sought to examine the biblical, theological and historical roots of the church's calling to spiri-

---

see Michael Gorman, *Cruciformity: Paul's Narrative Spirituality of the Cross* (Grand Rapids: Eerdmans, 2001).

[2]Herman N. Ridderbos, *The Epistle of Paul to the Churches of Galatia* (Grand Rapids: Eerdmans, 1953), p. 210.

tual formation, as sketched in this book. This volume emerged from the conference's dialogue about the theological shape of the contemporary discussion about spiritual formation, particularly within the evangelical Protestant community. While evangelicals have given renewed attention to this topic over the past two decades and have produced extensive literature that introduces spiritual disciplines to pastors and lay people, in-depth theological examination of what is involved in spiritual formation has remained less developed. Therefore, this volume is not designed to instruct people in *how* to go about practicing spiritual disciplines. Instead, it focuses on fundamental biblical-theological questions about the *purpose* of spiritual formation, *why* we pursue it, *where* we should locate spiritual formation in doctrinal terms and *what* critical theological convictions must be made operative in order for spiritual formation to take place individually and corporately. Accordingly, this volume provides substantive theological engagement with core issues such as:

- What do we mean by commonly used but laden terms such as *spiritual formation*, *spiritual direction* and *spiritual theology?*

- How does God bring about transformation into Christlikeness?

- How do our doctrines of God, salvation and the Holy Spirit inform our pursuit of godliness or the practices of piety? Does doctrine make a difference to devotion?

- What insights might we gain from a better awareness of some of the key traditions of the history of Christian spirituality?

- What theological convictions undergird some of the key "spiritual practices" or "spiritual disciplines" of the church?

This volume is divided into three major parts, followed by a reflection toward application. The first part, "Theological Contours," explores some major doctrinal underpinnings of any authentic pursuit of spiritual formation. Jeffrey Greenman's chapter sets the stage for the entire volume by offering a "theologically oriented" definition of spiritual formation: "Spiritual formation is our continuing response to the reality of God's grace shaping us into the likeness of Jesus Christ, through the work of the Holy Spirit, in the community of faith, for the sake of the world." His chapter not only expounds this definition, but also reflects on some particular evangelical challenges for spiritual formation that follow from four distinctive evangelical emphases. This discussion serves to locate this volume's discussions within the characteristic strengths (and limitations) of evangelicalism. Finally, Greenman offers a "spiritually oriented" definition of theology. Responding to the stereotypic idea that theology is nothing more than an arcane, abstract discussion of abstruse and impractical topics, he contends that theology, at its best, should be understood and practiced as "whole person formation for mission."

Greenman's essay is followed by Gordon Fee's argument that contemporary evangelical Christianity needs to give the Holy Spirit more prominence in our accounts of spirituality. He begins in the mode of lament, fixing our attention on the fuzziness of contemporary language of spirituality, the inadequacy of most English Bible translations of the key Greek words for *spirit*, *spirituality* and the *Holy Spirit*, and the church's neglect of the Holy Spirit by opting instead for what he calls a "functionally binitarian" doctrine of God. Fee underscores the vital importance of the historic, orthodox doctrine of the triune God for spiritual formation, including a robust doctrine of the Holy Spirit (pneumatology). He argues from the New Testament that Christians are "Spirit people," those who have been given new life by the Holy Spirit, and, therefore, "being saved" necessarily involves an utter dependence on the Spirit. Thus, says Fee: "Soteriologies that are insufficiently attentive to the decisive work of the Holy Spirit will be incapable of generating 'spiritual formation' in the Pauline sense." Fee also suggests that our Christology needs to recognize that Jesus, as fully human, was the "Spirit person par excellence," whose life and ministry were lived out in the power of the Holy Spirit. As we come to recognize Jesus' dependence on the Spirit, we will then be able to understand the New Testament admonition to become like Christ through the indwelling, empowering presence of the Holy Spirit.

The first part of the book concludes with a chapter by Dallas Willard, one of the most prolific and influential evangelicals currently writing in the area of spiritual formation. Willard explains and defends the provocative claim that there "is a prevailing understanding of salvation that poses almost insurmountable barriers to transformation of professing Christians into Christlikeness, which is the meaning of spiritual formation." He argues that our typical way of understanding what it means to be "saved" actually "has no conceptual or practical connection with such a transformation." Here the importance of the doctrine of salvation (soteriology) for spiritual formation moves front and center. Willard argues that spiritual formation, properly understood, is a "natural part" (that is, intrinsic component) of salvation, properly understood. What is needed, according to Willard, is a much greater emphasis on the Bible's teaching that the gospel of salvation in Christ involves the gift of new life, and therefore our participation in the divine life (cf. 2 Pet 1:14) in the here and now, as opposed to a more limited and largely transactional model of salvation whereby forgiveness is attained primarily as a "ticket to heaven" when we die.

The second part, "Historical Approaches," builds upon these theological arguments and attempts to put our contemporary concerns for spiritual formation into a larger historical context. In much the same spirit as the 2007 conference and its resulting volume, *Ancient Faith for the Church's Future*,[3] this section begins with a study of some influential traditions of spirituality found in the early church. George Kalantzis begins the section by focusing on the ascetical life and praxis of early Christians, paying particular attention to the move from prevailing classical Greco-Roman paradigms of philosophy as *askesis* and contemplation, to the late antique uniquely Christian redefinitions of spiritual formation and ascent, in what the Eastern Christian traditions call the process of *anagoge*—the process of being conformed to Christ. The "spirituality" early Christians inherited from both their Greco-Roman as well as their Jewish predecessors revolved around an understanding of materiality as incompatible with true spirituality, spiritual freedom and salvation, as the apostle Paul found out in his engagement with the Athenians on Mars Hill (Acts 17:16-34). Early Christian theologians

---

[3] *Ancient Faith for the Church's Future*, ed. Mark Husbands and Jeffrey P. Greenman (Downers Grove, Ill.: InterVarsity Press, 2008).

and apologists such as Justin (Martyr) and Origen of Alexandria struggled to articulate a properly Christian understanding of the relationship between the "new life of/from the Spirit" and life in the body, especially as that relationship bears witness to Christ. Kalantzis also shows how, as the church moved from the margins of society to the center, and its relationships with the state changed from persecution to official acceptance, the definition of *spirituality* also changed, now being expressed more clearly by the monastic movements of the fourth and fifth centuries. In the process, Kalantzis raises some often-forgotten aspects of monastic spirituality that lead away from individualistic and disengaged practices and redirect us in active service to the poor and marginalized.

The annual Wheaton Theology Conference often has been an ecumenical occasion. Given the prominence of the Roman Catholic tradition of spiritual theology and the rising levels of evangelical engagement with Catholic spirituality, it was important to hear from a highly distinguished interpreter of Catholic theology, Lawrence Cunningham. In his chapter, "The Way and the Ways: Reflections on Catholic Spirituality," Cunningham argues, referring to the teaching of Romans 8, that the Catholic tradition has held that "to live the Christian life is to live under the impulse of the Spirit, which converts us to the way of Christ." His chapter explores the meaning of the "way of Christ"—Christ is the way (cf. Jn 14:6). Cunningham provides an insightful treatment of the key features of varied Catholic "schools" of spirituality. These "schools" (such as the Franciscan, Dominican, Ignatian and others) are presented as diverse, valuable and alternative "ways of following the Way." Concluding with some reflections on ecumenical relations, Cunningham points to the common ground shared across confessional divides and offers some suggestions about how Catholics and Protestants can learn from each other in their shared pursuit of "life in the Spirit."

Following Cunningham's essay, Kelly Kapic examines the theology of "evangelical holiness" taught by an eminent Puritan divine, John Owen. Kapic not only corrects a variety of inaccurate stereotypes about Puritanism but also offers a detailed case study of a robust spiritual theology that is grace-centered, gift-oriented, Christ-centered, Spirit-enabled and nonmoralistic. The Christian life is depicted as focused on the believer's participation in loving communion with the triune God. According to Kapic, Owen's approach also provides a theological basis for a nuanced account of the imitation of Christ, a "real spirituality" that is "not fundamentally about self-improvement, but about an intimacy and communion with the triune God that transforms the believer's life." Kapic highlights how Owen's thought illuminates some particularly important implications of christological, trinitarian and pneumatological orthodoxy for vibrant Christian life.

In the final chapter of this section, "Seeking True Religion: Early Evangelical Devotion and Catholic Spirituality," Bruce Hindmarsh examines the roots of the distinctive evangelical devotion in the seventeenth and eighteenth centuries. He explains that early evangelicalism, as a movement aimed at fostering "true religion," drew extensively and eagerly on "a common core of classical Christian spirituality" represented primarily by Roman Catholic sources. Hindmarsh's chapter complements Lawrence Cunningham's, suggesting that early evangelicals were attempting to form a "school" of devotion, comparable in many ways to the Catholic "schools of spirituality" outlined by Cunningham. Hindmarsh provides a reception history of two key books. He shows that John and Charles Wesley, as well as George Whitefield, were deeply influenced by Henry Scougal's *The Life of God in the Soul of Man* (1677), a work that itself transmitted the spiritual teachings of major Catholic mystical writers such as François Fenelon, Madame Guyon and Teresa of Avila. Hindmarsh also points out the pervasive and powerful role that Thomas à Kempis's *Imitation of Christ* played on key evangelical leaders. This text was the evangelical introduction to the Catholic ascetical tradition. These strands of continental Roman Catholic tradition were received and "naturalized" (not uncritically) by early evangelical leaders. Showing that, from its inception, evangelical Protestantism has been open to engaging the Roman Catholic sources of the classical Christian tradition of spirituality, Hindmarsh argues that today's evangelical interest in learning from Catholic sources and spiritual traditions is not a new phenomenon and cannot be dismissed as somehow "unevangelical."

The third part of this book, "Spiritual Practices," addresses the need for theological reflection on some of the most formative spiritual disciplines, such as Bible reading, prayer, corporate worship, spiritual direction and social action. Christopher Hall's chapter, "Reading Christ into the Heart: The Theological Foundations of *Lectio Divina*," reflects on the author's experience of meditating on the Sermon on the Mount (with the help of his iPod). Hall describes the nature and purpose of the slow, attentive, transformational practice of "divine reading" of the sacred Scriptures that has been part of the Christian heritage since the early church and that has been an especially important component of monastic spirituality. It is a way of reading the Bible that is, quoting Jean Leclercq, "entirely oriented toward life, and not toward abstract knowledge." Hall explores the implications of his claim that "undergirding our reading of the [biblical] text is a fundamental theological proposition that is deeply trinitarian: the Eternal Word, sent by the Father, has become incarnate in Jesus Christ and continues to speak to us through the Holy Spirit." Through divine reading of the written Word, we feed on Christ, the incarnate Word.

The chapter by Susan Phillips, who is an experienced spiritual director, suggests that the ancient Christian art of spiritual direction is a "navigational aid to sanctification." Focused on listening, it is the practice of intentional spiritual "accompaniment" designed to help men and women walk according to the Spirit (Rom 8:4). Phillips writes that spiritual direction "helps people pay attention to God's presence and call in their everyday lives, and it rests in a paradigm of prayer and discernment." She explores how the doctrine of sanctification informs this practice, as men and women grow in grace (2 Pet 3:18) and become evermore rooted and grounded in love (Eph 3:17) through the church's ministry of "piloting" in the process of transformation toward maturity in Christ.

The practice of prayer is undoubtedly central to spiritual formation in all Christian traditions. While a thorough study of prayer is a worthy topic for an entire Wheaton Theology Conference and subsequent volume—maybe in the future—this book features a case study of the theological dimensions of the practice of centering prayer by James Wilhoit. Wilhoit focuses on the approach expounded by Father Thomas

Keating, a Trappist monk (b. 1923) who is widely considered the founder of the centering prayer movement in the contemporary church. Centering prayer is a controversial subject in evangelical circles. Wilhoit provides an evenhanded exposition of Keating's methods of prayer, drawing attention to Keating's belief that centering prayer builds upon the practice of *lectio divina* and is meant to be a way of deepening one's relationship with Christ. Keating's main focus is the importance of intention or "consent" wherein we consent to God's presence and action within us and with "mental engagement" in prayer (fending off distracting thoughts). Wilhoit states that the origins of centering prayer are trinitarian, and that for Keating, "the present indwelling of Christ in each believer is his theological touchstone." While Wilhoit finds that Keating's approach is significantly shaped by psychotherapeutic assumptions and has an underdeveloped account of sin and salvation, he is cautiously optimistic about the evangelical appropriation of some aspects of centering prayer.

Cherith Fee Nordling's chapter addresses one aspect of corporate worship, namely, congregational singing, as a spiritually formative experience. She explores the New Testament's rich language of worship and formative significance of the church's practice of singing psalms, hymns and songs of the Spirit (Eph 5:19; Col 3:16). She shows how such songs enable the Christian community to enter into, and experience afresh, the power of the gospel narrative. Nordling also strikes a chord of lament in her discussion of contemporary worship. She believes that the church's theological confusion and spiritual lethargy can be traced, at least in part, to "countless repetitions of anemic hymns and heretical choruses." She is especially worried whenever our human experience, not God, becomes the main subject of worship. Nordling focuses on the implications of a confident, healthy/orthodox Christology—most notably an affirmation of the real humanity of Jesus—for the transformative work of God in and through worship. Our "life in the Spirit" is a function of Jesus' life in the Spirit, shared with us and made possible by his saving grace. Her chapter is a challenging yet inspirational reading for anyone concerned with leading worship in congregational settings.

The final chapter in this section is by David Gushee, a prominent evangelical social activist, president of Evangelicals for Human Rights and a Christian ethicist. Too often neglected is the "outward discipline" of active commitment to compassionate service, especially practical care for the poor, needy and vulnerable. Gushee's chapter, "Spiritual Formation and the Sanctity of Life," argues that "a socially disengaged spirituality" is "inconceivable and inexcusable." He defines and describes the doctrine of the sanctity of life, the conviction that "the human being, created, sustained and redeemed by God in Christ, is infinitely sacred in God's sight." Given, then, the sacredness of human life, "Christian spiritual formation must yield Christian disciples who are absolutely and stubbornly impervious to any temptation or enticement to sacrifice the sacredness of any group of neighbors for any private or public purpose, however compelling it may seem at the time." For Gushee, a particularly important doctrinal consideration is the incarnation of Jesus Christ, which "forever elevates human bodiliness," and therefore, "what happens to human bodies (not just minds and spirits and souls, and not just the bodies of our friends but also our enemies) matters to God and must matter to us." Gushee shows that the challenge of cultivating an active, compassionate concern for our neighbors is an indispensible, nonnegotiable aspect of becoming like Christ. He concludes his chapter by reminding us that corporate worship has a crucial, irreplaceable role in forming disciples whose attitudes and instincts are attuned to the suffering and exploitation of others, near and far: "Worship of God is the ultimate origin of a true appreciation for life's sanctity—if we remember what kind of God it is we truly worship."

The book's final section is an epilogue, "Theology, Spiritual Formation and Theological Education," provided by Linda Cannell, one of the most incisive and creative theological educators in North America. Her chapter picks up from Jeffrey Greenman's concern for understanding theology as formation in chapter one and from Dallas Willard's critique in chapter three that most Christian institutions are failing to give sufficient emphasis to spiritual formation while choosing to be "doing something else." She addresses directly and honestly a topic that lies barely behind the surface of many of the chapters in this book, namely, the nature of knowledge itself. Many of the authors at least hint that our rationalistic and reductionistic ways of viewing the human mind and spirit, including our ways of reading Scripture and doing theology, have created obstacles to genuine Christian spirituality. Cannell traces the reasons why theology and spirituality are so commonly separated (even divorced from each other) in contemporary congregational and educational settings to the "rise of academic theology" and its institutionalization in "professionalized" theological colleges and seminaries. Cannell questions current assumptions about theological education from the "sapiential" standpoint, challenging the notion that what formation for ministry involves is "the nurture of the soul and growth toward wisdom." She proposes that some major (and possibly uncomfortable) rethinking and decisive organizational changes will be required if we are serious about refocusing our institutional efforts at developing the next generation of Christian leaders in more formative, holistic and spiritually nurturing directions.

The cover art for this book is by the renowned contemporary Chinese Christian painter, He Qi. During the 2008 Wheaton Theology Conference we were privileged to hear him describe his understanding of the connections between visual art and Christian spirituality, and to host on campus an extensive show of his work.

• • •

This book is dedicated to Dr. Duane Litfin, who retires in 2010 as the seventh president of Wheaton College. Coming to Wheaton from the pastorate, and having served previously as a seminary professor, during his seventeen-year tenure President Liftin has been an active supporter of the annual Wheaton Theology Conference. At the 2009 conference, Dr. Liftin's introductory remarks noted that the event's theme was especially apt for Wheaton College, since the college's mission statement speaks of nurturing "whole and effective Christians." He commented, "Spiritual formation is what Wheaton College is really all about." Under his leadership, Wheaton's Department of Biblical and Theological Studies has expanded and flourished. Beyond Wheaton, his Christ-centered vision for "fully" Christian higher education has highlighted

the centrality of biblical and theological reflection for every aspect of
the liberal arts curriculum.[4] Dr. Liftin has been a dedicated champion
of biblical faithfulness and doctrinal orthodoxy in evangelical theology
and has modeled gracious ecumenical engagement as well as open and
honest interfaith dialogue (particularly with the Roman Catholic and
Jewish communities). During his presidency Dr. Litfin's core theological convictions led him to take courageous stands on key social and
ethical questions of our time, including AIDS, poverty and climate
change. As a leading voice in North American evangelicalism, Dr. Litfin has enabled many to see the unparalleled importance of the Lordship of Jesus Christ over every aspect of human life. We dedicate this
volume to him with deep appreciation for his ministry and leadership,
for his persistent pleas for evangelicals to live Christ-centered lives and
for his sacrificial service to church and society worldwide in and through
Wheaton College.

---

[4]See Duane Litfin, *Conceiving the Christian College* (Grand Rapids: Eerdmans, 2004).

PART ONE
Theological Contours

Spiritual Formation in Theological Perspective

Classic Issues, Contemporary Challenges

JEFFREY P. GREENMAN

During the past thirty years, a widely recognized evangelical spiritual formation movement has taken shape and gained momentum. Richard Foster's 1978 landmark book, *The Celebration of Discipline*, is a clear marker of its birth. Foster's work has been followed by other pioneering writings from prolific authors such as Dallas Willard, James Houston and Eugene Peterson. These four writers together have played a principal role in shifting the focus of mainstream evangelical conversation from the traditional (but narrower) category of discipleship to the newer (and broader) category of spiritual formation. Each in their own way, these thinkers—as well as prominent evangelical theologians such as J. I. Packer, Robert Webber, Donald Bloesch, Alister McGrath and Simon Chan—have attempted to articulate evangelical spirituality afresh by providing a deeper biblical foundation, a stronger theological rationale and a wider historical awareness.

My purpose in this chapter is to offer a theological map of the landscape currently under discussion about spiritual formation, with particular attention to the ways in which evangelical theological convictions relate to a wider conversation. After offering a theologically oriented definition of spiritual formation, I examine some strengths and weaknesses typically found in evangelical spirituality and conclude with some suggestions about what this discussion means for our understanding of theology.

SPIRITUAL FORMATION THEOLOGICALLY DEFINED

The term "spiritual formation" has become popular, but since it is not a precise, technical term its actual meaning is sometimes unclear.[1] My proposal for a fairly comprehensive, reasonably succinct and theologically oriented definition is: Spiritual formation is our continuing response to the reality of God's grace shaping us into the likeness of Jesus Christ, through the work of the Holy Spirit, in the community of faith, for the sake of the world.

Spiritual formation is an ongoing process for Christians. It is not a program or project or course that is completed in a few weeks, but rather is a lifelong journey of transformation. While there can be decisive steps forward or dramatic spiritual insights in a moment, spiritual formation addresses the gradual and progressive movement of character development and personal growth. Faith in Jesus Christ sustains a lifelong pursuit of spiritual maturity or wholeness found in him. Despite the pressures of our activist, hurried culture, this process cannot be reduced to learning personal management techniques or how to "do things for the Lord" because it is primarily a matter of cultivating an intimate relationship with the triune God. This is a continuous challenge—running the race with perseverance (Heb 12:1). For this reason, my proposed definition refers to the dynamic of our "continuing response."

The process of spiritual formation is not defined by someone's search within themselves for spiritual health, but rather by a "continuing response to the reality of God's grace." By using the term *response* I want to emphasize that spiritual formation is not self-generated. It is not our attempt to cultivate inwardness for its own sake. Spiritual formation in its best sense cannot be reduced to the results of human techniques or personal willpower, but is primarily a matter of God's own initiative and God's vital action. This definition leaves no room for the sort of well-intended semipelagianism that is so prevalent, namely, the mistaken idea that we have the ability to seek God apart from God's prior movement of grace. In theological terms, *grace* speaks of the unmerited gift of God's love and mercy toward sinners, shown supremely in

---

[1] I am indebted to my former colleagues at Tyndale Seminary in Toronto for their input into the eventual shape of my proposed definition.

Christ's life, death and resurrection. Grace identifies God's decisive dealing with human sin through the cross of Christ, so that spiritual formation involves our reckoning seriously with the ongoing realities of human temptation and our continual struggle against corrupt desires. Rooted in a robust sense of sin and joyful confidence in the efficacy of the gospel, spiritual formation involves grace-based disciplines of confession, forgiveness and reconciliation.

My definition of spiritual formation seeks to reflect the biblical logic of divine grace that is exemplified in the truth that "we love because he first loved us" (1 Jn 4:19). Divine action takes priority over human action. God's gift precedes and makes possible the human task of discipleship, witness and service. As Christians, our vocation is to respond in faith, trust and obedience to the good news that we have received in Christ and to welcome God's transforming power into our lives. Spiritual formation necessarily involves intentional action and commitment, yet we recognize that divine grace is not opposed to human effort, but rather is opposed to earning divine favor.[2]

Divine grace speaks not merely of a past reality by referring backward to an experience of salvation; grace also is a present reality that informs the current experience of the Christian life. God's grace has shaped us, is shaping us from day to day, and will shape us in the future. What are we being shaped into? The goal of spiritual formation is to be transformed into the likeness of Jesus Christ (Rom 8:29; 2 Cor 3:18).[3] This also is our eschatological destiny as Christians, according to 1 John 3:2: "we know that when he appears, we shall be like him, for we shall see him as he is." Foster states that the "goal of the Christian life could be summarized as our being formed, conformed, and transformed into the image of Jesus Christ."[4] Because being "conformed to the image of his Son" is the ultimate purpose of God's saving work through

---

[2]This is a key theme in the writings of Dallas Willard. For example, see *The Great Omission* (New York: HarperOne, 2006), p. 61.

[3]None other than C. S. Lewis, that nonevangelical patron saint of evangelicals, concurs: "the church exists for nothing else but to draw men into Christ, to make them little Christs. If they are not doing that, all the cathedrals, clergy, missions, sermons, even the Bible itself, are simply a waste of time. God became Man for no other purpose." C. S. Lewis, *Mere Christianity* (London: Collins, 1952), p. 167.

[4]Richard J. Foster, "Becoming Like Christ," *Christianity Today*, February 5, 1996.

the cross and resurrection, "becoming like Christ" means participating in the salvation accomplished by Jesus—knowing Christ in the "power of his resurrection" and in "the fellowship of sharing in his sufferings" (Phil 3:10). Spiritual formation into Christlikeness therefore is an extension of the logic of the cross and is impossible apart from the reality of Christ's atoning work. Being "conformed to Christ" or "becoming like Christ" involves embracing a "cruciform" way of life with a distinctive shape expressed in obedience to God, which is marked by self-sacrifice and humble service for the sake of others, a way that Jesus demonstrated during his earthly ministry and commended to all his followers (Mk 10:42-45; Jn 13:12-17; Phil 2:1-11).[5]

My proposed definition explains that becoming like Christ happens "through the work of the Holy Spirit." It is God's own work, through the Spirit, to bring about Christ's character in us, and it is our calling to cooperate with God in this process as we share in the divine life given to us (2 Pet 1:4). For this reason Eugene Peterson writes: "Spiritual formation is primarily what the Spirit does, forming the resurrection life of Christ in us."[6] Participation in the life of Christ, by the Spirit, reproduces the character of Christ in his followers. The distinctive virtues of Christian faith are the fruit of the Spirit: "love, joy, peace, patience, kindness, goodness, faithfulness, gentleness and self-control" (Gal 5:22-23).

The wisdom of the church over two millennia is that this sort of transformation of heart, mind and spirit is not something that can be pursued satisfactorily by individuals in isolation. Spiritual formation involves personal spiritual disciplines, such as prayer, confession, fasting and biblical meditation as well as corporate participation in the congregation's shared life of worship, fellowship and teaching. The ecclesial practices of prayer and the Lord's Supper (or Eucharist) have a special prominence among the "means of grace" that God has appointed to strengthen our faith. For this reason, my proposed definition asserts

---

[5]Cf. Michael J. Gorman, *Cruciformity: Paul's Narrative Spirituality of the Cross* (Grand Rapids: Eerdmans, 2001).

[6]Eugene Peterson, *Christ Plays in Ten Thousand Places* (Grand Rapids: Eerdmans, 2005), p. 237.

that spiritual formation takes place "in the community of faith." Christians belong to one another as members of Christ's body, which becomes the communal context for mutual encouragement, mentoring and accountability in the journey toward Christlikeness. This commitment runs contrary to the highly individualistic and functionalist tendencies of contemporary North American culture.

My definition concludes with the affirmation that the necessary result of spiritual formation is active participation in serving God and sharing in God's work in the world.[7] The phrase, "for the sake of the world," reminds us that personal growth or spiritual depth involves not merely loving God, but loving our neighbors as ourselves (Lk 10:27). As people who are sent out into the world as witnesses to Christ (Jn 20:21), the mark of a genuine spiritual formation is our capacity to reflect Christ as "the salt of the earth" and "the light of the world" (Mt 5:13-14). Growth into the likeness of Christ accompanies our participation in Christ's mission to the world, in the power of the Spirit. Spiritual formation at its best involves a reciprocal dynamic between gathering and scattering, contemplation and action, silence and speech, being and doing, receiving and giving. Outward-focused spiritual disciplines such as hospitality and "works of mercy" complement inward-focused disciplines. In the words of Elizabeth O'Connor, "Just as we are committed to being on an inward journey for all of time, so we are committed to being on an outward journey, so that the inner and the outer become related to one another and one has meaning for the other and helps to make the other possible."[8]

My definition seeks to be fairly comprehensive, but above all it seeks to frame a God-centered way of speaking about spiritual formation as an alternative to ways of understanding spirituality that simply search for personal meaning or inner peace on one's own terms. There is much truth in the observation made by Eugene Peterson: "The great weakness

---

[7]Becoming like Christ as the purpose of God for the people of God—including becoming like Christ in his mission—was the theme of John R. W. Stott's final sermon before his retirement from public ministry in July 2007. See <www.langhampartnership.org/2007/08/06/john-stott-address-at-keswick/>.

[8]Elizabeth O'Connor, *Journey Inward, Journey Outward* (New York: Harper & Row, 1968), p. 28.

of North American spirituality is that it is all about us: fulfilling our potential, getting in on the blessings of God, expanding our influence, finding our gifts, getting a handle on principles by which we can get an edge on the competition. And the more there is of us, the less there is of God."[9] Contemporary discussion of spiritual formation as well as focused efforts in various settings to nurture mature Christian faithfulness, especially among evangelicals, should be able to find "more of God" through deeper biblical, theological and historical roots.

CONTEMPORARY EVANGELICAL CHALLENGES

One way to frame some contemporary challenges facing evangelicals is to reflect on some chief characteristics of the evangelical movement in general. David Bebbington's oft-used quadrilateral identifies central evangelical convictions and attitudes.[10] My proposal is that each of these four qualities points toward both strengths and weaknesses in the evangelical engagement with spiritual formation.

Biblicism. Evangelicals affirm the supreme authority of Scripture and generally hold the Bible in very high esteem. As John Stott says, "We evangelicals are first and foremost Bible people."[11] Perhaps the ecumenical charism of evangelicals is expository preaching and Bible study. A strength here is that evangelical churches and individuals are likely to be strongly interested in the biblical foundations for spiritual formation. Evangelicals typically ask, "What is the biblical basis for this contemporary emphasis on spiritual formation?" Clearly, the formational value of the standard evangelical practice of daily Bible reading is not to be underestimated nor taken for granted. A potential limitation is that typical patterns of evangelical engagement with Scripture can easily devolve into an information-oriented rationalism wherein the Bible is "word processed" in a mechanical way, rather than being ab-

---

[9]Peterson, *Christ Plays*, p. 335.

[10]David W. Bebbington, *Evangelicalism in Modern Britain: A History from the 1730s to the 1980s* (London: Unwin Hyman, 1989), pp. 2-17. For a nuanced revision of Bebbington's quadrilateral, see Timothy Larsen, "Defining and Locating Evangelicalism," in *The Cambridge Companion to Evangelical Theology*, ed. Timothy Larsen and Daniel J. Treier (Cambridge: Cambridge University Press, 2007), pp. 1-14.

[11]John Stott, *Evangelical Truth* (Downers Grove, Ill.: InterVarsity Press, 1999), p. 65.

sorbed and digested in a more deeply transformational manner. Biblical meditation in the style of ancient *lectio divina* is often hard for evangelicals to grasp and practice, having been schooled for generations in the procedures of inductive Bible study or the short "quiet time." This suggests a need for reaffirmation of the central place of the Bible in evangelical spiritual nurture and teaching, and an open-minded reexamination of the ways in which the Bible is studied and taught in and through congregations. One unfortunate, but common, consequence of the evangelical affirmation of the Bible as the supreme authority for faith and practice is that other promising sources of spiritual insight sometimes are unnecessarily denigrated, particularly historical sources drawn from various streams of the Christian tradition. In short: if we take the Bible sufficiently seriously, why bother knowing what the desert fathers were doing or what Teresa of Avila taught about prayer? Yet our evangelical forefathers never believed that the centrality of the Bible in individual and corporate life justified ahistoricism or any intentional disregard for the spiritual classics of previous centuries.[12]

Crucicentrism. Evangelicals understand the cross of Jesus as the focus of the gospel. The standard view is that "Christ died as substitute for sinful mankind."[13] The movement's most esteemed preaching and hymnody are expressions of a cross-centered instinct: "nothing in my hand I bring, simply to the cross I cling."[14] A clear benefit of this mindset is that it provides an objective, Christ-centered basis for personal piety. Crucicentrism acts as theological check against any tendency to reduce spiritual formation to self-centeredness or self-absorption. Yet evangelical spirituality sometimes has sentimentalized or trivialized the cross, and many contemporary evangelical songs and prayers operate without any reference to the reality of the atonement. In addition, it is hazardous to emphasize Christology and soteriology at the expense of pneumatology, a move that leads to a lopsided or diminished doctrine of the Trinity, which in turn undercuts the basis for authentic spiritual formation. Similarly, it is unwise to emphasize the doctrine of

[12]Bruce Hindmarsh's chapter in this volume argues this point compellingly.
[13]Bebbington, *Evangelicalism*, p. 15.
[14]Favorite words from Augustus Toplady's hymn "Rock of Ages."

salvation at the expense of the doctrine of creation, a move that can leave evangelical efforts at spiritual formation operating without sufficiently nuanced understandings of human creatureliness, embodiment or sociality.

Conversionism. Evangelicals assert that everyone needs to be converted to Christ. Therefore, their most recognized forms of ministry are altar calls and the "born again" experience. They are committed to the proclamation of the gospel through direct evangelism that calls each person to repent of their sins, trust in Christ and receive God's gift of salvation. Conversion is understood as a powerful, life-changing encounter with God involving intense commitment. Typically it is understood as a punctiliar event rather than an ongoing process. The strength here is that conversionism sets up spiritual growth as the deepening of an intentional personal relationship. The difficulty is when evangelicals focus so intently on the moment of conversion that little else matters. The gradual, progressive work of spiritual formation can be eclipsed by a conversionist mindset that prioritizes saving sinners in an "hour of decision" rather than shaping the lives of the saints over many years. It can lead to spiritual impatience in the long journey of transformation, a tendency made worse by the pressures of a culture of relentless hyperactivity. And if eternal salvation is achieved through a "decision for Christ" why does sanctification ultimately matter anyhow? If, as the bumper sticker says, "Christians aren't perfect, just forgiven," then why strive too hard for perfection?

Activism. Evangelicals believe in the active ministry of laity and clergy alike. In Bebbington's words, evangelicals recognize an "imperative to be up and doing."[15] All Christians are to help spread the gospel and serve the needs of the poor and needy, both at home and abroad. This activist impulse is the root of the global mission movement and the mother of countless parachurch ministries. Virtually all the evangelical heroes are activists: think of the way evangelicals appeal to the example of tireless (if not frenetic) figures such as John Wesley, William Wilberforce, Billy Graham or Chuck Colson. A clear strength here is the un-

---

[15]Bebbington, *Evangelicalism*, p. 12.

challenged assumption that genuine fellowship with Christ is meant to find active expression in God's service through some form of personal engagement in evangelism or social involvement. Evangelical spirituality is rarely jeopardized by an inert faith. If anything, evangelical activism poses a threat to spiritual formation when energetic service is emphasized at the expense of prayer, solitude and meditation. In addition, the activist impulse, when blended with our culture's thoroughgoing pragmatism, can devolve into a lazy anti-intellectualism that seeks little beyond a handful of prepackaged "simple steps to spiritual success." Unchecked activism typically encourages a bare-bones instrumental rationality that ignores or diminishes God's call for the renewal of our minds (Rom 12:1-2) and Jesus' command for us to love God with all of one's heart, soul, mind and strength (Mk 12:30).

CLASSIC THEOLOGICAL ISSUES

My proposed definition of spiritual formation and discussion of some strengths and weaknesses in evangelical spirituality has already identified some classic theological issues that are necessarily involved in the discussion of spiritual formation. These issues are not the exclusive domain of evangelical spirituality; in fact, they have their own form in every variety of Christianity. We have seen that a theologically shaped account of Christian spiritual formation will require us to consider a broad range of classic theological issues, such as:

- the shape of our creatureliness and sociality as "embodied souls";

- the nature of sin and its consequences;

- the meaning and significance of divine grace and the atonement;

- the work of the triune God, especially the distinctive work of the Holy Spirit;

- the meaning of "becoming like Christ";

- the relationships between conversion, regeneration, justification and sanctification;

- the appropriation of the "means of grace" in the Christian life, especially prayer and sacraments;

- the relationship between inward growth and outward service; and,

- the meaning of love, especially love for God with heart, mind, soul and strength, and love for one's neighbor as oneself.

My point is that Christian speech about discipleship, spiritual growth, spirituality or spiritual formation—whether at a popular level, or from the pulpit or in the rarefied theological air of scholarly debate—will necessarily involve a way of handling these complex theological topics, and probably a number of others not yet listed. Admittedly my proposed definition and analysis of evangelical spirituality involve a series of decisions about these matters, which mostly lurk implicitly beneath the surface of my argument. Limitations of space do not allow these decisions to be expounded. Similarly, in most cases, especially at the popular level, a host of interrelated theological convictions are taken for granted. Part of my purpose is to unearth these beliefs and suggest some of their implications. Teachers and preachers can help their congregants to discover more authentic spiritual formation by thinking through how their own theological frameworks shape their approach to formational ministries (e.g., "What is the theological basis for what we're doing?") and by considering how congregations can be helped to see the directly formational implications of basic Christian truths (e.g., "What difference do our core beliefs make in the pursuit of Christian maturity and faithfulness?").

THEOLOGY SPIRITUALLY DEFINED

Another new word for evangelicals in the past thirty years has been the term "spiritual theology." Although the popularity of the term is sporadic and remains somewhat strange to evangelical ears, the concept itself is anything but new. A commonly accepted definition is offered by Roman Catholic author Jordan Aumann:

> Spiritual theology is that part of theology that, proceeding from the truths of divine revelation and the religious experience of individual persons, defines the nature of the supernatural life, formulates directives for its growth and development, and explains the process by which souls advance from the beginning of the spiritual life to its full perfection.[16]

---

[16]Jordan Aumann, *Spiritual Theology* (London: Sheed and Ward, 1980), p. 22.

If we accept this definition, we can say that long-time evangelical favorites as various as John Owen, John and Charles Wesley, Jonathan Edwards and Charles Simeon each developed spiritual theologies. Diogenes Allen's description of spiritual theology proposes seven questions that represent the enduring "fundamental principles" expressed by classic texts on spirituality:

1. What is the goal of the spiritual life?

2. What is the path to the goal?

3. What motivates us to begin the spiritual life?

4. What helps us make progress in the spiritual life?

5. What hinders us?

6. How do we measure progress?

7. What are the fruits of the Spirit?[17]

It is certainly worthwhile for evangelicals to consider what a fully orbed, evangelically oriented, contemporary spiritual theology might look like. In this essay, I've made a number of proposals that could be developed further.

However, I want to conclude by observing that any examination of "spiritual formation in theological perspective" involves not only a complex set of assumptions about spiritual formation, but also a complex set of assumptions about the nature, task and purpose of theology. This is a huge topic. And I believe it is a necessary one since many people (and sometimes even pastors or Christian leaders) assume that theology is an abstract, specialized discourse that attempts to tidy up a series of arcane, speculative propositions that have no inherent usefulness to anybody. For too many people, theology is associated easily with utterly irrelevant questions such as how many angels can dance on the head of pin. For others, theology is just a clever game played by smart people who wish to avoid taking the Bible seriously. Therefore it might be helpful if I provided even a brief sketch

---

[17]Diogenes Allen, *Spiritual Theology: The Theology of Yesterday for Spiritual Help Today* (Cambridge, Mass.: Cowley, 1997), pp. 15-20.

of some of the implicit beliefs about theology that have informed my approach and suggested an alternative approach that runs directly counter to these popular stereotypes.

The corollary of a theologically oriented definition of spiritual formation would be a spiritually oriented definition of theology. Let me make two suggestions. First, in most basic terms, my view is that theology at its best seeks to inform, guide and nurture the whole person, since it equips the saints to obey the Great Commandment, loving God with all our being—heart, soul, mind and strength—and our neighbors as ourselves. When theology is construed merely as an academic exercise concerned to solve theoretical problems, without necessarily engaging the whole person, including matters of the heart or character, then we've already begun to define the whole enterprise in a way that greases the slide toward a one-sided intellectualism. But if theology concerns itself with the whole person, and every aspect of life, then there is a basis for a spiritually oriented approach to theology. Along these lines, we would need to say that theology's task is not merely to clarify *ideas* about loving God, but to inform, guide and nurture the *actual love* of God. Theology's work of analytical and critical reflection concerning texts, beliefs or concepts is not an end in itself, but actually an important means toward the greater end of assisting the transformation of persons toward Christian maturity. If so, authentic theology cannot be a "disinterested, impartial presentation of a variety of viewpoints" but involves a normative commitment to whole-person formation, in and through the community of faith.[18] If so, then theology is not primarily what is written in books or proclaimed in sermons, but what is "written" by faithful lives given over to the love of God.[19] As Ellen Charry has shown, this more directly and intentionally "sapiential" and "character-forming" approach is actually the view of theology that dominates premodern Christian thinking. It needs to be recovered in our day and embraced unapologetically.[20]

---

[18]This phrase comes from J. Andrew Kirk, *The Mission of Theology and Theology as Mission* (Valley Forge, Penn.: Trinity Press International, 1997), p. 21.

[19]A paraphrase of a remark by Kevin Vanhoozer, private meeting, April 13, 2009.

[20]Ellen T. Charry, *By the Renewing of Your Minds: The Pastoral Function of Christian Doctrine* (New York: Oxford University Press, 1997).

Second, theology at its best informs, guides and nurtures the church's fundamental vocation: to serve as God's representatives in the world, sharing in the mission of the triune God. The church is missionary by nature, sent into every sphere of society and into every corner of the world in the power of the Spirit to witness in word and deed to the reality of the kingdom of God. The earliest Christian writings, canonized in the New Testament, are documents written by missionaries in order to form and sustain communities engaged in witness to the world on behalf of Christ. Here we see that theology is not an end in itself, but a servant of the church that seeks to "equip the saints for the work of ministry" (Eph 4:12 NRSV) in its many forms. Thus, according to John Franke, "Theology that is faithful to its subject engages in the life and work of the church by articulating, assisting, promoting and participating in the missional vocation of the church."[21] From this perspective, the purpose of theology is formation for mission. Its goal is to help each generation of believers to live out their calling as faithful witnesses to Christ in their own contexts. Larry Crabb has stated, "a missional focus can only be sustained by a formational foundation."[22] Missional theology can devolve into little more than pragmatic, activist strategizing about techniques for the church's numerical growth if it is divorced from the formative impulse to foster qualitative growth in faith, hope and love nurtured in the community's worship and prayer. Thus, if we put together these two points, we conclude that the chief purpose of theology is whole-person formation for mission. Because it addresses the whole person, theology is inherently spiritual. Because it concerns God's mission to the world, theology is inherently missional. There is no opposition between these two emphases; they are two inseparable dimensions of the church's vocation as God's chosen people, a royal priesthood, a holy nation, God's special possession (1 Pet 2:9).

---

[21]John Franke, *The Character of Theology: An Introduction to Its Nature, Task, and Purpose* (Grand Rapids: Baker Academic, 2005), p. 166.

[22]See Doreen L. Olson, "Spiritual Formation Forum: A Brief Reflective," <http://www.covchurch.org/formation/spiritual-formation-forum>.

2 On Getting the Spirit Back into Spirituality

GORDON D. FEE

I want to begin by making some observations about the language of spirituality, one from the current meaning of the word *spiritual* and one from the place of its origins in the New Testament. First, then, as to its meaning in common English parlance, if we begin outside the church, the current reality is that almost anything under the sun that is not related to our physical bodies comes under this language, and much of it is simply too off the charts to deserve notice. Unfortunately, things are not terribly different inside the church, so that both the noun *spirituality* and its cognate adjective *spiritual* have become what a British scholar, in another setting, once dubbed as "concertina words," words whose meaning is related to how much air one pumps in or out of them.

My second observation is that the adjective *spiritual* is one of the more abused words in the English language, both in and outside the church, so that my *Random House Dictionary* offers nine shades of meaning for the word in English, and its derived Christian meaning comes in seventh: "of or pertaining to sacred things or matters; religious; devotional; sacred." And, of course, its original meaning in Greek doesn't appear in the New Testament at all. And how can I be so sure of that? The answer is because the word had its origins in the Greek world as a way of saying that something was related to "wind or air" and thus without material substance.

What should cause any thinking Christian a bit of alarm about these two realities is that they are totally unrelated to the *only* meaning the word has in the New Testament. So here are the data, which I wish to make as my starting place for this presentation; and at this point my actual point of departure will be from the entry in the Bauer-Danker Lexicon of the Greek New Testament, since Fred Danker himself seemed to be a bit wary of the Holy Spirit. His first entry, legitimately so, has to do with its usage in classical Greek, namely, "pertaining to spirit as inner life of a human being," a meaning which appears (and only possibly so) in Ignatius of Antioch, a full two generations after the word's appearance in the New Testament.[1] Its New Testament usage, the singular interest in this paper, is basically limited to Paul, where it is always and singularly an adjective, sometimes turned into a substantive. (It does appear twice elsewhere, in a decidedly Pauline way, in 1 Peter 2:5, where believers are to be a "spiritual house" and they are to bring "spiritual sacrifices.") Hence the reason for the title of this chapter, and all the more so, since the concept of "spirituality" itself, which once defined by us is then used by us to press the biblical text into service of a meaning that does not in fact derive from biblical language at all.

MISLEADING TRANSLATIONS

So I begin, and hopefully without belaboring this point, with the most likely reason for this failure on the part of the contemporary church to use the adjective *spiritual* in a biblical way. And that seems to me to be the fact that even though orthodox Christianity has maintained (strongly so) its trinitarian way of speaking about, and even sometimes of thinking about, God, in everyday life believers are practicing binitarians, in almost all areas of Christian life, except in the creeds themselves. Thus in their practical life in the world, there is very little self-conscious awareness of one's life being filled with, or led by, the Holy Spirit. And the same seems generally to hold true in the church's worship and theological life, although in both cases there is a generally consistent doffing the hat toward the Spirit, as it were; but at the base

---

[1]Walter Bauer and Frederick W. Danker, *A Greek-English Lexicon of the New Testament and Other Early Christian Literature* (Chicago: University of Chicago Press, 2001).

there seems to be a general unease about Spirit talk. And it is precisely this tendency toward wariness regarding the Spirit that has allowed the biblical language to gravitate toward (I would say, degenerate into) a usage that is totally without a biblical foundation.

So what I aim to do in this chapter is to look once more at Paul's usage of this adjective (and less frequently, adverb) to point out that any talk of Christian spirituality that is genuinely biblically based must take the word's origins into account in a much more self-conscious way. And I begin with its single occurrence in the New Testament as an adverb, namely 1 Corinthians 2:14, which, as I pointed out in my commentary over two decades ago, is one of the more abused moments in the entire Pauline corpus. There he is arguing that the person without the Spirit doesn't have a clue as to what God is doing through a crucified Messiah, because such "foolishness" on God's part can only be discerned by the person who has the *Spirit* of God. In the process, however, Paul switches from the noun to the adjective, and at that point the unfortunate history of translation into English takes place. It begins with the King James Version, which reads: "But the natural man [read, the person without the Spirit] receiveth not the things of the Spirit of God, . . . neither can he know them, because they are *spiritually* discerned" (1 Cor 2:14 KJV). And in this the translators of the KJV have been followed by the vast majority of later English versions (RSV, NRSV, NASB, NIV, NAB).[2] Only the TNIV, REB and NJB have got it right at this point. Indeed the TNIV has got it right altogether, by rendering the first word not as "the natural man," but as the context demands, that "the person without the Spirit does not accept the things that come from the Spirit of God . . . because they are discerned only through the Spirit" (1 Cor 2:14 TNIV)—which is yet another reason why, as a friend has put it, the English Standard Version should not become the standard English version, given that the translators have been generally quite insensitive to the role of the Spirit in Pauline theology.

---

[2]The following English Bible translations are under discussion: Revised Standard Version (RSV), New Revised Standard Version (NRSV), New American Standard Bible (NASB), New International Version (NIV), New American Bible (NAB), Today's New International Version (TNIV), Revised English Bible (REB), New Jerusalem Bible (NJB) and English Standard Version (ESV).

When we turn from this (often abused) passage in Paul to other significant moments, we find much the same tendency either to downplay or to ignore altogether Paul's own emphasis of the role of the Spirit in all aspects of everyday life. And all of this is the result of turning Paul's own adjective *(pneumatikos)* that refers universally and unequivocally to the Holy Spirit into the bland English adjective *(spiritual)* that has almost no meaning at all, because it is open to so many different, and almost always incorrect, understandings.

I begin with its singular usage in Galatians, a letter that has more Spirit talk per line of text than any other document in the New Testament, and that because Paul recognized so clearly what most later Christians do not, that the only God-given antidote to legalism (as a way of securing one's relationship with God) is a full and thoroughgoing reliance on the Spirit. So at the very end of the letter, where the Holy Spirit is mentioned some eighteen times, he urges those who are "spiritual," meaning, as the TNIV rightly has it, those "who live by the Spirit," to restore a brother or sister who is "caught in a sin" (Gal 6:1 TNIV). This unfortunate chapter break in the English Bible tradition has caused this admonition to be totally separated from all the Spirit talk that has immediately preceded it, which includes the so-called fruit of the Spirit. It is by the Spirit's gentleness (sixth in the listing of the "fruit") that others are to restore such a person within the believing community. So how do most translations handle it? By rendering it (lowercase), "you who are spiritual." The NRSV is the notable exception, while the NAB is the most offensive of all—"with a gentle spirit"—since its translation of the word is simply biblical nonsense.

When we turn to Colossians, where the adjective appears twice, the same kind of abuse of Paul occurs in the majority of English translations. Thus in the well-known prayer in Colossians 1:9, Paul says that he prays that "God [might] fill you with the knowledge of his will through all the wisdom and understanding that the Spirit gives" (TNIV, which again [nearly alone] rightly translates it). To translate this as (lowercase) "spiritual wisdom and understanding" is especially offensive in this case, since the prayer follows hard on the heels of the thanksgiving that ends with "who told us of your love in the Spirit" (which

English translations have almost universally got right). But then in the follow-up, when mention of the Spirit appears as an adjective, the same translations render it "all spiritual wisdom and understanding." Few readers would have thought of "all spiritual wisdom" as a direct reference to the wisdom that comes from the Spirit, mentioned in the preceding sentence.

Similarly, later in the same letter, and in an especially well known moment (Col 3:16), Paul encourages them, while in the community gathered for worship, to encourage one another "through psalms and hymns and Spirit songs" (TNIV, "songs from the Spirit"), which has rather universally been rendered as "spiritual songs." But the only way the average reader could get at what Paul is doing is by means of a commentary, whereas a translation sensitive to Pauline usage will at least do what the TNIV did, or go in the (less precise) direction of the New Jerusalem Bible, with its "inspired songs."

Before drawing this harangue to a suitable conclusion, I offer a final example from the companion letter that ended up as "to the Ephesians" (although originally it apparently had no addressee and was thus intended to be a circular letter to the churches in the province of Asia that ended up in the capital city). Much in keeping with Colossians, but now at the very beginning of the letter, Paul begins by "blessing" God the Father who in Christ has blessed them "with every spiritual blessing in the heavenly places" (Eph 1:3 NRSV). As it turns out this is also the only place where the TNIV translators chose to stay with the English tradition regarding this adjective. But one must ask, what can this phrase possibly mean to the average English reader? What exactly is a "spiritual blessing"? Is it something to be seen in contrast to a "material blessing"? And if so, what would that mean when fleshed out in some way? To make one more godly? To receive more "spiritual gifts"? To be blessed in the inner person as opposed to in a material way?

If one were to use the word in its Pauline way, and not in the way of modern readers, it would mean precisely what one reads elsewhere in Paul and should expect of him here. Namely, that he simply cannot help "praising" God (which is what "blessing God" means ultimately) for the manifold ways that God has chosen to bless his people by means of his Holy Spirit. Thus the emphasis lies not with the "character" of the "blessings" themselves, but with their divine origins within what the later church came to call the "blessed Trinity," blessings which have been lavished upon God's people through the Holy Spirit.

THE HOLY SPIRIT IN PAULINE SPIRITUALITY

So in light of the New Testament evidence, the only real question that should be raised *biblically* about "spirituality" has to do with who the Spirit is and what the Spirit is doing. And at this point we could go to several of our biblical writers, especially Luke and John. But since my long-time interest has been with Pauline theology, I will belabor this concern yet one more time. While Paul does speak of the Holy Spirit as the "Spirit of Christ" (Rom 8:9; Gal 4:6; Phil 1:19) he more typically refers to the Holy Spirit as the "Spirit of God." The theological point is that both phrases emphasize that the Spirit is conveying the activity of either God or Christ to the believer. In Paul's theology, the presence of the Spirit is the reality of God's personal presence in the midst of his people. Thus for Paul, the Spirit is always understood as a person, not some merely impersonal force or influence or power. The Spirit is God's own personal presence in our lives, individually and corporately.[3] What does the Holy Spirit do? He acts as a divine personal agent in myriad ways. The Spirit searches all things (1 Cor 2:10), knows the mind of God (1 Cor 2:11), teaches the content of the gospel to believers (1 Cor 2:13), dwells among or within believers (Rom 8:11; 1 Cor 3:16; 2 Tim 1:14), accomplishes all things (1 Cor 12:11), gives life to those who believe (2 Cor 3:6), cries out from within our hearts (Gal 4:6), leads us in the ways of God (Rom 8:14; Gal 5:18), bears witness with our own spirits (Rom 8:16), has desires that are in opposition to the flesh (Gal 5:17), helps us in our weakness (Rom 8:26), intercedes on our behalf (Rom 8:26-27), works all things together for our ultimate good (Rom 8:28), strengthens believers (Eph 3:16) and is grieved by our sinfulness (Eph 4:30). Moreover, the fruit of the Spirit's indwelling are the personal attributes of God (Gal 5:22-23). From this list, it is obvious that

---

[3]For more detail, see Gordon D. Fee, *God's Empowering Presence* (Peabody, Mass.: Hendrickson, 1994), chap. 13.

if the Holy Spirit is left out of our account of Christian spirituality, then a very great deal will have been lost. Spirituality without the Holy Spirit becomes a feeble human project. As I argue in my *God's Empowering Presence*, a book of a thousand pages in which every reference to the Holy Spirit in Paul's letters is given full commentary treatment, there is scarcely an aspect of genuinely Christian life that is not "spiritual" in the Pauline sense, of being lived in and by means of the so-called third person of the Trinity.

In the first place, this is simply because of the meaning of salvation in Christ.[4] For Paul, salvation is explained with reference to the character and agency of the triune God. Salvation originates in the Father's redeeming love; it is in Christ, brought about by his death and resurrection; and it is realized in the life of the believer by the Holy Spirit, the empowering presence of God. For this reason Paul describes what happens to the believer in conversion with reference to the decisive activity of the Holy Spirit, such as in Romans 8:9, "If anyone does not have the Spirit, that person does not belong to Christ at all." This means that the newly constituted people of God, saved through Christ's death and resurrection, have been given life by the life-giving Spirit (2 Cor 3:3, 6; Gal 5:25). Therefore, the people of God are Spirit people: they walk by the Spirit and are led by the Spirit, since Paul's understanding of "getting saved" first of all means "receiving the Spirit." From this standpoint, it is easy to see that soteriologies that are insufficiently attentive to the decisive work of the Holy Spirit will be incapable of generating "spiritual formation" in the Pauline sense. If conversion is essentially the work of the Spirit, believers are not "white-washed sinners" who are still sinful, but accepted by God nevertheless. Rather, in conversion the believer has been invaded by the life-giving Spirit and thereby transformed from within. In Pauline terms, there is no such thing as Christian conversion that does not have the coming of the Spirit into the believer's life as the crucial ingredient.

This sets the stage for understanding the meaning of "life in the Spirit." In Pauline perspective, to "get saved" means joining the people

---

[4]For more detail, see ibid., chap. 14.

of God by the Spirit, and to "be saved" means "to live the life of the saved person." Conversion by the Spirit involves a commitment to a life of walking in the Spirit, being led by the Spirit, sowing to the Spirit. It means being a Spirit person, first and foremost, since the Holy Spirit is the absolutely essential constituent of the whole of the Christian life.

From this exposition of Pauline Christianity, you can see why I find it utterly tragic that most expressions of the Protestant tradition have ended up being trinitarian in name only, but not in practice. As a former student, who once came to my office regarding this matter, said to me, "God the Father I understand, Christ the Son I know, but the Holy Spirit is a gray oblong blur." And he has spoken for the large majority of Protestant students I have known over the years. They come from church communities where the only mention of the Spirit is the clause toward the end of the creed, "and I believe in the Holy Ghost/Spirit." And so they "believe" in the Spirit, but come from church communities where the Spirit is kept in the creed, lest he become a vital—and perhaps sometimes threatening—part of the church's ongoing life. Thus in belief Protestants maintain their trinitarianism, but in practice many of them are thoroughgoing binitarians.

I cannot offer any easy remedies. I would make a general plea to church leaders to throw away the boxes in which they have kept the Spirit securely under their own control, and to trust the Spirit to guide the whole community to a life in the Spirit that leads to genuine *Spirituality* in the believers' daily lives. And even more so this plea would be for a similar genuine *Spirituality* in the gathered believing community that remains open to the Spirit to do things his way rather than to be invited in to be the silent partner of the Trinity so that we may continue to "do church" our often ineffective and powerless way. One critical aspect of our coming to terms with a more biblical understanding of "spirituality" might be for evangelical believers to be done with their latent—I think at times almost rampant—tendencies toward the heresy of Apollonarianism, in which the deity of Christ is so strongly superimposed over the historical Jesus that he is basically a "little God" walking among us. The biblical texts, on the other hand, are quite clear that his miracles and insights into people's lives were the direct result of his living by the Spirit; or to put it in Lukan terms, "who went around doing good . . . because God was *with* him." Looking just at Luke, we see that Jesus is the Spirit person par excellence. Jesus is prophesied to be filled with the Spirit from birth (Lk 1:15). At his baptism, the Holy Spirit descends upon him to empower his future ministry (Lk 3:22). Full of the Holy Spirit, he is led into the wilderness to be tempted (Lk 4:1), returns to Galilee in the power of the Spirit (Lk 4:14) and announces his "manifesto" with the recognition that the Spirit is upon him (Lk 4:18). He is filled with joy through the Holy Spirit (Lk 10:21). If evangelicals were more attuned to the centrality of the Holy Spirit in the life and ministry of Jesus, we might be able to hear Paul himself a bit better, so that "living in/by the Spirit" likewise means for us to "do what is good for, and to, one and all."

So I conclude by going back to the beginning, and that is to make a plea that we more consciously allow the Spirit to have a much more major and focused role in our thinking about "spirituality." As long as we continue to use this word in the way it has evolved, and thus totally separated from its very singular origins in the person and work of the Holy Spirit, we will keep on talking about "spiritual exercises" rather than about genuine *Spirituality* related to what Paul calls "living in and by the Spirit." Paul means by this that the Spirit is both the "locus" and the "enabler" of our lives as believers. In an explicitly Christian context, where *Spirituality* has often deteriorated into a lifeless series of scripted or traditional routines undertaken by sheer human willpower, I would press for a meaning that is more closely related to our becoming more aware of the person and role of the Spirit in every aspect of Christian life.

3 Spiritual Formation as a Natural Part of Salvation

Dallas Willard

There is a prevailing understanding of salvation that poses almost insurmountable barriers to transformation of professing Christians into Christlikeness, which is the meaning of spiritual formation. Simply put, as now generally understood, being "saved"—and hence being a Christian—has no conceptual or practical connection with such a transformation. There is plenty of talk about transformation in the New Testament (Rom 5:1-5; 12:2; 2 Cor 3:18; Eph 4:14-16; Col 3:4-17; 2 Pet 1:2-11; 3:18, etc.). It is presupposed in the Bible's extensive descriptions of normative behavior. And it shines in the lives of acknowledged "great ones" in the way of Christ and in the literature spun off by the church through the ages. But all of this appears to the ordinary Christian today like distant galaxies in the night sky: visible, somehow, but inaccessible in the conditions of life as we know them. Hence, you will rarely meet an individual Christian who is seriously engaged in the transformation (spiritual formation) depicted in the Bible and in church history, or who even has a hope for anything like it this side of heaven. And while you might think that Christian organizations would have such transformation as their central focus, that simply turns out not to be true. They are doing something else.

So let us start out with some clarification of *spiritual formation*. As I have explained in various writings, spiritual formation in Christ as portrayed in the Bible and seen in the "great ones" is not primarily behavior modification, though modification of behavior certainly is an outcome of it. Especially, it is not being trained into one or another outward cultural form of the Christian religion: Lutheran, Benedictine, Quaker, etc. That is how it has often been approached, but to suppose that it is identical with such training will only result in another form of "the righteousness of the Scribes and Pharisees" (see Mt 5:20) which leaves untouched the inward character of the person, the "heart," the source of action and outward bearing (Mk 7:21-23). It is appropriate to regard this inner dimension of the self as the "spiritual" side of the human being, and then to think of "spiritual formation" as the process of reshaping or redeveloping it until it has, to a substantial degree, the character of the inner dimension of Jesus himself. This is a process in which the agency of the Holy Spirit is indispensable, along with other instrumentalities of God and his kingdom. One can think of the process as formation *of* the human spirit as well as formation *by* the divine Spirit, for it indeed is both.

What this looks like is indicated in various ways in the teachings of Jesus and his early followers. When asked by a scribe to state the foundational commandment of all, Jesus replied in terms of recognition of Jehovah as the One God, and of our loving him "with all your heart, and with all your soul, and with all your mind, and with all your strength," and loving "your neighbor as yourself" (Mk 12:29-31). This would be the outcome or "product" of the process of spiritual formation in Christ. In various wordings, that is the uniform testimony of the New Testament. Some high points are Romans 5:5, 1 Corinthians 13, Colossians 3:14 and 2 Peter 1:5-7.

The behavioral outcome of such a spiritual formation is assured. "He who has My commandments and keeps them, he it is who loves Me. . . . He who does not love Me does not keep My words" (Jn 14:21, 24 NKJV). Paul remarks that "love does no wrong to a neighbor; therefore love is the fulfillment of the law" (Rom 13:10 NASB). John says bluntly: "The one who says, 'I have come to know Him,' and does not keep His commandments, is a liar, and the truth is not in him" (1 Jn 2:4 NASB). But one must understand the order that is in these sayings, or otherwise they will throw us into a legalistic frenzy—as has happened over and over in the history of Christ's people. Accordingly, the practical aim of the person who takes obedience seriously is not to obey, but to become the kind of person who easily and routinely does obey as a result of devotion to Jesus and consequently of taking him as Lord, teacher and friend. The practical aim is to know him, to be devoted to him, in this inclusive manner.

What, then, does "being saved" have to do with such a transformation? We should perhaps start with recognition that, for almost everyone today in Western Christendom, being saved has *nothing* essentially to do with it. We might find "being saved" and such transformation conjoined in an individual here or there, and that might be regarded as admirable; but it is not normative for being a Christian, and when it does happen it has to be accounted for in terms other than the basic nature of the salvation presumed. All notable theological and ecclesiastical positions with which I am familiar in the contemporary world hold that you can be right with God in ways that do not require transformation and in ways that do not routinely support and advance transformation. These ways may involve (1) professing right doctrine, (2) a specified form of association with a denomination or group, or on the more liberal side (3) a kind of vague—or even intense—sympathy with what one takes Jesus to stand for. There are, of course, many ways in which this can be spelled out, which I have tried to deal with in more detail elsewhere.[1] But together these three paths—frequently overlapping—pretty much take in the ways in which North Americans, at least, along with many Europeans, think of themselves as "Christian." This seems to me to be a merely descriptive point.

Now within this broad range of Christians, a narrower group—many Roman Catholics, Eastern Orthodox and evangelical Protestants—think of "salvation" or "being saved" as strictly a matter of having one's sins forgiven and of having heaven "nailed down" as a result. The problem we are addressing then arises from a soteriology that identifies being saved with having your sins forgiven. And our question then comes down to how having your sins forgiven relates to spiritual formation as

---

[1]Dallas Willard, *The Divine Conspiracy* (San Francisco: HarperSanFrancisco, 1998), chaps. 1-2.

process and as outcome. The background assumption is that justification is the entirety of salvation, that is, if you are justified—your sins
forgiven—then you are saved and you will be okay after your death. I
submit to you that this is what is offered, in still more specific forms, by
most current efforts ("evangelism") to convert people to Christianity,
and it is what people generally understand to be essential to the trans-
action. It is how many people come into the church. Other words may
be used—such as "giving your heart to Jesus," or "taking him into your
heart" or even "accepting Jesus as Lord of your Life"—but what is essential, no matter the words, is receiving forgiveness by counting on the
merits of Christ to cover your sin-debts.

To get the complete picture you have to explain how grace is understood in this context. Salvation is by grace through faith. That is a
foundational truth. But it is usually understood to mean that nothing
you do contributes to salvation. With this, a pervasive passivity enters
the scene. You will even be told by some that your very faith in Christ
as the sacrifice for your sins is not something you do, but something
God just produces in you (or not). It is not just that grace is "unmerited
favor," but that it is something exterior to you—an event involving God
in heaven, a transfer of merit from Christ to your account.

Now when that is done it is done. "Salvation" is complete. On some
soteriologies you have to service the account in various ways if you are
going to make it in—faithfulness to the sacraments, for example, or
periodic repentance and efforts to do better, or even rebaptism—but
only in very few cases is there an insistence that you have to be significantly transformed into Christlikeness to "get in." In one tradition it is
said that *gratitude* for forgiveness will in fact make you adhere to Christ
in such a way that transformation and obedience will follow. That has
happened, and perhaps still happens in some cases. But if you simply
observe the groups that propose this, you will see that the rate of radical
transformation in them is quite low, and usually no higher than in
groups that do not hold their view.

The conclusion I draw from all of this is that a view that takes salvation
to be the same thing as justification—forgiveness of sins and assurance of
heaven based upon it—*cannot* come to see spiritual formation as *a natural*

part of salvation. The result of that will be the routine omission of spiritual formation unto Christlikeness as a serious objective of individuals and groups who hold a mere "justification" view of salvation. Further, it seems to me, adherence to this view of salvation is what accounts for the transformation of evangelical Christianity into a version of nominal Christianity over the course of the twentieth century, even though, historically, evangelicalism has strongly opposed nominal Christianity.

But is there a recognizably Christian view of salvation—one prominent in Scripture and history—that *does* have spiritual formation as a natural part or outgrowth of "salvation," understood to be an identifiable *status* (sometimes, at least, associated with a specific *event*)? There is such a view, and it comes in the form of the theological concept of regeneration. This is the event of *a new type of life* entering into the individual human being. The kind of life that the human being has on its own—its "natural" life, so to speak—is a kind of "death" compared to the type of life that begins to move in us at "regeneration." Once this is mentioned, I believe the person familiar with the New Testament writings will recognize the passage from "death" to "life" as a constant biblical theme, where "life" is a real and powerful presence in the regenerate individual (Eph 3:20; 2 Tim 2:1).

John the apostle states as a sure indication that we have "passed out of death into life, [that] we love the brethren. He who does not love abides in death" (1 Jn 3:14 NASB). And also: "He who has the Son has life" (1 Jn 5:12). *Life* is perhaps John's favorite term for what happens when one comes to Christ. It is the entire point of "the birth from above" as discussed in John 3—a passage that is desecrated by the usual reading of it as focused upon forgiveness of sins. There the "life" is associated with seeing and entering the kingdom of God. Birth and life of course go together. Paul describes the action of God in saving us: "For He rescued us from the domain of darkness, and transferred us to the kingdom of His beloved Son" (Col 1:13 NASB). To enter the kingdom is to have the life "from above." That life is the principle of kingdom inclusion. Paul otherwise describes it as sharing in the resurrection life of Jesus himself. "You have died and your life is hidden with Christ in God" (Col 3:3 NASB). Again: "You were dead in your tres-

passes and sins. . . . But God . . . even when we were dead in our trans-
gressions, made us alive together with Christ (by grace you have been
saved), and raised us up with Him, and seated us with Him in the heavenly places in Christ Jesus" (Eph 2:1, 4-6 NASB). That is what the birth
"from above" does. Simple inductive study of the New Testament will,
I believe, convince anyone that its primary way of understanding salvation is in terms of a divine life that enters the human being as a gift of
God. There is then a new psychological reality that is God acting in us
and with us. Eternal life is said by Jesus to be knowledge. Knowledge
in biblical language is an interactive relationship, and in this case with
"Thee, the only true God, and Jesus Christ whom Thou hast sent" (Jn
17:3 KJV). Eternal life in the individual does not begin after death, but
at the point where God touches the individual with redeeming grace
and draws them into a life interactive with himself and his kingdom. A
new, nonhuman activity becomes a part of our life. Our life is now in-
terwoven with his and his with ours. (Amazing grace indeed!) Speaking thus we must make it clear that we are not just "talking something
up," but referring to the concrete reality of regenerate existence.

What is life? What is a *new* life? I won't attempt here a definition of
life, but observation will show that life is self-initiating, self-directing,
self-sustaining activity, of *some* kind and *some* degree. That is what distinguishes living things from nonliving things, and things that are still
alive from things that have died. An important part of the activity that
is life consists of the living thing's interaction with its environment,
and, indeed, the kind of life that is in a thing determines what counts
as its environment. The life that is in a plant makes soil, water and
sunlight the major factors of its environment, and when it dies it ceases
to interact with those factors by appropriate activity. A kitten has a different kind of life in it and interacts with different types of things in
different ways: small rubber balls, mice and other kittens, for example.
A dead kitten is totally indifferent to those things, as the plant is indifferent to them while it is alive. And so on through the scale of living
things. A human being, in comparison to other living things, has a real
or possible environment of fantastic proportions not yet revealed (Is
64:4; 1 Jn 3:2).

The human being is by nature meant to function on the basis of interaction between itself and God at the very center of its life. The sufficiency of God to the human being (Rom 8:31-39) is adequate to the "fantastic proportions" of human abilities and aspirations. To lose that central reality is what it means to be "dead in trespasses and sins." Life activity of a sort continues on in the human being for a while but is defined in terms of the reverse trinity of the world, the flesh and the devil (Eph 2:2-3). But that activity draws from limited, chaotic and self-destructive resources. Its condition of *spiritual* death ends in *total* death (Rom 8:5-6).

God alone has life in himself (Jn 5:26), and it is he who gives life to all things (1 Tim 6:13). He alone can say, "I am that I am" (see Ex 3:14). Life in anything other than God is always dependent. Its self-initiating, self-directing, self-sustaining activity is always limited and dependent on other things—ultimately upon God. In regeneration God, utilizing various instrumentalities, imparts his own life to the fallen life of the human being apart from God. The self-initiating, self-directing, self-sustaining activity of God now penetrates the darkened world of the human soul and begins to act in it and around it. It has rarely if ever been better said than by Charles Wesley in his famous hymn "And Can It Be That I Should Gain":

> Long my imprisoned spirit lay
> Fast bound in sin and nature's night;
> Thine eye diffused a quick'ning ray,
> I woke, the dungeon flamed with light;
> My chains fell off, my heart was free;
> I rose, went forth and followed Thee.

Salvation, being saved, is then not a meager, merely human existence here, but life with a heavenly account flush in the transferred merits of Christ. It is a human existence, to be sure—meager as it may be—but one in which the currents of divine life have at least begun to pulsate. It is "Christ in you, the hope of glory" (Col 1:27). It is "He who began a good work in you will perfect it" (Phil 1:6 NASB). It is "God who is at work in you, both to will and to work for His good pleasure" (Phil 2:13

NASB). It is becoming "partakers of divine nature, having escaped the corruption that is in the world by lust" (2 Pet 1:4 NASB). It is "Your life is hid with Christ in God" (Col 3:3 KJV).

Life also has a natural development. This is the absolutely crucial point for our discussion here. The activity that is life is poised for a specific order of development. It can be deflected or stunted, but its natural course is set by the kind of life it is. The same is true with the new life "from above" that enters the human being, however degraded, upon regeneration. The first clear manifestation of heavenly life in the individual is recognition, hearty confidence, that Jesus really is the Anointed One, Christ, Lord. This is not primarily a profession. It is a gripping realization of what is the case. It is not possible for the unaided human being to arrive at such a condition. When it gripped Peter, the Lord told him that only divine assistance could have brought it to him, not "flesh and blood" (Mt 16:16-17 NASB). That was not a point upon which error could be tolerated. Jesus went on to say that the rock of this realization would be the foundation upon which his triumphant *ekklesia* would prevail and stand, with access ("keys") to the resources of the kingdom of the heavens. Paul, in helping the Corinthians come to an understanding of where God was really present, pointed out, "No one can say, 'Jesus is Lord,' except by [assistance from] the Holy Spirit" (1 Cor 12:3). When one understands the realities involved here it will be clear why: "If you confess with your mouth Jesus as Lord, and believe in your heart that God raised Him from the dead, you will be saved" (Rom 10:9 NASB). (To "confess" is to own up to a condition of your soul; to profess is to put forth an understanding of something.) Confidence in Jesus as absolute master of the universe is the first indication of regeneration. It is this, not a mere credit transfer, which constitutes a "personal relationship with Jesus."

The natural consequence of this confidence is apprenticeship to Jesus in kingdom living. We will not say that failure to become the apprentice or disciple of Jesus is a metaphysical impossibility for one who has confidence that he is Lord of the universe. A certain degree of understanding of "what comes next" is presupposed, and in the midst of confused teaching and example, things might not proceed as they naturally would. Life in all its forms permits distortion within limits, of not becoming what it was meant to be. But in the nature of the case, one who really understands who Jesus is sees their own situation in a realistic light and wants to take measures to remedy their condition by staying as close to Jesus as possible. Discipleship is a natural part of confidence in Jesus as he really is.

What exactly is a "faith" that does not naturally express itself in discipleship to Jesus? It would be that of a person who simply would *use* something Jesus did, but has no use for him. This is the person I have outrageously called the "vampire Christian." "I'll take a bit of your blood, Jesus—enough to cover my debts—but I'll not be staying close to you until I have to." Wouldn't heaven be hell for a person stuck forever with the company of someone (the magnificent Jesus and the triune God) whom they did not admire or even like enough to stay close to them? There is no way you can say that such a person has faith or confidence in Jesus Christ. This is not the faith that works by love (Gal 5:6), or the faith though which Christ dwells in the heart (Eph 3:17). It is not the faith that is a natural part of regeneration as life from above.

Discipleship may be loosely described as staying as close to Jesus Christ as possible. It is life *with* him, his life *with* us. As his disciples we are learning from Jesus how to live our life here and now in the kingdom of the heavens as he would live it if he were in our place. Now the locus of our life with him as disciples is precisely obedience where we are. Our obedience, to start with, will be ragged, messy and inadequate, but we are not trying to be "righteous" anyway. All hope in that direction has been abandoned and we do not deal with ourselves or with others on the basis of "righteousness." Our faith in Christ, now that we understand what it is, is that upon which our interactive relationship with God in Christ is based. Abraham believed God and it was reckoned to him as righteousness (Rom 4:3). That is to say, God based his relationship to Abraham upon Abraham's confidence in God, not on Abraham having always done "the right thing." So it is with us. Obedience to Jesus Christ is not how we earn anything; it is simply the place where the kingdom of God is in relation to us. It is where we know it and where we know him. Merit is not the issue. Life is the issue: life beyond merit.

Our relationship with God enables us to get grace right. Grace is God acting in our life to bring about, and to enable us to do, what we cannot do on our own (2 Tim 2:1). Inductive study of Scripture, once again, will make this unmistakably clear. Grace is inextricably bound up with discipline in the life of the disciple or apprentice of Jesus. Discipline in the spiritual life is doing something in our power that enables us to do what we cannot do by direct effort—because in this way we meet the action of God (grace) with us, and the outcome is humanly inexplicable. This is what it means to speak of discipline as "a means to grace." Thus Jesus tells his puzzled and frightened friends that, if they love him they will keep his commandments, and God will give them "another Helper" that will always be with them (Jn 14:15-16). Loving him, keeping his commandments and trinitarian cohabitation are inseparable parts of the life into which regeneration "naturally" develops (Jn 14:9-28).

Thus the famous statement of Jesus about truly being his disciples: "If you abide in my word, then you are truly disciples of mine, and you will know the truth, and the truth will make you free" (Jn 8:31-32 ESV). The "abiding" here is "dwelling in" or living in. It is the same basic term used in the great teaching of John 15:1-7—abide in me, as the branch dwells in the vine. But what does it mean "to abide in his word"? It means to put his words into action, to act according to them. When we do that we inhale the reality of the kingdom. That is what it means to be his "disciples indeed." And one who does this will come to know the truth, the reality, of the kingdom and of God's action with them, and that in turn will enable them to live free from the bondage of sin. This is exactly the situation that Paul is spelling out in Romans 6:14 (NASB): "For sin shall not be master over you, for you are not under law, but under grace." "Grace" here is an active agency in the psychological and biological reality of the disciple.

So we think like this: Being a disciple (apprentice, student) of Jesus is the status into which regeneration naturally brings us because of the nature of the belief in Christ through which regeneration expresses itself. Discipleship to Jesus has as its natural outcome transformation of character—the hidden realities of heart, mind, soul, body—in such a way that conformity to his commands becomes the easy, routine, standard way the well-developed disciple comports himself or herself. (We are not talking about legalistic perfection, or perfection in the way it has been taken in most of the battles over that subject. And, of course, when we say "natural" here, we mean it in such a way that it does not exclude, but actually requires, the *super*natural—as should be clear from what we have already said.)

It should be clear that we, with all our faults and failures, have an indispensable role in both discipleship and in spiritual formation. "Be on the alert, stand firm in the faith, act like men, be strong" (1 Cor 16:13 NASB). Once we are clear that the issue is no longer merit, but life—and that grace is not opposed to effort but to earning—this responsibility should cause no problem. We are quite prepared to hear the ceaseless admonitions to action set down in Scripture, to welcome them and to undertake the corresponding actions—as best we can, learning as we go. Paul's admonitions to "put off the old person and put on the new" now present themselves as something we are to do! James's directive to "prove yourselves doers of the word, and not merely hearers who delude themselves" (Jas 1:22 NASB) is completely appropriate. Jesus' own picture of the foolishness of those who hear him but do not do what he says (Lk 6:49) makes utter sense. "The grace of God which brings salvation" does not offer us a cushion, but "instructs us to deny ungodliness and worldly desires and to live sensibly, righteously and godly in the present age . . . zealous for good works" (Tit 2:11-14). That looks like the only way for a believer in Jesus to go anyway.

The key to it all, from the point of view of action, is indirection. We want to obey Jesus, and we know that we cannot do this just by trying to do what he said. We understand that we are broken—not only wrong but wrung, twisted, with parts that do not connect up right. We realize that our feelings, embedded in our body and its social context, are running and ruining our life, and producing godless and destructive actions under the direction of false ideas and images and messed-up patterns of thinking. We know that we must, instead of just trying to obey, find a way to become the kind of person who does, easily and routinely, what Jesus said—does it without having to think much about it, if at all, in the ordinary case. It is here that disciplines come to our rescue, always encompassed by grace. In engaging disciplines we go to the root of the tree of our life, the sources of behavior. We do the things that will transform our minds, our feelings, our will and our embodied and social existence, even the depths of our soul, to "make the tree good, and its fruit good" (Mt 12:33 NASB). We cultivate and fertilize the tree (Lk 13:8). We don't try to squeeze fruit out of the ends of its branches. In doing this we use tried and true methods of Christ's people, as well as any sensible means at our disposal, including "professional help." And in this way we become, by divine grace, the kind of person who does the things Jesus said to do and avoids what he said not to do. From the point of view of our assemblies of disciples, we teach disciples to do everything Jesus commanded (Mt 28:20).

So all of this can give us a practical hope when we look at remarkable New Testament passages such as 1 Corinthians 13, Colossians 3 and 2 Peter 1:1-11, or at the landmark literature of discipleship and spiritual formation generated by the lives of disciples throughout the Christian ages (Francis of Assisi, Hudson Taylor, Amy Carmichael, etc.).

In 2 Peter 1 the writer addresses "those who have received a faith of the same kind as ours, by the righteousness of our God and Savior, Jesus Christ" (1:1 NASB). He then prays, "Grace and peace be multiplied to you in the knowledge of [interactive relationship with] God and of Jesus our Lord" (1:2 NASB). He cites the fact that "through true knowledge of Him who called us by His own glory and excellence . . . divine power has granted to us everything pertaining to life and godliness" (1:3 NASB). All of this means that "He has granted to us His precious and magnificent promises, so that by them you might become partakers of the divine nature, having escaped the corruption that is in the world by lust" (2 Pet 1:4 NASB). This brings fully before us the picture of salvation as leading a life that is caught up in the kingdom of the heavens, or in what God is doing in human history. It is a life in which "God works all things together for good to those who love him and are absorbed into his purposes" (Rom 8:28). It is "resurrection life": a life already beyond death (see Jn 8:51-52; 11:25-26; Col 3:1-4).

And then comes, as a "natural part" of such life, the active response of discipleship and spiritual transformation. "Now for this very reason," 2 Peter continues—or, "Because all of this is so"—"also, applying all diligence, in your faith achieve moral excellence [virtue], and in your moral excellence achieve knowledge, in your knowledge achieve self-control, in your self-control achieve endurance, in your endurance achieve constant adoration, in your adoration achieve kindness to others [brotherly love], and in your kindness to others achieve divine love *[agape]*" (2 Pet 1:5-7 NASB).

We do not have time and space here to discuss each of these in turn, but an adequate course in discipleship and spiritual formation would go into each of these "additions" and explore how each lays a foundation for the later ones, and how each of the later ones enriches and strengthens the earlier ones. Also, such a course—should it not be the standard curriculum of our local congregations and denominations?—would go into detail as to how, starting from faith, one achieves virtue, from virtue one achieves knowledge, and so forth, always presupposing divine assistance, grace, in the human progression. This would be done in a way that includes practical directions, training sessions and disciplines, not just "information"—though the relevant information is crucial and currently is sorely lacking. Such details were not laid out in the New Testament because they were conveyed by the examples and practices of the communities arising out of the original fellowship of Jesus and his apostles.

Peter, in any case, clearly assumes that "these qualities are [to be] yours and are increasing," and that "they render you neither useless nor unfruitful in the true knowledge of [interactive relationship with] our Lord Jesus Christ" (2 Pet 1:8 NASB). That would be the natural progression and outcome of spiritual formation in the disciple. Diligence in this direction makes one sure of his "calling and election" (1:10), because "as long as you practice these things, you will never stumble," and because "in this way the entrance into the eternal kingdom of our Lord and Savior Jesus Christ will be abundantly supplied to you" (2 Pet 1:10-11 NASB). We should not assume that this latter "entrance" refers primarily to the famous "gates of splendor"—though that entrance is certainly grand and important, and is also included in the package. It too is a "natural part" of the life in question. Rather, the eternal kingdom mentioned, as the context should make clear, is the one Jesus announced as already "at hand," from which the regenerate person is drawing "the life that is life indeed" (see 1 Tim 6:19).

Now with all of this before us we can perhaps make good practical sense of the parting admonition of 2 Peter: "Grow in the grace and knowledge of our Lord and Savior Jesus Christ" (3:18). *Grace*, we have said, is God acting in our life to bring about results beyond human ability, and *knowledge*, biblically understood, is interactive relationship with what is known. Grace and knowledge are two aspects of one reality in the concrete existence of the disciple of Jesus living out the process of spiritual formation. But for our purposes here it is vital to understand that we can, by our attitudes and actions, actually increase the amount of grace and knowledge of Christ that is in our lives. "Be strong in the grace that is in Christ Jesus," Paul instructs Timothy (2 Tim 2:1). To increase in grace and knowledge is to open our life ever more fully to the presence/action of God with us in all we are and do. This is something we intentionally undertake and learn to do as we go. In Old Testament language it is to acknowledge him in all our ways (Prov 3:5-7). It is increasingly to humble ourselves under the mighty hand of God. On prevailing understandings of grace and salvation, however, 2 Peter 3:18 seems to remain in the category of pretty words without practical implications. "Christian education" now has the mandate to change that.

So, to review and reemphasize: regeneration, entry of God's nature and life into our real existence and identity, has as a natural progression or part entry into the status of discipleship to Jesus Christ in the power of the new life. Living in the status of disciple has as a natural part and progression spiritual formation in Christlikeness. Progression in spiritual formation in Christlikeness leads to easy, routine obedience to the commandments Christ brought to us, and to living the public life—from the inside out—as any sincere and thoughtful person would expect from the biblical record and the track record of the "great ones" in Christian history. In practice all of this is, no doubt, more ragged and messy than I have, for the sake of simplicity, made it look here, but the basic structure is clear and holds up in the demands of actual human existence.

But this leaves us with difficult practical problems facing the project of spiritual formation in Christlikeness in our local congregations and in the larger units of Christian organization—even, indeed, in the "Christian" atmosphere of thought still pervading the Western world. We have to deal with a massive population of churched and unchurched people who think of "being saved" or "being right with God" merely in terms of some picture of justification, not regeneration. Being "born again" is usually understood now not in terms of being animated by a "life from above," but in terms of a profession of faith—often a profession of faith in the death of Christ as bearing the punishment for sin that otherwise would fall on us. This understanding usually prevails in ways that do not involve—may not even make mention of—participation in divine life. (And, of course, one can mention it without engaging it.) Then, of course, the otherwise natural progression into discipleship and its spiritual transformation naturally does *not* occur, and the churches and surrounding society are flooded with nondiscipled Christians whose lives seem not to differ profoundly, if at all, from non-Christians. Because of human hunger for something deeper than a strictly physical existence, we then see multitudes who say that they are not *religious* (not "churched," they usually mean) but they nonetheless are "very *spiritual*." Most often these are people who think they have seen, and seen through, the authentic Christian way. (Ironically, the "spirituality" they practice commonly has little or no bearing on their character, for they despise "morality" almost as much as they do "religion," and morality now is often lumped together or confused with religion, and treated as "the same thing.")

For evangelical Christians, turning around the ship of their social reality and restoring the understanding of salvation that characterized evangelicalism from its beginnings in Luther, and periodically after him, will be very difficult if not impossible. It would primarily be a work of scriptural interpretation and theological reformulation, but modification of time-hardened practices will also be required. Radical changes in what we do in the way of "church" will have to be made.[2] This in turn will demand the utmost in loving character, humility of mind and dependence upon the hand of God in a "with God" life.[3] But that is the way it is supposed to be anyway, is it not? It can be done and has been done, providing some of the most brilliant periods in the history of Christ's people.

I will suggest two steps on the way forward. One is that responsible leaders at all levels of Christian activity begin to exemplify and teach, in their official activities, spiritual formation in Christlikeness as something essential to the condition of "being saved"—not as a *pre*condition but as a natural development. How that is to be worked out, avoiding "works righteousness" and legalism, is something that must be carefully elaborated in scriptural, theological, ecclesiastical and psychological terms. The other is that efforts in evangelism and toward increasing "church membership" be very purposively reoriented toward bringing people to the point of regeneration and discipleship. The work of turning people to Christ is not done until that point. If we continue to make "converts" or "Christians," instead of disciples animated with the life from above that comes at "new" birth, spiritual formation and obedience to Christ (doing "all that he commanded") have little prospect other than that of a passing fad, which will certainly disappoint or fade into diverse legalisms and vacuous "spiritualities"—things that fall entirely within human abilities, described in the Bible as "the flesh."

The future of vital Christian life lies in the hands of the pastors and others who teach for Christ—especially including those who teach pastors. What will they do? The greatest field open for discipleship evangelism today is the North American and European churches and seminaries or divinity schools. They are full of people hungering for the real life, which is offered in companionship with Christ in his kingdom.

---

[2]I have tried to outline some of the basic changes in chaps. 12 and 13 of Dallas Willard, *Renovation of the Heart*, American ed. (Colorado Springs: NavPress, 2002).
[3]Richard Foster, *Life with God* (San Francisco: HarperOne, 2008).

PART TWO
Historical Approaches

4   From the Porch to the Cross

Ancient Christian Approaches to Spiritual Formation

GEORGE KALANTZIS

*But there is a danger for the solitary life . . . the first
and paramount danger is that of self-pleasing.*

ST. BASIL *LONGER RESPONSES* 7.3.26

Nowhere have I found a better description of Christian spirituality than the one offered by Charles Kannengiesser in the introduction to his collection on early Christian spirituality: "Christian spirituality reflects the radiance of Christian faith in daily life."[1] It is the charism (or gift) of the Holy Spirit and its aim is "a life transfigured, redeemed from evil and freed from death, a life in God."[2] As such, Christian spirituality derives its essence from the theology of the church and is nurtured by her practices, that is, her *askesis*. This section of our book, then, provides a brief historical look at some examples of Christian spirituality, spiritual theology and practices, as the transformative move and call to faith in daily life developed from the first centuries of the life of the church to our time.

---

[1]Pamela Bright and Charles Kannengiesser, "Early Christian Spirituality," in *Sources of Early Christian Thought* (Philadelphia: Fortress, 1986), p. 1.
[2]Ibid.

In this chapter I focus on the ascetical life and praxis of early Christians, paying particular attention to the move from prevailing classical Greco-Roman paradigms of philosophy as *askesis* and contemplation, to the late antique Christian redefinitions of spiritual formation. In so doing, I attempt to show both continuity as well as dissonance and to examine some often-forgotten aspects of monastic spirituality, such as the service to the poor and marginalized.

In our discussion of ancient concepts of spirituality, then, we ought to remember that neither the practice of asceticism nor the search for the life of (even in) the Spirit were uniquely Christian phenomena. Countless works have described the thirst for the spirit's ascent to behold the transcendent. Almost all the philosophical schools of Greek, Roman and late Roman antiquity understood the transitory nature of cosmic existence and sought to understand and engage "what really exists." Among all others, Plato looms large. Thirty-five dialogues and thirteen letters provided the framework of much of classical theory of knowledge and virtue. His lasting legacy on the Ideas—singularly perfect and unchangeable in this world of time and sense that is constantly in flux and, therefore, always and only illusory—forms the background of most of the philosophical trajectories in the search for truth, beauty and goodness, the ascent (*anagōge*) of the spirit, or mind, from mere gnosis, the cognition of the phenomena of the universe, to episteme, the transcendent knowing that is actual participation in the eternal forms themselves.

However tempting the urge to engage these pluriform traditions of spiritual ascent and enlightenment that have framed our world views, equally ancient and modern, I will resist and take it as my task to limit this essay to the Christian tradition, especially the late antique movements of anachoresis, the search for a fuller spirituality and union with God.

FROM THE PORCH TO THE CROSS

In his famous *Dialogue with Trypho*, the second century philosopher and Christian apologist Flavius Iustinus (ca. 100-165 C.E.) better known by his later surname, "Martyr," shows himself to be the quintessential example of someone on the classical quest for the divine, enlightenment and transcendence beyond the mere limits of the material. Born in Flavia Neapolis (modern Nablus) to a traditional Roman family, Justin's thirst for God meant he threw himself into *philosophia*, for "philosophy is indeed," as Justin explains it, "one's greatest possession, and is most precious in the sight of God, to whom it alone leads us and to whom it unites us, and in truth they who have applied themselves to philosophy are holy men."[3] In the telling of his own story Justin takes us along on this journey to spiritual fulfillment and enlightenment through the customary options of his time, namely, the philosophical schools prevalent in Greco-Roman antiquity:

> When I first desired to contact one of these philosophers, I placed myself under the tutelage of a certain *Stoic*. After spending some time with him and learning nothing new about God (for my instructor had no knowledge of God, nor did he consider such knowledge necessary), I left him and turned to a *Peripatetic* who considered himself an astute teacher. . . . I left him because I did not consider him a real philosopher [that is because he asked for tuition from Justin!]. . . . Since my spirit still yearned to hear the specific and excellent meaning of philosophy, I approached a very famous *Pythagorean*, who took great pride in his own wisdom. [He, too, was a disappointment to Justin.] . . . at my wit's end, it occurred to me to consult the *Platonists*, whose reputation was great. Thus it happened that I spent as much time as possible in the company of a wise man who was highly esteemed by the Platonists and who had but recently arrived in our city. Under him I forged ahead in philosophy and day-by-day I improved. The perception of incorporeal things quite overwhelmed me and the Platonic theory of ideas added wings to my mind, so that in a short time I imagined myself a wise man. So great was my folly that I fully expected immediately to gaze upon God, for this is the goal of Plato's philosophy. (*Dialogue* 2.2-6)

One day, on a morning walk by the seashore, where Justin could find "absolute solitude, devoid of human distractions" (*Dialogue* 3.1), he came across an old man. The man conversed with Justin and challenged him with a simple question: "How then, can the philosophers

---

[3]St. Justin Martyr *Dialogue with Trypho* 2.1, trans. Thomas B. Falls, ed. Michael Slusser (Washington, D.C.: Catholic University of America Press, 2003).

speculate correctly or speak truly of God, when they have no knowledge of him, since they have never seen nor heard him?" (3.7). Leading
the young seeker to see the inconsistencies in his vain search for knowledge of God apart from God's self-revelatory act in Moses and the
Prophets, the old man encouraged Justin to "beseech God to open to
you the gate of light, for no one can perceive or understand these truths
unless he has been enlightened by God and his Christ" (7.3). This was
the moment of enlightenment for Justin: "But my spirit was immediately set on fire, and an affection for the prophets, and for those who
are friends of Christ, took hold of me; while pondering on his words, I
discovered that his was the only sure and useful philosophy. Thus it is
that I am now a philosopher" (8.1-2). Justin's sequential conversion from
the porch to the academy found its final resting place at the cross for, as
Robert Wilken puts it so elegantly,

> The intellectual effort of the early church was [not preoccupied with
> ideas, but was] at the service of a much loftier goal than giving concep-
> tual form to Christian belief. Its mission was to win the hearts and
> minds of men and women and to change their lives. Christian thinkers
> appealed to a much deeper level of human experience than had the reli-
> gious institutions of society or the doctrines of the philosophers. . . .
> The church gave men and women a new love, Jesus Christ, a person
> who inspired their actions and held their affections. This was a love un-
> like others.[4]

PHILOSOPHY AS *ASKESIS*

This was a love unlike any other, to be sure, and as one continues to
read past the captivating account of Justin's conversion, one quickly dis-
covers that his claim to be a philosopher affirmed not simply a *noetic*
assent to an epistemology, but a holistic way of life better described by
the word *asceticism*.[5] The concept of asceticism is older than Christian-

[4]Robert Louis Wilken, *The Spirit of Early Christian Thought: Seeking the Face of God* (New Haven: Yale University Press, 2003), pp. xiv-xv.
[5]When faced with the question of the limitations of an embodied soul to perceive God, Justin
initially responded in true Platonic fashion: "'Even while it is in the human body,' I replied, 'it
[the soul] can see God by means of the intellect, but especially after it has been released from
the body, and exists of itself, does it perceive God whom it always loved'" (*Dialogue* 4.5).

ity. Among the Greco-Romans, asceticism found philosophical support and fertile ground especially among the Stoics of either Greek or Roman lineage and the Neoplatonists. Plotinus and Porphyry were themselves some of the best-known examples of the *philosophical* way of life that sought after the "life of the spirit" unencumbered by physical attachments. In the opening line of his biography of Plotinus, Porphyry describes his teacher as a model philosopher, not only detached from worldly cares, but in full contempt of his material condition: "Plotinus, the philosopher of our times, seemed ashamed of being in the body."[6] Asceticism was not a foreign concept to the Jewish mind of this time either. On the contrary the solitary life of the Nazirites (e.g., John the Baptist) in the desert or the communal groups of the Essenes in the Judean desert and the Therapeutae in Egypt are well-known examples of long-standing ascetic traditions among the Jewish populations of Roman antiquity. Among the Christians too, Origen (ca. 185-254) used repeatedly the athletic images of *askesis*, which he saw not so much rooted in Plato, I would argue, as in Paul: "Athletes exercise self-control in all things; they do it to receive a perishable garland, but we an imperishable one. So I do not run aimlessly, nor do I box as though beating the air; but I punish my body and enslave it, so that after proclaiming to others I myself should not be disqualified" (1 Cor 9:24-27 NRSV) and the so-called hard sayings of Jesus:

> Then someone came to him and said, "Teacher, what good deed must I do to have eternal life?" And [Jesus] said to him, ". . . If you wish to enter into life, keep the commandments." . . . The young man said to him, "I have kept all these; what do I still lack?" Jesus said to him, "If you wish to be perfect, go, sell your possessions, and give the money to the poor, and you will have treasure in heaven; then come, follow me." When the young man heard this word, he went away grieving, for he had many possessions. Then Jesus said to his disciples, "Truly I tell you, it will be hard for a rich person to enter the kingdom of heaven." (Mt 19:16-23 NRSV)

---

[6]Porphyry, *On the Life of Plotinus and the Order of His Books* 1, in *Plotinus*, trans. A. H. Armstrong, Loeb Classical Library 440 (Cambridge, Mass.: Harvard University Press, 1966), p. 3.

Or, and of much greater consequence in Origen's case, Jesus said to his disciples,

> Not everyone can accept this teaching, but only those to whom it is given. For there are eunuchs who have been so from birth, and there are eunuchs who have been made eunuchs by others, and there are eunuchs who have made themselves eunuchs for the sake of the kingdom of heaven. Let anyone accept this who can. (Mt 19:11-12 NRSV)

Origen was no ordinary Christian. Eusebius tells us that even as a young boy Origen was clearly marked by "divine and heavenly Providence." His brilliant mind and inquisitive spirit were nurtured by his father who trained his firstborn not only in the usual Greek liberal education, but "he drilled him in sacred studies" as well, requiring him "to learn and recite every day Divine Scriptures from childhood."[7] Origen's "youthful wisdom and his genuine love for piety," as Eusebius calls it, was first exhibited during the local but fierce persecution of 202 in his city of Alexandria. Upon learning of his father's arrest and impending martyrdom, Origen wished to rush to his side and share in his father's fate. Though prevented by his mother from doing so, the seventeen-year-old was led by "a zeal beyond his age" that would not suffer to simply stay home but sent to his father "an encouraging letter on martyrdom, in which he exhorted him, saying, 'Take heed not to change your mind on our account.'"[8] Well educated in the divine Scriptures and Greek literature, Origen was best fitted to take over the catechetical school of Alexandria that was headless during this time of turmoil—which he did, at the age of eighteen. But Origen's piety and devotion to divine Providence was not limited to his erudition. Eusebius is eager to emphasize that Origen also exhibited abundant evidence of a genuine philosophic and ascetic life, proof of his inner qualities of purity and divine grace:

> For they say that his manner of life was as his doctrine, and his doctrine as his life. . . . For many years he lived philosophically in this manner,

---

[7]Eusebius *Ecclesiastical History* (hereafter *H.E.*) 6.2.7-8, in *Eusebius, Ecclesiastical History*, trans. J. E. L. Oulton, Loeb Classical Library 265 (Cambridge, Mass.: Harvard University Press, 1932).
[8]Eusebius *H.E.* 6.2.6.

putting away all the incentives of youthful desires. Through the entire day he endured no small amount of discipline; and for the greater part of the night he gave himself to the study of the Divine Scriptures. He restrained himself as much as possible by a most philosophic life, sometimes by the discipline of fasting, again by limited time for sleep. And in his zeal he never lay upon a bed, but upon the ground. Most of all, he thought that the words of the Savior in the Gospel should be observed, in which he exhorts not to have two coats (Mt 10:10) nor to use shoes nor to occupy oneself with cares for the future (Mt 6:34). With zeal beyond his age he continued in cold and nakedness; and, going to the very extreme of poverty, he greatly astonished those about him. And indeed he grieved many of his friends who desired to share their possessions with him, on account of the wearisome toil, which they saw him enduring in the teaching of divine things. But he did not relax his perseverance. He is said to have walked for a number of years never wearing a shoe, and, for a great many years, to have abstained from the use of wine, and of all other things beyond his necessary food, so that he was in danger of breaking down and destroying his constitution.[9]

MARTYRDOM AS IMITATIO CHRISTI *(MIMESIS CHRISTOU)*

Origen was no ordinary Christian indeed. The result of his life and example was that "by the divine Power working with him he aroused a great many to his own zeal."[10] Yet Origen was not alone in his zeal. During these formative centuries for Christian identity and community, this transformative zeal, this "love unlike others," seems to have had only a superficial resemblance to the Greco-Roman mimetic relationship between teachers and pupils. For, unlike their contemporaries, the One whom Christians were called to imitate was Christ himself. Of course, this mimesis was nowhere more clearly manifested than in the examples of the ones who, like Origen, were "deemed worthy of martyrdom." In these first few centuries of Christian history it was martyrdom itself that was the *culmen perfectionis*, the ultimate proof of true spirituality and the seal of true piety on those who had chosen to follow Christ without regard for self or kin.

---

[9]Eusebius *H.E.* 6.3.7-12.
[10]Eusebius *H.E.* 6.3.7.

These "noble athletes of piety," as Eusebius called them,[11] were indeed the paradigmatic Christians who identified with the victory of Christ on the cross and whose struggles and valor bore witness to the power of God and to "trophies won from demons, and victories against unseen adversaries, and the crowns at the end of all."[12] The accounts of the *Martyrs of Vienne and Lyons*, the *History of the Martyrs in Palestine*, *The Passion of Perpetua and Felicitas* and countless others from the Acts of the Martyrs were examples of such divine empowerment and steadfastness in the face of the enemy.[13]

While the primary adversary—or instigator of persecution—was invariably no other than Satan himself (*Historiae Ecclesiasticae* 5.1.5; also 11.1.1), the role of the martyrs was to serve as examples of resistance and steadfastness for the rest of the Christian community.[14] Martyrdom was almost always interpreted in theological terms. It was an anticipation of the *eschaton*, to which the power of the Holy Spirit bore witness through visions and prophetic utterances and the supernatural empowerment of "weaker vessels" such as women and slaves (or better yet, slave women such as Blandina, "the most honorable martyr of Lyons"). It was the second baptism, this one of blood, which brought forgiveness of sins; it was an *anamnesis*, a reenactment of the Eucharist, in which one drank the cup of sufferings of Christ.[15] Against a Gnostic denial of martyrdom, this emphasis on martyrdom "according to the will of God" was an imitation of Christ in which one shared "in the sufferings of Christ and was brought into direct contact with the Lord,

---

[11]Eusebius *H.E.* 5.3. In an analogy that followed the imagery of Eph 6:10-17 the warrior saints were referred to as *miles Christi* or *miles Dei*. Jerome (*Letter 14 to Heliodorus,* in PL 22,348) compares the graces received in baptism to a *donativum*, while Cyprian had written of the *milites Christi* in their *divinis castris* (c.f. PL 4,254). See also John Petruccione, "Prudentius, Portrait of St. Cyprian: An Idealized Biography," in *Revue des Études Augustiniennes* 36 (1990): 225-41.

[12]Eusebius *H.E.* 5.4.

[13]For an excellent essay on the topic see Everett Ferguson, "Early Christian Martyrdom and Civil Disobedience," *Journal of Early Christian Studies* 1, no. 1 (1993): 73-83.

[14]Eusebius *H.E..* 5.1.23 and 27; *M. Apoll.* 47; *M. Fruct.* 7.2; *M. Agap.* 1.2.4; Hermas, *Sim.* 8.3.6; Origen *Mart.* 42; and *C. Cels.* 8.44.

[15]Ignatius *Rom.* 4.1-3, ANF 1:75 "Suffer me to become food for the wild beasts, through whose instrumentality it will be granted me to attain to God. I am the wheat of God, and let me be ground by the teeth of the wild beasts, that I may be found the pure bread of Christ . . . I may be found a sacrifice [to God]."

and the glory of Christ himself was manifested in the martyr."[16]

It would be rather inappropriate, however, to assume that these accounts served to promote martyrdom. On the contrary, almost all writers make it fairly clear that these were quite extraordinary people.[17] They were "steadfast pillars" who attracted the wrath of the persecutors, thus saving the weak (*H.E.* 5.1.6). By their example, the faith of the rest was strengthened (*H.E.* 5.1.35) and their stories became the threads that continued to weave across the centuries and form the interpretive patterns for Christian spirituality: "Yesterday was a martyr's day," exclaimed John Chrysostom in late fourth-century Antioch, "yet today too is a martyr's day. If only we were always celebrating a martyr's day!"[18]

THE HOLY ONES OF GOD: FROM MARTYRS TO MONKS

The era of the martyrs, whose blood is the seed of the church,[19] came to somewhat of an end with Galerius' Edict of Toleration in 311, and Christianity became a legitimate religious option for the empire with the joint declaration (by Constantine and Licinius) known as the Edict of Milan in 313. The changes in Christianity's legal status brought with them massive conversions during the fourth century that were seen as a mixed blessing by many of the faithful. By the end of the century the transformation from a popular but still marginal *superstitio*, as the Romans designated Christianity, to *the* official religion of the empire was completed with another joint edict, issued by Theodosius I and Gratian in February 380, requiring all their subjects to profess "the

---

[16]Ferguson, "Early Christian Martyrdom," p. 75.

[17]The *Martyrdom of Polycarp* (*M. Polyc.*) 4 uses the example of Quintus, a Phrygian, to deter others from voluntary, impulsive martyrdom: "when he saw the wild beasts [he] became afraid. This was the man who forced himself and some others to come forward voluntarily [for trial]. The proconsul, after many entreaties, persuaded [him] to swear and to offer sacrifice. Wherefore, brethren, we do not commend those who give themselves up [to suffering], seeing the Gospel does not teach so to do" (ANF, 1:40). See also, Ps-Cyprian, *laud. mart.* 23; *M. Polyc.* 14; 20; *M. Carp.* 41; 42; *M. Perp.* 21.11; *M. Cyp.* 2.1; *M. Mar.* 2.3; 3.4; *M. hen.* 5.2; Clement of Alexandria, *Stromateis* 4.12; Hippolytus *Dan.* 3.26; Cyprian *mort.* 17.

[18]John Chrysostom, *A Homily On the Holy Martyrs* 1, preached in Antioch (date uncertain: either 386, or 390-91, or 397, in *Let Us Die That We May Live: Greek Homilies on Christian Martyrs from Asia Minor, Palestine, and Syria (C. AD 350-AD 450),* ed. Johan Leemans et al. (London: Routledge, 2003), p. 118.

[19]Tertullian *Apologeticus* 50.13 *(semen est sanguis Christianorum).*

faith of the Bishops of Rome and Alexandria."[20] And in 399, the Western emperor Honorius closed the pagan temples forever. The world had changed, and with it also the church. Mass baptisms and political exigencies meant that not only was the church in the world, but, now more than ever, the world was in the church. Augustine wrote:

> How can the just man be directed, then, except in secret? For now that the Christian name has arrived at the zenith of its glory, the very actions people admired in the first stages of Christianity, when worldly powers crushed the saints beneath persecution, do but serve to foster the growth of hypocrisy and pretense in people who are Christian in name but prefer to please humans rather than God. Amidst the confusion of such hypocrisy, how, I ask, is the just man to be directed except by the God who searches hearts and reins, who looks into our thoughts, here designated by the word "heart" and our pleasures, here called "reins"?[21]

And so, as the era of the martyrs as the archetypes of spirituality and Christian perfection was coming to an end, the era of the monks as examples of Christian perfection was just beginning. Throughout the first three centuries of the Christian era there is abundant evidence of a steady trickle of people out of the urban centers and into the desert in Egypt as well as in Syria and Palestine. People went there for a variety of practical reasons, but mostly they sought security of one kind or another. They included deserters, those who could not cope with the heavy taxation, debtors, rebels, criminals as well as victims of political and religious persecution.[22] From the mid-third to mid-fifth century the trickle became a steady stream. In Egypt, Syria and Palestine, the process known as *anachoresis* ("withdrawal" or "retreat") replaced the old forms of martyrdom. With the end of official persecution, the ideal of *askesis* culminating in literal martyrdom was transferred from the public

---

[20]*Codex Theodosianus* 16.1.2; Sozomen *Ecclesiastical History* 7.4. See Michele R. Salzman, "'Superstitio' in the *Codex Theodosianus* and the Persecution of Pagans," in *Vigiliae Christianae* 41, no. 2 (1987): 172-88.

[21]Augustine *Discourse on Psalm 7*, 9 (on Ps 9:10), in. *St. Augustine on the Psalms*, Ancient Christian Writers series 29, ed. Scholastica Hebgin and Felicitas Corrigan (Westminster, Md.: Newman, 1960), pp. 85-86.

[22]Yizhar Hirschfeld, *The Judean Desert Monasteries in the Byzantine Period* (New Haven: Yale University Press, 1992).

arena to the area of private life. This motivation was quite openly acknowledged and is often mentioned in monastic literature.[23] The new ascetics were not the philosophers like Origen and Justin whose piety was made manifest in the arena, but those who chose to move away from the safety of family and city and do battle in the desert in search for a fuller spirituality and union with God.[24] The adjective *monachos* (meaning "alone") became their name in both Greek and Latin literature; it did not describe *how* they were, but *who* they were: *Monachoi*.

The monks chose voluntarily to go beyond the expected and the ordinary, beyond the precepts, to the extraordinary, and to live their lives in search for God, mortification of the body and imitation of the *abbas* and the *ammas*. They followed the examples of those great and wondrous figures such as the prophets, John the Baptist and Jesus into the deserts of Egypt and the Sinai, Arabia, Syria and Palestine, as far east as Cappadocia and Persia, and as far south as Nubia and the highlands of Ethiopia.[25] There, amid the wild, desolate landscape, they could retreat from the settled world and dedicate themselves to "a radically simplified and poor lifestyle of disciplined work, celibate chastity,

---

[23]The *Acta Martyrorum* were now routinely replaced by hagiographies, biographies of the saints and monks who served as the new examples of Christian spirituality, such as Athanasius' *Life of Anthony*, and collections of anecdotes written by monks, the *Apophthegmata Patrum* or *Saying of the Fathers*, who lived in these areas during the Byzantine period. For the Judean desert see the writings of *Cyril of Scythopolis* (ca. 560; tells the stories of seven monks, spread throughout the prior 150 years [*Euthymius, Sabas, John Hesychast, Cyriac, Theodosius, Theognius and Abramius*]), the collection of stories *John Moschus* (late sixth century), the biography of *Chariton*, (second half of the sixth century), the biographies of *Gerasimus* and of *George of Choziba.*

[24]Which, of course, was in complete and utter opposition to the Greco-Roman concept of perfection and the relationship between the State and the individual, for the human being is a political animal, as Aristotle declared, meant by nature to be in community. The one who chooses to move away from those relationships by design would surely be either a bad person, lawless or above humanity: Aristotle *Politics* 1,1253b.9-13: "Hence it is evident that the state is a creation of nature, and that man is by nature a political animal. And he who by nature and not by mere accident is without a state, is either a bad man or above humanity; he is like the tribeless, lawless, heartless one, whom Homer denounces—the natural outcast is forthwith a lover of war; he may be compared to an isolated piece at draughts. . . . The individual, when isolated, is not self-sufficing. . . . But he who is unable to live in society, or who has no need because he is sufficient for himself, must be either a beast or a god: he is no part of a state. . . . But justice is the bond of men in states, for the administration of justice, which is the determination of what is just, is the principle of order in political society."

[25]From the fourth century on urban monasticism also appeared in the great centers of Rome and Constantinople, and after the fifth century, Western monasticism also increased substantially in Gaul, Italy and Britain.

and study of the sacred writings of the prophets and saints who had preceded them."[26] The monastic and mystical theologies that are the product of this period present a distinctively Christian spirituality that was based, to a large degree, on the Origenist traditions of scriptural exegesis and his theology of purification of the soul and its ascent.[27]

The Threefold Ascent: Praxis, Theoria and Gnosis

The *Apophthegmata partum* or *Saying of the Fathers* and numerous biographies—or rather, hagiographies—preserve for us the treasure of those early monastics and their transformation from ordinary men and women to heroes, now not in the war with the state but, by the power of the Holy Spirit and a life of discipline, in the war with the flesh. Their task was neither the defense of the faith to the interested interlocutor (e.g., Justin's *Dialogue with Trypho*, or Tertullian's *Prescriptions* and Irenaeus's *Against Heresies*), nor an apology to the state that would prevent persecution and bloodshed (e.g., the *Epistle to Diognetus*), but rather a radical discipleship in life's aim for union *(henosis)* with God and deification *(theosis)*.

The descriptions of piety and "life in the Spirit" that permeated the earlier accounts of Christian philosophers like Justin and Origen were now applied to these new examples of Christian spirituality and were reinterpreted as an even more radical *askesis* and a new metaphor for purification and the Way of Life:

> [Antony] fasted continually, his clothing was hair on the inside, while the outside was skin, and this he kept to his dying day. He never bathed his body in water to remove filth, nor did he as much as wash his feet or even allow himself to put them in water without necessity. No one ever saw him undressed, nor did anyone look upon his bare body till he died and was buried.[28]

---

[26]John Anthony McGuckin, *The Book of Mystical Chapters: Meditations on the Soul's Ascent, from the Desert Fathers and Other Early Christian Contemplatives* (Boston: Shambhala, 2003), pp. 4-5.

[27]Regardless of the anti-Origenist sentiments of later monastics such as Jerome and Pachomius who wrote against Origen because of the condemnation of his more provocative theological speculations in, for example, *De Principiis*. Origen's scriptural exegesis continued to be of formative influence in both East and West, and it was his biblical interpretation that prevailed at the end.

[28]Athanasius *The Life of Antony* 47, in *The Life of Antony and the Letter to Marcellinus*, trans. Rob-

Fasting, disregard for the body and for material comforts, unceasing prayer and solitary meditation marked these new "battles of the faith" (*Life* 47). Asceticism was not simply an escape. It was the soul's thirst for repair amidst the world's inarticulate woe, a search tempered by the language and imagery of "battle," unceasing battle with the demonic forces and, therefore, unceasing watchfulness for the adversary. Those who left the early communal dwellings to venture deeper into the desert were most often seen as God's new "holy ones." In the writing of their contemporaries (even highly educated and sophisticated writers like Theodoret or Suplicius Severus) we find lives of extraordinary obedience through whom God was made manifest. "To them it was not incredible that God worked miracles again for those who put their whole selves in his hands, as he had in biblical times, and it was certainly regarded as virtuous to believe it."[29]

And much of the spiritual direction and understanding of the Christian life in both East and West has followed their example for centuries. Evagrius of Pontus (345-399), for example, identified the eight *logismoi*, evil or obsessive thoughts as he called them in his *Antirrhetikos*. Unlike normal thoughts, these obsessive thoughts are fostered by demons and attack Christians on the spiritual journey, in general, and monks, in particular, and destroy one's inner calm: gluttony, sexual indulgence (lust), love of money (avarice), sadness, anger, acedia, vainglory and arrogance (pride). These eight also became the basis of Latin spirituality through John Cassian and were later rearticulated by Gregory the Great into the well-known "seven deadly sins." The monastics must undertake the ascetical practices of obedience and mortification of the body by which they are strengthened in virtue in their fight against the demons. Through practical obedience, the hermits root out weaknesses, ridding themselves of these *logismoi*.

Yet, practical obedience was only the first step in this long journey to deification. In the monastic traditions, at least in the Greek East, there is a strong emphasis on human freedom in the work of salvation.

---

ert C. Gregg, Classics of Western Spirituality (New York: Paulist, 1980), pp. 66-67.
[29]Stuart G. Hall, *Doctrine and Practice in the Early Church* (Grand Rapids: Eerdmans, 1992), p. 178.

This is how St. John Chrysostom put it: "We must first select good, and then God adds what appertains to His office; He does not act antecedently to our will, so as not to destroy our liberty."[30] This co-operative relationship between human and divine wills, however, is not a union of equals. Chrysostom again: "You do not hold of yourself, but you have received from God. Hence you have received what you possess, and not only this or that, but everything you have. For these are not your own merits, but the grace of God. Although you cite faith, you owe it nevertheless to His calling."[31] This *synergeia* between the human and divine wills (and not our intellectual assent or psychological satisfaction) undergirds the process by which our human will is surrendered and conformed to the will of God. This is the chief means of union with God.[32] A monk of the Eastern church suggests, "both the distinction between the human will and divine grace and their interpenetration [the *perichoretic* relationship] help us understand how, in the spiritual life, the ascetical and mystical elements can differ and mingle."[33] Christian spirituality, therefore, is based on God's action on the soul and is a synthesis of the "ascetical" and the "mystical," where, unlike modern psychological interpretations or poetic uses of language, the former denotes the life of discipline and personal virtue, while the latter concentrates on the gifts of the Holy Spirit. The threefold movement towards deification from *praxis*, to *theoria*, to *gnosis* is the culmination of this synthesis.

Even from the early fourth century the attempt was made very early to distinguish ascending stages in the spiritual life. In the West they have been divided into purgative, illuminative and unitive. In the East, Evagrius's description of Christian spirituality in the *Praktikos* and

---

[30]John Chrysostom *Homily 12* on *Hebrews*. See also George Kalantzis, "'The Voice so Dear to Me': The Epistle to the Romans in the Antiochene Tradition," in *Reading Romans with the Greek Fathers*, ed. Kathy Ehrensperger and R. Ward Holder, Romans Through History and Cultures, vol. 8 (New York: T & T Clark, 2009).

[31]John Chrysostom *Homily 12* on *1 Cor*. Adapted from Nicene and Post-Nicene Fathers (NPNF) First Series, vol. 12, ed. Philip Schaff (Buffalo, N.Y.: Christian Literature, 1889). Revised and edited for New Advent by Kevin Knight <www.newadvent.org/fathers/220101.htm>.

[32]See Moine de l'Eglise d'Orient, *Orthodox Spirituality: An Outline of the Orthodox Ascetical and Mystical Tradition* (Crestwood, N.Y.: St. Vladimir's Seminary Press, 1978), pp. 23-40.

[33]Ibid., p. 25.

Chapters on Prayer has been most influential. The initial stage of practical obedience, the *praktike*, is the stage of spiritual *askesis* during which the initiate, or *eisagogikos*, is mainly concerned with the practice of virtue *(praxis)* which leads to control of the passions of the soul and true awareness of the nature of the world.

Led by *pure* prayer, which Evagrius calls "the continual intercourse of the spirit with God," the monk's progress in the practical life will lead to *apatheia*, "passionlessness," that can only be achieved by freedom even from mental representations that are associated with passionate attachments.[34] In this middle stage *(mesos)* the ascetic reaches a "state of deep peace and inexpressible joy," which enables one to engage in right prayer, the prayer of contemplation, seized by true love and understanding of the world *(theoria)*. Not synonymous with high intellectual speculation or insight, this contemplation is simultaneously acquired and infused: acquired by personal effort and infused by divine grace apart from human effort. But most of all, it is contemplation that springs from the depths of simplicity.

Beyond his middle stage of contemplation lies the last stage of the perfection, the *teleiotes*, which cannot be achieved in this life but is the true experimental knowledge *(gnosis)* of God himself *(theologia)*. For Gregory of Nyssa this was a dramatic shift from "profane philosophy" of Plato and his intellectual ascent to the *Ideas*, who like the childless and barren daughter of Pharaoh is always in labor but never gives birth, to Scripture, the natural mother and giver of life.[35]

"WHOSE FEET ARE YOU WASHING?": CHARITY AND THE SOLITARY LIFE

Stuart Hall insists, "the learning of Evagrius and those like him did not appeal to those who made ignorance and simplicity a virtue."[36] The sanctified optimism of monastic literature, however, was tempered by

---

[34]Evagrius *Prayer* 3, in Robert Edward Sinkewicz, *Evagrius of Pontus: The Greek Ascetic Corpus* (New York: Oxford University Press, 2006), pp. 192-209. Later, it would be Cassian's biblical virtue of *agnotes*, "purity of heart," that superseded the Stoic term *apatheia* in spiritual literature.

[35]Gregory of Nyssa *The Life of Moses* 2.10-11, HarperCollins Spiritual Classics (San Francisco: HarperSanFrancisco, 2006), p. 34.

[36]Hall, *Doctrine*, p. 177.

the real life circumstances of ascetic communities throughout the Christian world. As one moves past the literary embodiment of the various *Lives* and *Sayings* with increased awareness of the complexity of both sources and their origin, one becomes all the more aware that the diverse ascetic paths of late antiquity cross much more often than previously thought. Ecclesiastical strife and party politics seem to have replaced all too often the *hesychastic* (i.e., quiet meditation) life of the monks and their search for spiritual purity.

As evidenced by the Meletian controversy in Egypt, for example, and the Athanasian appeal to the monks both for political as well as theological (even ideological) cover, the new *militia Christi* was called upon to defend bishops and creeds without hesitation. Such stories of loyalty and orthodoxy were preserved in the *Life of Antony* and the *Vita Prima* (a precursor to the Greek *Life of Pachomius*), as well as in many of the *Sayings*. But as Jerome discovered in Palestine and Basil in Cappadocia, not all monastic communities were on the path to transformative union with God. For some, their anchoritic status and way of life was becoming an excuse for pride and self-centeredness: "I blush to say it," wrote Jerome, "but from the caves which serve us for cells we monks of the desert condemn the world. Rolling in sackcloth and ashes, we pass sentence on bishops. What use is the robe of a penitent if it covers the pride of a king? Chains, squalor, and long hair are by right tokens of sorrow, and not ensigns of royalty" (*Ep.* 17.2).[37]

In Cappadocia Basil was fighting the twin fight to Jerome's. While deeply supportive of the monastic quest for contemplation and a measured solitude, Basil became sharply critical of the anchoritic (or hermetic) life, which he saw as deeply individualistic and a distortion of the Christian message. In the *Long Rule*, the most famous section of the *Asketikon* (his collection of treatises on monasticism) Basil roots his vision of the monastic life and practice in the Scriptures and articulates a coherent monastic spirituality based on the example of Christ. He warns against the danger of self-pleasing in the anchoritic life and calls

---

[37]Ibid., p. 178.

for the monks to be God's hands and feet in the world:

> There are other dangers in the solitary life besides those we have already described. The first and greatest danger is that of [self-pleasing]. For if a man has no one to examine his actions, he will think that he has already achieved the perfect fulfillment of the commandments, and, since his conduct is never tested, he neither notices his shortcomings, nor perceives any progress which he may have made, for the very reason that he has deprived himself of all opportunity for fulfilling the commandments.
>
> For how will he practice the virtue of *humility* if there is no one to whom he may show himself humble? How will he show *pity* if he is cut off from the society of others? Or how will he show *forbearance* if there is no one to oppose his wishes? But if some one says that instruction in the Holy Scriptures is sufficient for right conduct, he is like one who learns how to weave, but never weaves anything, or is taught the smith's art, but never deigns to put into practice what he has learnt. To such a man the Apostle would say, *"Not the hearers of the law are just before God, but the doers of the law shall be justified"* [Rom 2:13]. For we see that our Lord Himself, from his exceeding great kindness, did not rest content with words or precepts, but expressly set before us an example of humility in the perfection of His love. For indeed *He girded Himself and washed His disciples feet* [Jn 13:5]. *Whose feet will you wash? To whom will you be a servant? Among whom will you be the last of all, if you live alone by yourself?* How can that *good and joyful thing, the dwelling together of the brethren,* which is likened by the Holy Spirit to the precious *ointment that ran down from the high-priest's head* [Ps 132:1-2], be accomplished in the life of the solitary?
>
> The dwelling together of the brethren [Ps 132:1] is indeed a field for the contest of athletes, a noble path of progress, a continual training, and a constant meditation upon the commandments of the Lord. It has for its one aim and end the glory of God, according to the commandment of our Lord Jesus Christ, who says, *"Let your light so shine before men that they may see your good works, and glorify your Father which is in heaven"* [Mt 5:16].[38]

---

[38]Basil, *Regula Fusius Tractatae* 7:34-36 [emphasis added]. The critical edition of the *Long Rule* is found in Anna Silvas, *The Asketikon of St Basil the Great*, Oxford Early Christian Studies (Oxford: Oxford University Press, 2005). Here I am using the translation by E. F. Morison, *St. Basil and His Rule: A Study in Early Monasticism* (London: H. Frowde, 1912), pp. 43-44, because I find that his translation presents Basil's passionate plea in a richer language.

Basil was no mere theorist. He was a priest and bishop at work. Basil used his great skills and resources as administrator to change the cities in his ecclesiastical jurisdiction. Orthodoxy was not his only concern. Through his *Rules* he led the monks in this choreography of communal practices in which the life of prayer was animated by their care for the poor. Basil was deeply interested in "practical religion, in developing a sense of social responsibility among Christians."[39] In the funeral oration commemorating Basil's life, his friend and colleague Gregory of Nazianzus tells us how he "united the solitary and the community life" by founding cells for ascetics that were connected to one another and in such proximity to the cenobitic communities that the "contemplative spirit might not be cut off from society" but instead work together for the glory of God.[40] In Caesarea Basil encouraged care for the poor and needy, as evidenced by the Basileiados, a range of buildings for the care of the sick and for the distribution of surplus food to those in need. He established hospitals for the poor and hospices for Christian pilgrims, as well as a series of what would be called urban monasteries, whose task was to provide charity throughout the city. It was Basil and his monks who spearheaded a large-scale relief effort in Cappadocia in the aftermath of the famine of 369.

Basil insisted that absence of generosity is a major sin. He believed that the chief and visible social sign of Christian conversion, life and perfection would be economic in form, not just spiritual. For Basil, salvation might have been personal (or, "within the confines of one's soul"), but it was never an individual experience. Basil taught his monks that the *culmen perfectionis*, the utmost manifestation of true Christian spirituality, is none other than the *culmen caritatis*, the utmost exercise of charity. No one was exempt, not even the monks.

CONCLUSION

In this chapter we have followed the development of the concept of spirituality and the practices of *anagoge* from its Greco-Roman prede-

---

[39]Philip Rousseau, *Basil of Caesarea* (Los Angeles: University of California Press, 1994), p. 136.
[40]Gregory of Nazianzus *Oratio* 43.62 (SC 384:260; trans. NPNF 7:415-16).

cessors to the Christian monastics—the movement from philosophy to martyrdom to self-imposed spiritual martyrdom in imitation of Christ, and from the private to the public arena, albeit in the desert cells and mountaintops. Yet, it seems that what St. Basil identified as a danger lurking behind some of the practices of late antiquity, namely the dangers of isolationism, individualism and self-pleasing, still remain. The temptation of our own time seems to be the same, a spirituality focused on the self as its ultimate *telos*. In the struggle for "spiritual discipline" and "perfection," the need to be with the "other" remains paramount. As the ancient rules and catechisms taught, the true virtue of humility is not found in isolationism or abandonment of the self, regardless of whether the such is cloaked in language and practices of piety and self-imposed martyrdom, but, as Basil and Pachomius taught us almost from the beginning, in the language and praxis of love. For, unlike Aristotle's magnanimous man who seeks to outshine others in virtue, the Christian lives by *caritas*, God's charity towards us; and having thus been a recipient of God's *caritas* that stems from the cross, the Christian naturally now turns to the neighbor in love.

5   The Way and the Ways

Reflections on Catholic Spirituality

LAWRENCE S. CUNNINGHAM

INTRODUCTION

There is something almost intractable about pinning down exactly what the word *spirituality* means.[1] Getting the term right is made all the more difficult because it is, in common discourse, bandied about in such a promiscuous fashion and without much in the way of precision. It is also the case that many today use the term in a rather flaccid way to mean something vaguely uplifting as opposed to the alleged rigidity of institutional religion; that is the way in which the cliché (and it is a cliché), "I am spiritual but not religious" is usually taken. It is not my purpose here to ponder that phrase and what is behind it although I have unburdened myself on the topic on other occasions.[2]

Nonetheless, within Christian circles in general and Catholic circles in particular there has been intense resurgence of interest in spirituality as a way of fleshing out traditional academic theology into a closer relationship with the lived experience of the Christian life. That interest can be summarized as a desire to mend the breach between theology

---

[1]Still useful is the essay by Walter Principe, "Towards Defining Spirituality," *Studies in Religion/Sciences Religieuses* 12 (1983): 127-41. For further considerations of definitions, methodologies, etc., see *Minding the Spirit: The Study of Christian Spirituality*, ed. Elizabeth A. Dwyer and Mark S. Burrows (Baltimore: Johns Hopkins University Press, 2005).

[2]Lawrence S. Cunningham, "Spirituality and Religion: Some Reflections," in *Business, Religion, and Spirituality: A New Synthesis* (Notre Dame, Ind.: University of Notre Dame Press, 2003), pp. 168-83. For a book length treatment, see Robert C. Fuller, *Spiritual but Not Religious* (New York: Oxford University Press, 2001).

and spirituality traditionally understood. Healing the breach between theology, understood as formal seminary or university intellectual education, and the lived experience of Christians has been keenly discussed by Roman Catholic theologians of such stature as Hans Urs von Balthasar and Karl Rahner in their attempt, differently articulated, to bring together into some kind of whole vision the way theology was once understood, for example, in both the patristic period and in the monastic theology that reigned before the rise of scholastic theology in the high Middle Ages. It is tempting to sketch out that separation but time does not permit; let me satisfy myself simply by saying that in the twentieth century there has been an ongoing project to mend the historical rift.[3]

I will simply stipulate here that the traditional Catholic understanding of spirituality roots itself in the famous contrast that Paul makes in Romans 8 between those who live "in the Spirit" and those who live "in the flesh." It is worthwhile to note that Paul contrasts *Spirit* and *flesh*, not Spirit and body; Paul was no Manichean. To live the Christian life is to live under the impulse of the Spirit, which converts us to the way of Christ. Every conversion, of course, implies an aversion, which is why the turning to Christ, of necessity, means that one is also turning away from something else; that something else is, in Pauline language, the flesh. The later Christian tradition uses various titles for those who live in the Spirit and one of the most common of these is the Greek term *pneumatikos*—a person of Spirit. In the West, Augustine of Hippo, to cite a conspicuous example, will refer frequently to those who, in his estimation, have read and lived the Scriptures faithfully as the "spiritual men" *(viri spirituales)* or verbal equivalents with obvious reference to the language of Romans 8.

In the Catholic tradition the way of the Spirit is sometimes called the way of holiness. Scripture teaches us that holiness is almost a synonym for God—God alone is holy (which is to say, totally other) and everything else and everyone else is holy only to the degree that there is a nexus to God. Holy persons, places, times, objects, communities, etc.,

---

[3]The nexus between theology and spirituality has been neatly summarized by Mark McIntosh in *Mystical Theology* (Oxford: Blackwell, 1998), pp. 1-38.

get their denomination only in reference to God. In that sense being spiritual is another way of saying being holy.[4] Holiness and spirituality are thus intimately connected, if not synonymous.

To undertake the way of holiness in the Spirit may also be understood as following the way of Jesus who has said, "I am the Way." It will be a fundamental notion in this chapter that while Jesus is "the Way" there are many ways to follow Jesus; that discipleship is the Way, but the ways of discipleship are various. It is worth noting, in passing, that the term *disciple* and its cognates occur over 150 times in the New Testament and in almost eighty of those places the term is linked with some form of the verb "to follow."

The Way and the Ways

The eminent Peruvian theologian Gustavo Gutiérrez has pointed out that the earliest name for the Christians was, according to Acts, "followers of the Way." In fact, the Greek *hodos* often appears in the New Testament as a quasi-technical term to mean the way of Jesus.[5] Some of you may be familiar with the ancient icon of the Blessed Virgin who holds Christ in her left arm while with her right, she points to Jesus; that icon is what is known in the Christian East as the *hodoteria*—"She who points the Way." It is a powerful shorthand way of making Gutiérrez's larger point.

"The Way" is a useful concept in that it means that while we are on this earth we are on a way that will have a finality, beatitude. It also means that we have not yet arrived so that our Christian life has a decidedly eschatological character to it. To be a Christian is to undertake a way of life and that way of life points to an end.

The notion of choosing the correct way has a very ancient pedigree. Already in the Old Testament we find examples of a sharp contrast between the way of Torah in Deuteronomy (30:15-20) as a

---

[4]Lawrence S. Cunningham, "Holiness," in *The New Dictionary of Catholic Spirituality*, ed. Michael Downey (Collegeville, Minn.: Glazier/Liturgical, 1993), pp. 479-87. For a comprehensive view of this theme, see *Holiness: Past and Present,* ed. Stephen C. Barton (London: T & T Clark, 2003).

[5]I borrow here from Gutiérrez's *We Drink from Our Own Wells* (Maryknoll, N.Y.: Orbis, 1983), which makes this argument at length.

way of life and the way of death; in the wisdom psalm which opens
the psalter (Ps 1) the way of the just is contrasted to the way of the
evildoer; one finds the same notion in the prophet Jeremiah (21:1;
21:8) as well as the theme of the "way of the Just" described in Proverbs 4:18. Interestingly enough, the prologue to the *Didache*, an ancient Christian text from circa A.D. 100, opens with a prologue that
may be an ancient baptismal homily describing the "Way of Life"
and the "Way of Death" between which, the text says, is a "vast gulf."
It is worth noting that the "Way of Life" and the "Way of Death" in
the *Didache* actually amount to a catena of biblical texts or close
paraphrases.[6] St. Augustine, in one of his Christmas sermons, puts
that matter charmingly in commenting on the donkey of Isaiah mentioned in the Christmas gospel: "Be in attendance at the manger; do
not be ashamed of being the Lord's donkey. You will be carrying
Christ; you will not go astray walking along the way because the
Way is sitting on you."[7]

This concept of the Way then will be the template that I will use in
this paper to argue that, fundamentally, Catholic spirituality is the way
of Christ to the Father under the guiding impulse of the Holy Spirit.
Catholic spirituality is, at its most fundamental, a trinitarian enterprise. It is in that context that I argue there is one Way but many ways
of following the Way. And, further, that "following" is best described
in trinitarian terms. My assumption, further, is that authentic Christian spirituality is foundationally trinitarian; all of our liturgical prayers
are "To the Father, through the Son, in the Holy Spirit" and that for-
mula is as good as any to describe the Christian life simply. It is why we
Catholics almost always open our prayers with the sign of the cross: "In
the name of the Father, and of the Son and of the Holy Spirit."

THE MANY WAYS

What the Catholic spiritual tradition, when viewed broadly, shows is
that over the centuries individuals or small communities got a certain

---

[6]The exhaustive commentary in the Hermeneia Series, *Didache*, ed. Kurt Niederwimmer (Minneapolis: Fortress, 1998) dates this text from ca. A.D. 100-110.
[7]Sermon #189.4.

insight into the gospel that led them to adopt a certain way of living, which they saw as a particular following of Christ. If that way of living seemed possible and desirable it became a way of living within the larger church community. It may not have been everyone's way but it was accepted as one possible way among many. If that way persisted over time it became known as a school of spirituality.

We should linger a moment over the word *school* since that word had its own significance in late antiquity. As Pierre Hadot has brilliantly shown, the ancient world saw the pursuit of philosophy not as an academic study but as the adoption of a way of life that often involved a certain manner of dress, a certain practice of asceticism and a single-minded pursuit of wisdom.[8] Hadot ends his study by noting that late antique Christianity took over this concept and adopted a way of life, which became the love of that true wisdom *(philosophia)* who is Jesus Christ—the Logos. Thus it was not uncommon for the Cappadocians to describe their lives of biblical study, retirement from the world, ascetic practice, ministerial practice and so on as the true philosophy.

The Cappadocians exalted, then, a certain way of life that was one form of what we would begin to call *monasticism.* Monasticism itself took on various modalities but it is a very ancient way of life that over the centuries more or less crystallized into an Eastern Christian form and a Western one with the latter best exemplified by the Rule of Benedict.[9] It is well beyond the scope of this paper to outline the evolution of monasticism but I single it out as one way within Catholicism that has a definite shape and a character clear enough to be known as a "school of spirituality" within the Catholic tradition. The persistence of monasticism in the Catholic and Orthodox world is a testimony to both its attractive character and, indirectly, to its value as one way to follow the Way.[10]

---

[8]Pierre Hadot, *Philosophy as a Way of Life* (Oxford: Blackwell, 1996).

[9]The literature on monasticism is staggering. For an excellent survey relative to its beginnings, see William Harmless, *Desert Christians: An Introduction to the Literature of Early Monasticism* (New York: Oxford University Press, 2004).

[10]The most successful attempt to integrate the monastic tradition into evangelical Protestantism is, of course, the Taizé community. For a sympathetic account by a Protestant, see Jason Brian Santos, *A Community Called Taizé* (Downers Grove, Ill.: InterVarsity Press, 2008).

Schools of Spirituality

I have used the term "schools of spirituality" to indicate ways of living the Christian life within the Catholic tradition. I have further indicated that one of those schools is the monastic one. There are, of course, many others like the Franciscan school or the Ignatian or the Salesian. At this point, however, it would be helpful to indicate the generic characteristics of schools of spirituality more specifically. Apart from their longevity within the tradition, there are four salient characteristics that deserve a bit of comment.

A canon within the canon of Scripture. What occurs in the history of the tradition is that a charismatic leader or a small group of serious persons sees in the Scriptures a clue or an indication of how to follow Christ in a better way. Such a group might attempt to enflesh their insights into a way of living. For St. Francis of Assisi and his followers it was the cluster of texts in the Synoptic Gospels where Jesus told his disciples to give up all worldly goods to follow him in providential poverty in order to preach the good news to the poor. For the early monks it was the picture of the primitive church holding all things in common as described in the early chapters of Acts. For the modern lay movement known as the Catholic Workers it was the great eschatological sermon of Jesus in Matthew 25 where he tells his disciples that those who will be saved are those who see him in the poor, the hungry, the naked and so on.

These core texts and the response to them do not neglect the rest of the biblical canon but they privilege certain scriptural imperatives as a kind of shaping ideal that guide the way they live as persons of the Spirit. Those texts become, for them, what Hans Urs von Balthasar once felicitously called *ganze im fragment*—everything in a little.

The accumulation of a tradition. The community, which embarks on this perceived way of life, soon develops a tradition both oral and written. Rules of life begin to emerge; foundational stories begin to be told; theological and devotional literature expanding on the way of life come into being; small forms of legislation or casuistry accumulate as the followers attempt to discern what is compatible or incompatible with their chosen way of being; holy exemplars of the tradition are remembered in biographies and so on that serve to model the tradition.

The accumulated tradition of a given school serves as a resource for keeping the school faithful to its original inspiration and further serves as a "memory bank" so that the school can retrieve the roots of its original impulse. It is a mark of a living school that it has the energy to look back (in a process known by the French word *ressourcement* from the old Latin cry *ad fontes*—back to the sources!) to reform itself. Let me give one example to make this point. Most of you have heard of Trappist monks. The word *trappist* derives from a seventeenth-century abbey in France called La Trappe that tried to get back to its old Cistercian roots. The Cistercians, in turn, were a reform of the Benedictines in the twelfth century while the Benedictines, rooted in the Rule of Saint Benedict, were a restatement of older monastic models (Benedict says so explicitly in his *Rule*) going back to the fourth century. Not to put too fine a point on it: Trappists are a seventeenth-century reform of a twelfth-century reform of a sixth-century reform of a Rule whose roots go back to the fourth century. Incidentally, contemporary Trappists have been engaged in a reform of their own practices for the better part of the last fifty years.[11]

A pedagogy of prayer. While all members of all schools of spirituality are devoted to the life of prayer, each has its own way of prayer and, more importantly, each has a pedagogy of prayer.[12] Monastic prayer is not the same as Ignatian prayer just as Carmelite contemplative prayer is not the same as Franciscan prayer. All schools are shaped by the public worship of the church but each has its own particular take on how to develop the life of prayer. Monks have traditionally prayed the psalms in community while encouraging members to pray privately by an intense rumination over Scripture. The Ignatian tradition, by contrast, has, at its core, the making of the Spiritual Exercises of Saint Ignatius of Loyola which focuses on a close prayerful consideration of the life of

---

[11]Kees Waaijman's *Spirituality: Forms, Foundations, Methods* (Leuven: Peeters, 2002), pp. 116-210, has the most comprehensive study of schools of spirituality of which I am aware, although I am not in total agreement with all of its judgments.

[12]The literature on prayer is enormous. For a useful survey, see Michael Casey, *Towards God: The Ancient Wisdom of Western Prayer* (Liguori, Mo.: Triumph, 1996). Casey has as his main focus the patristic and medieval masters on prayer.

Jesus in order to help the practitioner make an election for the greater glory of God.[13]

Now, it is the case that the Catholic spiritual tradition has given pride of place to those who follow one or other of the classical schools of spirituality by dedicating their lives to the monastic way or being trained in the Jesuit or Franciscan or Dominican schools of spirituality. Everyone in the Catholic Church, obviously, does not join such schools in the sense of actually joining a given religious community, but there has always been a tradition of the schools influencing ordinary Catholics' lives by the "spillover" effect of the learned traditions of the schools. Those effects take many and various forms. Many Catholics make "retreats" by setting aside time for a day or days of spiritual reflection, a practice deriving directly from the practices of the Jesuits. Many read the biblical text as a form of prayer according to the ways set down by the monastic tradition that encourages this practice, best known under its traditional name of *lectio divina* ("sacred reading"), while still others practice such popular devotional exercises as the recitation of the rosary (encouraged by the Dominicans) or making the "Stations of the Cross" (preached by the Franciscans) or pursuing the quiet of contemplative prayer (fostered by the Carmelites).

Now if all of those various practices (I have mentioned only a fraction of them) are ancillary to the core practice of Catholics, which describe the essence of being a Catholic? What is at the core of Catholic spiritual practice? What is a generic "way of life" that can be called Catholic? I will satisfy myself with mentioning the triad enumerated by Pope Benedict XVI at the end of his first encyclical titled *God Is Love* (Latin: *Deus Caritas Est*).[14] Toward the conclusion of that letter Benedict enumerates three core principles of the church and, by extension, three fundamental duties of each Catholic: (1) Proclaiming the Word of God and giving witness to it; (2) full celebration of, and participation in, the sacramental and liturgical life of the church and (3) exercising

---

[13]I have explored the notion of "schools of spirituality" further in my book *Roman Catholicism* (Cambridge: Cambridge University Press, 2009), chap. 7.

[14]There are many editions; I have followed the text in *God Is Love* (San Francisco: Ignatius, 2006). The encyclical itself was dated Christmas Day, 2005.

the ministry of charity.[15] The spiritually motivated Catholic is called upon to live out the power of the gospel and give witness to it; to worship God by full participation in the public worship of the church; and to extend that love that Jesus demands of his followers. It is Benedict's understanding that these three tasks are not discrete but symbiotic. Again, these three functions are not to be conceived of as acts of the will but the fruits of God's grace by which we are prompted by the Holy Spirit to accept and show forth God's revelation in Christ; to worship in the name of the Holy Trinity;[16] and to be obedient to the second great commandment of love of neighbor—a demand that can only be done under the power of grace.

The conversion of life. Finally, it should be emphasized that all schools of spirituality have as their primary aim not the acquisition of knowledge, but conversion of life. Catholics understand conversion as an ongoing process in which the followers of Christ, in the Spirit, conform themselves more closely to the person of Christ. The various schools may understand this conversion process in a particular fashion or by using a precise language peculiar to that school, but all schools have in mind cooperation with the grace freely given by God in the following of Christ. The Ignatian tradition may privilege "election" in following the will of God while the Franciscan may encourage imitating the poor Christ, etc., but all orient themselves to conversion more intimately to Christ.

SOME PARTICULARS OF THE CATHOLIC SPIRITUAL TRADITION

Asceticism. While the Greek term *askesis* meant something like athletic training, asceticism in religious terms may be defined as the "voluntary, sustained, and, at least, partially, systematic program of self-discipline and self-denial in which immediate, sensual or profane gratifications are renounced in order to attain a higher spiritual state or a more thorough absorption into the sacred."[17] All the great religious traditions

---

[15]Benedict XVI, *Deus Caritas Est,* II.25a—the pope uses ancient Greek terms to describe this triad: (1) *kerygma-martyria* and (2) *leitourgia* and (3) *diakonia.*

[16]The well-known Catholic practice of the "sign of the cross" is a gestural act of faith both in the saving power of the cross and the trinitarian character of God.

[17]W. Klaeber, "Asceticism" in *The Encyclopedia of Religion,* ed. Mircea Eliade (New York: Macmillan, 1987), 1:441-45. For more particular studies, see *Asceticism,* ed. Vincent L. Wimbush

have some forms of asceticism but the classic ones as described in Matthew 5–7 are fasting, almsgiving and prayer. Those classical practices, of course, are part of the ordinary Catholic repertoire of practice.

What the various strands of the Catholic spiritual tradition have done is to enhance the basic gospel demands into various forms of the ascetical life: voluntary celibacy or the virginal life; giving up of individual possessions by taking up the life of poverty; strategies for living a life of constant prayer and so on. These enhancements have taken on concrete form in the so-called Evangelical Counsels of poverty, chastity and obedience, which are at the core of the various religious orders and communities within the Catholic tradition.

In the long tradition of Catholic spirituality there has also been an "institutionalization" of the practice(s) of almsgiving from the simple functions of the office of deacon, whose task it was to provide from the common purse. We know that in the same century as the Constantinian peace there were already formal institutions for the care of the elderly, the sick, the traveler, the orphan, the leper and abandoned children. In the course of time these caregiving places were, depending on place, under the care of lay confraternities or religious communities of men or women whose purpose was directly oriented towards a specific task. It is worthwhile to take note of this long history if only to remember that many of the present-day institutions have behind them a long history going back as far as the patristic period. Such impulses are structured around given communities even today; thus the lay group known as the Catholic Workers dates back to the late 1930s while the Missionaries of Charity, founded by the late Mother Teresa of Calcutta, is a religious community founded in 1950 with a special vow to serve "the poorest of the poor."[18] Thus, the various religious communities combine in their lives an ascetic spirit of almsgiving with a commitment to fulfilling the evangelical counsels of poverty, chastity and obedience.[19] Most of the religious communities of women present in

and Richard Valantasis (New York: Oxford University Press, 1995).

[18] A community of brothers was subsequently established as well as a contemplative branch dedicated to prayer.

[19] Obviously, not all lay people live a celibate life; they are enjoined to practice chastity according to their "state in life."

this country, for example, were founded to carry out one or other of the standard forms of almsgiving, as that notion is broadly understood.

The mystical tradition. It was earlier observed that every school of spirituality developed a pedagogy of prayer. Over the course of the centuries that pedagogical interest brought with it an enormous literature, some of it highly technical, on the theology of prayer as well as books on the "methods" of prayer and guides for the life of prayer. Conspicuous among such works were those that discussed mystical prayer.

The terms *mystic* and *mysticism* are modern words unknown to the ancient church, but it did know the term *mystical theology*. First coined by the fifth-century Syrian monk known as the Pseudo Dionysius, *mystical theology* simply meant the "hidden discourse about/to God." Dionysius meant his eponymous treatise to be read as a counterpoint to his other work, known as *The Names of God*.[20] Dionysius says that there are some words culled from Scripture by which we name God (Father, etc.) but such naming does not exhaust or even approach what and who God is. God is inexpressible mystery[21]—a "hidden God." Using a trope rooted in the Sinai experience of Moses, Dionysius, borrowing his idea from Gregory of Nyssa's *Life of Moses*, argues that in the silence of prayer, when words are no longer sufficient to describe the reality of God, we fall into a hidden silence simply being in the presence of God.

Dionysius was translated into Latin in the early Middle Ages and his work had a profound influence on the later tradition of Catholic spirituality (as it did, following a different trajectory, in the Christian East) that can be traced from many contemplative writers—the Carthusians as well as other strands of Catholic contemplative practice. Perhaps the best-known theoretician of mystical theology was the sixteenth-century Carmelite, Saint John of the Cross. The fifteenth-century polymath writer Jean Gerson (died 1429) surveyed all of the writings he could find on this subject and then developed his massive two-volume *De Theologia Mystica*, in which he defined this kind of prayerful experience as "an experiential knowledge of God that comes

---

[20]His complete works may be found in *Pseudo-Dionysius: The Complete Works*, ed. Colm Luibhead (New York: Paulist, 1987).

[21]*Mystery* and *mystical* derive from the same Greek root.

through the embrace of unitive love."[22] By "experiential knowledge" Jean Gerson made the assumption that love itself as a form of knowing (the old Latin tag for this going back to Pope Gregory the Great is *amor ipse notitia est*) so that the deepest form of prayer was that which emerged from the love of God and not merely fear of God. Tacit in this understanding was the conviction that one had already converted from a life of sin and, further, that God drew the person closer to God's self through a free gift (grace) from God. It was further assumed that such experiences were, as it were, a small anticipation of the beatific vision of God enjoyed by those who were in heaven. Although it was wrongly assumed that such prayer is for the elite few, it is in fact the common teaching of Catholic theologians that such prayer is open to all who are predisposed to answer God's call to a closer union with him in Christ through the Spirit.

RECOVERING SPIRITUALITY

It has been frequently remarked on that the older notion of spirituality, rooted in patristic, monastic and medieval sources, took a turn in the early modern period away from its fundamental orientation toward God to a more refined preoccupation with one's own interior dispositions; thus, as Michel DeCerteau has shown, both the term *mysticism* and the word *spirituality* came to refer to interior experiences detached, to a lesser or greater degree, from their roots in the religious experience of participation in the liturgical life of the church.[23] One can look to this "turn" as the remote source of the phrase "I am spiritual but not religious," to which we alluded at the very beginning of this paper.

The serious debates about the nature of Catholic Spirituality today, many of them energized by the pioneering work of Hans Urs von Balthasar, have brought a precise focus upon fundamental tropes rooted in

---

[22]The most accessible survey of mystical theology in English is William Harmless's *Mystics* (New York: Oxford University Press, 2008). Gerson is discussed on pp. 4-5. The comprehensive history of the Western Christian mystical tradition is Bernard McGinn's four (with a fifth to come) volumes on the history of Western mysticism under the general heading *The Presence of God* (New York: Crossroad, 1990-).

[23]This turn has been worked out in some detail by Mark McIntosh's *Mystical Theology* (Oxford: Blackwell, 1996).

the appropriation of the biblical tradition: What does it mean to live in Christ? How does one die to be reborn again? How do we appropriate notions such as dying to the self in order to live in Christ? Those kinds of questions have inevitably led serious students of the subject back to those sources before the "turn" to interior dispositions became the center of attention. Curiously enough—and a moment's reflection indicates that we should not be surprised by this—it is the fundamental building blocks of the Catholic way of living in the Spirit that have been most important: How does one participate in the life-giving liturgy of the church? How does one move beyond "Bible study" to a profound sense of being transformed by the Word of God *(lectio divina)?* How does one integrate an obligation of charity and the demands for justice into a coherent whole without falling into some kind of jejune style of social gospel? What ways can we recover the wisdom of the ascetic/monastic forms of spirituality without the tacit demand that those who are not called to those forms of life become fellow travelers with them? These are all ongoing discussions.

Catholic Spirituality and Ecumenism

Some years ago, Alister McGrath remarked that a lack of solid works on spirituality was so pressing in the evangelical tradition that it led many young evangelicals to go back to the older classics and, in the process, he warned somewhat ominously, those same youngsters became infected with what he called "Roman fever." Out of that fear he turned his attention to the theme of Christian spirituality and produced, in quick time, his own book on the subject.[24] Of course, he is hardly alone in writing in this area, as a quick glance at the catalogs of Brazos, Zondervan, Baker and InterVarsity Press will show.[25]

I have followed the publication record of such presses with some care and have tried to review such books in Catholic venues when they appear. Obviously, these works are trimmed to fit an evangelical audience

---

[24]Alister McGrath, *Christian Spirituality: An Introduction* (Oxford: Blackwell, 1999).
[25]I have in mind such useful works as Simon Chan, *Spiritual Theology* (Downers Grove, Ill.: InterVarsity Press, 1998); Rodney Clapp, *Tortured Wonders: Christian Spirituality for People, Not Angels* (Grand Rapids: Brazos, 2004), and most recently, the massive survey of Evan B. Howard, *The Brazos Introduction to Christian Spirituality* (Grand Rapids: Brazos, 2008).

with a rather thin approach to liturgical and sacramental practice, but that is hardly to be faulted. Sturdy Protestants from the late seventeenth century on read Thomas à Kempis's *The Imitation of Christ* to their benefit even though most of those Protestant editions quietly excised Thomas's deeply felt devotion to the real presence of Christ in the Eucharist, which he so fervently expresses in book four of that classic. By contrast, we Catholics traditionally read none of the great Protestant works of spirituality either because they were on the Index of Forbidden Books—volumes condemned by the Roman authorities—or, more commonly, simply because they were Protestant.

The *ressourcement* now so evident in evangelical circles is a truth to be noted and praised, but for my purposes it is far more important to underscore the evident healing and deeper rapprochement reflected in these developments.

First, the great classics of Catholic spirituality were all rooted in a profound appropriation of sacred Scripture as the Word of God. The recent efflorescence of interest in the classics of Catholic spirituality would be unthinkable except against the background of the biblical renewal that was prior to and found its best expression in the teachings of the Second Vatican Council. The dogmatic constitution on divine revelation *(Dei Verbum)* devotes its final chapter to urging Catholics to meditate and absorb the Word of God not only as it is proclaimed in the liturgy and via instruction in catechetics but as a profound listening to the Word of God as God speaks to us through his Word. To the degree that Catholics became more biblically centered; they grew more capable of entering into fruitful exchanges with those for whom the Bible is at the center of their faith and its expression.[26]

Second, and by contrast, the more Protestants in general and evangelicals in particular come into contact with the rich heritage of Catholic spirituality the more it becomes plausible to see that such seemingly strange practices as monasticism, the ascetic life and so on—all hall-

---

[26]Shortly after the end of the council, the young German theologian, Josef Ratzinger, pointed out that Catholics were only dimly aware of the riches in the final chapter of *Dei Verbum* as a source for spiritual renewal; see his comments in *Commentary on the Documents of Vatican II* (New York: Herder and Herder, 1969), 3:262-72.

marks of Catholic spirituality—are strategies for working out the imperatives found in the Scriptures that may have been underplayed or ignored, or even thought to be unscriptural in Protestant circles. That is not only a gain for Protestants but it is also a corrective check for Catholics since not everything in the Catholic spiritual tradition is above reproach. Indeed, some elements that run like a thread in the tradition need correction or, better, benign neglect. One must also be on guard against an overblown Platonism and even Gnosticism within certain historical Catholic circles. Some devotional works and practices barely escape the charge of magic, while others seem rather undernourished in their theology of grace. The fact that the Vatican has not condemned a book does not mean that it is a good book; indeed, I could cite books often read in the not so distant past which are, in fact, bad books. Some of them are even published today.

Third, and finally, many readers will be more familiar than I am with the three "alones" of the Reformation: *sola scriptura, sola fides, sola gratia*—Scripture alone, faith alone and grace alone. Let us remind ourselves, however, that these are derivative and secondary theological statements since they lack a direct object, which is, of course, Jesus Christ. It is in his grace, by faith in him and through the witness of Scripture that we come to Christ.

If, as I have argued in this paper, authentic Catholic spirituality is rooted following Christ, who is the Way, then we have to say that the criterion for an authentic spirituality is this: do we follow Christ by this practice, or by reading that book, or by participating in the liturgy, or by seeing Christ in others? By the use of that criterion we can then judge whether this vast panoply of Catholic devotional, ascetic, spiritual, liturgical and diaconal practices, nourished and sustained in the Catholic tradition, are worthy of attention.

Evangelical Holiness

*Assumptions in John Owen's
Theology of Christian Spirituality*

KELLY M. KAPIC

INTRODUCTION

J. I. Packer always shows enthusiasm for the Puritans in general, and
for John Owen (1616-1683) in particular:

> For the Puritan, everything everywhere in every respect must become a
> specific instance of holiness to the Lord. Arguably, Puritanism repre-
> sents the most complete, profound, mature and magnificent realization
> of biblical religion that the world has yet seen, one that few since the
> seventeenth century have matched and none have surpassed. But be that
> as it may, it was this Puritanism that from start to finish was John Ow-
> en's personal way of life.[1]

[1]J. I. Packer, "A Puritan Perspective: Trinitarian Godliness According to John Owen," in *God
the Holy Trinity: Reflections on Christian Faith and Practice*, ed. Timothy George (Grand Rapids: Baker Academic, 2006), pp. 91-108. For other studies on different Puritan approaches to
spirituality, see Simon K. H. Chan, *The Puritan Meditative Tradition, 1599-1691: A Study of
Ascetical Piety* (Ph.D. diss., University of Cambridge, 1986); Charles Hambrick-Stowe, *The
Practice of Piety: Puritan Devotional Disciplines in Seventeenth-Century New England* (Chapel
Hill: University of North Carolina Press, 1982); Charles Hambrick-Stowe, "Puritan Spiri-
tuality in America," in *Christian Spirituality: Post-Reformation and Modern*, ed. Louis Depré
and Don Saliers (London: SCM Press, 1990), pp. 338-53; E. Brooks Holifield, *The Covenant
Sealed: The Development of Puritan Sacramental Theology in Old and New England, 1570-1720*
(New Haven: Yale University Press, 1974); Kelly M. Kapic and Randall C. Gleason, *The Devoted Life: An Invitation to the Puritan Classics* (Downers Grove, Ill.: InterVarsity Press, 2004);
Richard C. Lovelace, "The Anatomy of Puritan Piety: English Puritan Devotional Literature,
1600-1640," in *Christian Spirituality: Post-Reformation and Modern*, ed. Louis Depré and Don
Saliers (London: SCM Press, 1990), pp. 294-323; Irvonwy Morgan, *Puritan Spirituality* (London: Epworth, 1965); J. I. Packer, *A Quest for Godliness: The Puritan Vision of the Christian Life*

While not all will agree with Packer's exceptionally high praise of the Puritans and John Owen, his strong endorsement should at least cause us to listen to some of these neglected voices, and in particular to Owen.

Having explored aspects of Owen's spirituality elsewhere, I focus here on a new route into his theology of spiritual formation; it seems promising to organize some of his main concerns around an evocative phrase he uses with some regularity: "evangelical holiness." Although this phrase occasionally appears in other seventeenth-century authors, it is very rare, and Owen alone seems to utilize it frequently.[2] It occurs most commonly in his extended treatments of justification and sanctification, but it appears in almost every work he writes. An exploration of the ideas and concerns behind the phrase illumines the path of spiritual formation as Owen envisioned it.

EVANGELICAL HOLINESS IS NOT SIMPLY MORAL VIRTUE

Consistently Owen stresses that Christian spirituality, or Christian righteousness, as he occasionally puts it, is not simply about doing right actions. He distinguishes evangelical holiness from what he calls "a life of moral virtue" or "philosophical virtue."[3] Owen often uses "moral vir-

---

(Wheaton, Ill.: Crossway, 1990); G. S. Wakefield, *Puritan Devotion: Its Place in the Development of Christian Piety* (London: Epworth, 1957).

[2]Not surprisingly, I have yet to find this phase in any sixteenth or seventeenth-century Roman Catholic authors. Somewhat surprisingly, I have found it only a few times in Protestant authors, although the ideas behind the phrase are fairly widely endorsed. I have only discovered three other Protestant authors from around this time who employ this phrase: Thomas Goodwin, Petrus de Witte and William Twisse. Each of these authors use this phrase with almost singular rarity, e.g., Petrus de Witte, *Catechizing upon the Heidelberg Catechism* (1652; reprint, Amsterdam: Gillis Joosten Saeghman, 1664), p. 464. Goodwin and Twisse references are noted below. For a full treatment of sanctification that builds on the ideas related to evangelical holiness, see the later Puritan Walter Marshall (1628-1680), *The Gospel Mystery of Sanctification* (London: Printed for T. Parkhurst, 1692). Later authors use this language as well, although it can take on different meanings in their different contexts: e.g., John Wesley, "Sermon 9: The Spirit of Bondage and of Adoption," in *Sermons on Several Occasions* 1717 (text from the 1872 edition); Jonathan Edwards, *Religious Affections* (New Haven: Yale University Press, 1959), p. 456. By the end of the eighteenth century, this phrase is widely used and plays a key role in the popular and somewhat controversial Angelical work by James Hervey, *Meditations Among the Tombs: Tending to Reform the Vices of the Age, and to Promote Evangelical Holiness* (London: Printed for J. and J. Rivington in St. Paul's Church-yard and J. Leake at Bath, 1746), which went through twenty-five editions.

[3]E.g., *Works*, 3:467, 473, 502. All references to *Works* come from John Owen, *The Works of John Owen*, ed. William H. Goold, 24 vols. (1850-1855; reprint, Edinburgh: Banner of Truth Trust, 1965-1991). The Libronix Digital edition of Owen's works is much stronger than the older

tue" in a negative sense, contrasting it with the gift and action of holiness in the life of the believer.[4] The former focuses on self-generated effort, the latter arises out of divine life.[5]

Contrary to the stereotypes of wooden and legalistic religiosity often attributed to Puritanism, Owen tries to deliver his readers from such burdens that commonly arise when mere human diligence is confused with genuine spirituality. His work frames the Christian life completely in terms of God's grace. He recognizes and guards against our tendency to construct substitutes for real spirituality, which normally take the shape of external or civil morality. Owen firmly warns against those who think "all they have to do with God consists in their attendance unto moral virtue!"[6] Improved moral compliance may be better for one's state or family, but it does nothing to overcome the chasm between the holy Creator and the rebellious creature. Morality is not spirituality. Owen sees that this confusion leads straight to Pelagianism, for it seeks to generate righteousness out of mere human power, believing that the burden (and ability) lay with humanity to increase their holiness by their own effort.[7]

EVANGELICAL HOLINESS IS DEPENDENT ON THE GIFT OF THE GOSPEL

As Owen distinguishes law from gospel he describes the place of virtue in the Christian's life. The law guides, directs and even commands how we should live, but the law itself gives no aid to do so; the law makes demands, truly righteous demands, but it provides no power to fulfill those demands. Owen does not view the law as merely negative, much less as intrinsically bad; rather, it was never intended to give life. On the one hand, the law clearly outlines God's expectations and, in light of sin, it then reveals our guilt and shortcomings, which is, in fact, its good and proper office, but not a life-giving one. It is the gospel, once rightly revealed and enjoyed, that channels God's grace and actually

---

Ages version.

[4]E.g., *Works*, 3:10-11. Owen does not universally use it as a negative term, as for example when he discusses the Spirit giving moral virtues in the Old Testament (*Works*, 3:149).

[5]Cf. ibid., 3:478.

[6]Ibid., 3:200.

[7]Ibid., 3:201.

brings spiritual strength.[8] This is why the law provokes fear and dread
when it comes to sinners with its warnings and threats. On the other
hand, the gospel gives life, "cheerfulness, courage, and perseverance";
grace animates, revives and relieves the soul "in all its work and duty,
keeping it from faintness and despondency."[9] Christ has made "an end
of sin" and thus has removed the curse and condemnation of the law.
While Christ has fulfilled the law, it nonetheless remains a true guide
for believers who are still commanded to love God and neighbor. But
believers—because they experience union and communion with God—
are now empowered to respond to the law in the freedom and power of
the gospel.[10]

Unlike worldly attempts at moral virtue, according to Owen, evangelical holiness arises out of the good news of God. All gospel duties
flow out of the love of the Father, the mediation of the Son and the
"ready assistances of the Holy Ghost." The work of the triune God
weaves its way through the experience of believers and gives them "the
highest assurance of final success and victory."[11] Simply put, for Owen,
Christian spirituality is a gift from God. While we are the ones who
live in and out of this gift, we can understand it only if we see it as gift,
which is another way of saying, "grace."[12]

By *evangelical* Owen means that which is "peculiar to the gospel
alone."[13] In fact, even though his preferred phrase seems to be "evangelical holiness," he somewhat regularly substitutes this phrase for
"gospel holiness."[14] God, in gracious condescension, liberates his people

---

[8]Ibid., 7:547.

[9]Ibid., 7:551.

[10]Ibid., 5:382.

[11]Ibid., 7:551.

[12]Cf. Thomas Goodwin, "A Discourse Of Election," in *The Works of Thomas Goodwin*, 12 vols.
(Edinburgh: J. Nichol, 1683), 9:414-20, where he deals with the idea of believers' children as
evangelical and thus truly holy, stressing the fact that this holiness is not ceremonial or moral,
but it is a gift of the gospel.

[13]*Works*, 3:278.

[14]E.g., *Works*, 5:433-35; 7:162-82; 19:276; 24:296. At one point he clearly states that "gospel
holiness" is "evangelical obedience" (*Works*, 7:164). Cf. Gould notes (*Works*, 7:162; 5:386). The
language of "gospel holiness" is much more common later in the work of Jonathan Edwards.
E.g., Jonathan Edwards, *Ecclesiastical Writings*, ed. David D. Hall (New Haven: Yale University Press, 1994), pp. 320, 356-57, 364, 374; Jonathan Edwards, *Ethical Writings*, ed. Paul
Ramsey (New Haven: Yale University Press, 1989), p. 95; Jonathan Edwards, *Religious Affec-*

not only by bringing them into a holy state, but calling them to holy actions. The "comprehensive difference," Owen clarifies, "between a spiritual life unto God by evangelical holiness, and a life of moral virtue" is that the former requires the Son and Holy Spirit, while the latter draws upon mere will power.[15]

While the Son is normally linked with the atonement and the Spirit with sanctification, both associations mean that none other than God himself rescues and renews his people. "Evangelical holiness is purchased for us" by Christ under the covenant, and it is "communicated unto us by his Spirit."[16] Natural reason alone cannot understand or experience holiness, and only those who have experienced the good news have "evangelical grounds and motives" that are "suited" to obey God.[17]

Christ alone is our "actual sanctification" by his sacrificial death and by his ongoing intercession.[18] Saints receive this sanctification as a gift conveyed to us by the Spirit. All evangelical holiness is "a fruit or effect in us of the Spirit of sanctification," which makes believers alive unto Christ, which is the heart of the "spiritual life."[19] As we will see later, Owen's emphasis on divine gift does not nullify, but is the basis for the call to action by the believer, always understanding that such action depends on the life given to us by the Spirit. Real spirituality, therefore, is not fundamentally about self-improvement, but about an intimacy and communion with the triune God that transforms the believer's life.

Believer's Commune with the Divine Persons

One of Owen's great contributions to western spirituality, his book *Communion with God*, outlines how the believer has "peculiar" fellowship with the Father, Son and Holy Spirit. The entire treatise rests on the lavish Pauline benediction: "The grace of the Lord Jesus Christ and the love of God and the fellowship of the Holy Spirit be with you all" (2 Cor 13:14 esv). Owen explains our communion with God according to the benedic-

---

tions, ed. John E. Smith (New Haven: Yale University Press, 1959), p. 474.
[15]*Works*, 3:467, 523, 526.
[16]Ibid., 3:506.
[17]Ibid., 3:372; 5:380; cf. 3:406, 610.
[18]Ibid., 3:506.
[19]Ibid., 3:372, 10. Cf. 3:490-91, 523.

tion's structure, linking the Father with love, the incarnate Son with grace and the Spirit with sanctification. We are drawn into fellowship with the three persons of the One God in their eternal and loving communion.

God in Christ by his Spirit has extended himself to us, drawing us into his loving embrace, into a divine giving and receiving, and this divine movement necessarily has a trinitarian shape. Owen's premise is fairly simple: we have communion with God, and yet there is no God but the divine persons. All our approaches to God are always approaches to a divine person: this movement does not take us away from God since this is the only way we actually worship him.

Worshiping the Father, Son and Spirit does not involve us in three different acts of worship, but reflects one fluid motion of praise before the triune God. In Owen's language, "the divine nature is the reason and cause of all worship; so that it is impossible to worship any one person, and not worship the whole Trinity."[20] We do not make requests three times to three separate persons; rather, we approach the Father through the Son in the Spirit, glorying in the persons as we find ourselves in the presence of God.[21] So in our prayers, though we often pray to God the Father and end our prayers in the name of the Son, "the Son is no less invocated and worshipped in the beginning than the Father . . . in the invocation of God the Father we invoke every person."[22]

The triune movement of the Father through the Son by the Spirit relates a "distinction of the persons, as to their operations, but not at all as to their being the object of our worship."[23] Owen thus holds the Act and Being of God together. "For the Son and the Holy Ghost are no less worshipped in our access to God than the Father himself."[24] When God reveals himself to us and encounters us in his triunity, the believer worships; and when believers are "led to worship . . . any person, we do herein worship the whole Trinity; and every person, by what name so ever, of Father, Son, or Holy Ghost, we invoke him."[25] Such an em-

---

[20]Ibid., 2:268.
[21]Ibid., 2:269.
[22]Ibid.
[23]Ibid.
[24]Ibid.
[25]Ibid.

phasis on the persons protects Owen from the danger of positing a hidden god behind God's revelation of himself in three persons.[26]

We are to worship and glorify God's Spirit just as we do the Father and Son. Owen, like other Puritans, endorsed prayers to each of the divine persons, including the Spirit, according to the logic that, when we are drawn to worship the Spirit "he is not worshipped exclusively, but the whole Godhead is worshipped."[27] Those who experience the Spirit's empowering presence see his effects and know his comfort as they are stirred and provoked "to love, worship, believe in, and invocate him."[28] Drawn near to the divine Spirit, saints are simultaneously directed by the Spirit to "the other persons."

Here Owen's formulations roughly parallel Gregory of Nazianzus's dictum, which he quotes: "No sooner do I conceive of the One than I am illumed by the Splendour of the Three; no sooner do I distinguish Them than I am carried back to the One."[29] For Owen, like Gregory long before him, Christian spirituality never moves beyond but always toward God's triunity, and this movement is always a gift of grace.

EVANGELICAL HOLINESS IS CHRIST-CENTERED

Owen appears to sense no contradiction when he assumes that trinitar-

---

[26]Colin Gunton was often concerned with this problem, placing much of the blame for such tendencies at the feet of Augustine. He worried that Augustine so elevated the oneness of God that the divine persons merely pointed to the real God, rather than God being encountered in the divine persons. See, e.g., Colin E. Gunton, *The Promise of Trinitarian Theology*, 2nd ed. (Edinburgh: T & T Clark, 1997), especially pp. 30-55; Colin E. Gunton, "God the Holy Spirit: Augustine and His Successors," in *Theology Through the Theologians* (Edinburgh: T & T Clark, 1996), pp. 105-28. For responses to Gunton, begin with Lewis Ayres, "'Remember That You Are Catholic' (Serm. 52.2): Augustine on the Unity of the Triune God," *Journal of Early Christian Studies* 8, no. 1 (2000): 39-82; Lewis Ayres, *Nicaea and Its Legacy: An Approach to Fourth-Century Trinitarian Theology* (New York: Oxford University Press, 2004). Whether or not Augustine is guilty of the charges—and they do not seem to stick—the potential theological confusion remains real.

[27]Kelly M. Kapic, *Communion with God: The Divine and the Human in the Theology of John Owen* (Grand Rapids: Baker Academic, 2007), pp. 163-64. For general background on the Puritans' view of the Spirit and prayer see Geoffrey F. Nuttall, *The Holy Spirit in Puritan Faith and Experience*, 2nd ed. (1946; reprint, Chicago: University of Chicago Press, 1992), pp. 62-74. Owen's quote from *Works*, 2:269.

[28]*Works*, 2:270.

[29]Cited in Greek in Owen's original footnote, in *Works*, 2:10. Gregory of Nazianzus, *Oration 40: The Oration on Holy Baptism*, Nicene and Post Nicene Fathers [NPNF] 2 7:375; Patrologia Graeca [PG] 36, col. 417B.

ian spirituality is necessarily Christ-centered. In his mind, to be Christ-centered does not compromise the Father or Spirit, but rather it reflects biblical revelation and Christian experience. His two mature treatises *Christologia* (1678) and *The Glory of Christ* (1684) display this conviction powerfully, but it reverberates throughout all his writings.[30]

God is most clearly known in his Son, and in Christ we discover how we are restored to communion with him. The incarnate Christ is "the great representative of the nature of God and his will unto us," and apart from him God would have been eternally hidden and invisible: "we should never have seen God at any time, here nor hereafter."[31] Simply put: we see God in Christ. The incarnate Son "becomes the great representative of God unto the Church" so much so that "in the face of Jesus Christ we see his glory."[32]

To revere Jesus as an example for spiritual living, or an ethical teacher, and then go no further misses his identity altogether. He is God, the revelation of God. In Jesus the very love, grace, holiness, justice, freedom and power of God are made manifest.

> He, and he alone, declares, represents, and makes known, unto angels and men, the essential glory of the invisible God, his attributes and his will; without which, a perpetual comparative darkness would have been on the whole creation. . . . This is the foundation of our religion, the Rock whereon the church is built, the ground of all our hopes of salvation . . . namely, the representation that is made of the nature and will of God in the person and office of Christ. If this fail us, we are lost for ever; if this Rock stand firm, the church is safe here, and shall be triumphant hereafter.[33]

To speak of Christian spirituality is to bask in the glory of Christ, to find in him forgiveness, hope and love. Believers do not look to Christ

---

[30]During the final decade of his life, Owen's writing career, which had begun in 1643, often focused on studying the Son and the Spirit. In this decade he wrote his massive studies on the person and work of the Spirit, his two monographs (see above) on Christ, as well as most of his extensive commentary on Hebrews, which explores the centrality of Jesus in the story of redemption.

[31]*Works*, 1:294.

[32]Ibid.

[33]*Works*, 1:294-95.

only when they first believe, but gazing upon and following their Messiah perpetually defines their entire lives.

The Spirit of Christ Makes Us Evangelically Holy

With Owen's view of Christ in mind, it is not surprising that one of his tests to discern whether the Holy Spirit or a false Spirit is at work in a person is that person's view of Jesus. God's Spirit always directs people to Christ, whereas a false spirit tries to draw focus and worship away from the incarnate Lord. This need for such a test grew out of Owen's wrestling with the growing "Enthusiasts" phenomenon in the seventeenth century.[34] He believed Enthusiasts pit the Spirit against the Son and the Scriptures, and so like Jonathan Edwards after him, he found it necessary to differentiate the Spirit of God from false spirits or natural human impulses.[35] Drawing especially from 1 John and John's farewell discourse (Jn 13:31–16:33), Owen concludes that, since the Spirit brings us to Christ, we can recognize him by that work. Elsewhere Owen explains, "His [the Spirit's] whole work is to glory and exalt Jesus Christ."[36] This does not diminish the Spirit, but rather rightly reflects his presence and power as he draws people to the Son, and thus enfolds them into communion with the triune God.[37]

---

[34]For historical background on the Enthusiasts movement, see Michael Heyd, *Be Sober and Reasonable: The Critique of Enthusiasm in the Seventeenth and Early Eighteenth Centuries*, Brill's Studies in Intellectual History (New York: E. J. Brill, 1995); Michael Heyd, "The Reaction to Enthusiasm in the Seventeenth Century: Towards an Integrative Approach," *Journal of Modern History* 53 (1981): 258-80; Geoffrey F. Nuttall, *Studies in Christian Enthusiasm: Illustrated from Early Quakerism* (Wallingford, Penn.: Pendle Hill, 1948); R. A. Knox, *Enthusiasm: A Chapter in the History of Religion*, Oxford Scholarly Classics (Oxford: Oxford University Press, 2000). For an example of this tension as Owen encountered it, see Toon's treatment of two young Quaker women who came and tore their clothes as they walked through Oxford calling the students of theology to abandon their books and trust the inner light of the Spirit: Peter Toon, *God's Statesman: The Life and Work of John Owen: Pastor, Educator, Theologian* (Exeter, U.K.: Paternoster, 1971), pp. 76-77.

[35]It is worth noting that one of the few authors Edwards cites in this work is Owen, drawing particularly from his *Pneumatologia*. Edwards, *Religious Affections*, esp. pp. 250-51; 372-73.

[36]*Works*, 7:234. It should not be surprising that J. I. Packer, a serious student of Owen, speaks of the "floodlight ministry" of the Spirit: he is "the hidden floodlight shining on the Saviour," J. I. Packer, *Keep in Step with the Spirit* (Old Tappan, N.J.: F. H. Revell, 1984), pp. 65-66.

[37]Owen develops other tests: e.g., that the true Spirit delights in creation and does not belittle it. The Spirit is the Spirit of creation, and the Spirit of Christ that brings new creation does so by affirming our humanity, reshaping us in the image of God; see Kelly M. Kapic, "Worshiping the Triune God: The Shape of John Owen's Trinitarian Spirituality," in *Communion with the*

Believers, secure in their justification, are called to live by the Spirit in response to his motions and grace. By the indwelling of the Spirit they receive continuous supplies of grace for growth in sanctification. Behind the Spirit's sanctifying movement then is the promise to re-shape believers ever more into conformity with their Savior. "Nothing less than the entire renovation of the image of God in our souls will constitute us evangelically holy."[38] God's Spirit brings about "a universal conformity unto him as he is the image of the invisible God."[39] We should not miss in this Owen's attempt to formulate a holistic spirituality. He used terms like "entire renovation" and "universal conformity" to describe God's work in all aspects of the redeemed person. The Spirit illumines the mind, frees the will and enlarges our affections, drawing our entire being into renewed communion with God.[40] "The Holy Ghost in our sanctification doth work, effect, and create in us a new, holy, spiritual, vital principle of grace, residing in all the faculties of our souls"; he sustains and grows his people "by effectual supplies of grace from Jesus Christ."[41] No faculty, to use seventeenth century language, will be left out of this sanctifying work.

EVANGELICAL HOLINESS DEPENDS ON UNION WITH CHRIST

What differentiates natural moral virtue from evangelical holiness is the saint's relationship to the triune God, and this occurs only through union to Christ. Such a union is established by the Father's love, secured through the Son's mediation and enjoyed in fellowship with the Spirit. Only in and through this unique union to Christ by the Spirit are "real supplies of spiritual strength and grace" experienced, and only here is a saint's holiness "preserved, maintained, and increased," for these things are "constantly communicated unto them" out of this union.[42] Because this holiness comes purely by gift, he calls it "evan-

Triune God: A Classic Work by John Owen, ed. Kelly M. Kapic and Justin Taylor (Wheaton, Ill.: Crossway, 2007), pp. 42-45.
[38]*Works*, 3:523.
[39]Ibid., 3:509.
[40]Ibid., 3:493.
[41]Ibid., 3:496; cf. 3:436-67.
[42]Ibid., 3:513-14.

gelical grace" and opposes it to moral virtue, which attempts self-improvement without these gifts. Christ is the head, the fountain and spring of all holiness and life in the church.[43] He describes holiness here in terms of gift, and this giving occurs only within the union that believers have with Christ.[44]

In Owen's brief *Lesser Catechism* written in 1645, he asks, "what are the privileges of believers?" His answer includes six things in this order: union with Christ, adoption, communion of saints, right to the seals of the new covenant, Christian liberty and the resurrection of the body to eternal life.[45] Union with Christ is the foundation of all that follows: all of the blessings flow out of the reality of this relationship. Here Owen mirrors Calvin with his very strong doctrine of union:

> We must understand that as long as Christ remains outside of us, and we are separated from him, all that he has suffered and done for the salvation of the human race remains useless and of no value for us. Therefore, to share with us what he has received from the Father, he had to become ours and to dwell within us.[46]

Elsewhere in Owen's massive volume on the *Perseverance of the Saints*, he observes in detail some of the biblical imagery used to paint this theological idea of union. Such metaphors include the natural connection between a head and members of the body, the bond between a husband and wife and the organic connection of a tree made up of roots, trunk and branches.[47]

In *The Greater Catechism*, which expands on *The Lesser*, Owen slightly unpacks what he means by this union: "An holy, spiritual conjunction unto him, as our head, husband, and foundation, whereby we are made partakers of the same Spirit with him, and derive all good things from him."[48] Further, Owen adds some wonderfully suggestive footnotes to amplify his definition of union. For example, when he mentions this

---

[43]Ibid., 3:514.
[44]Cf. ibid., 3:518.
[45]Ibid., 1:469.
[46]John Calvin, *Institutes of the Christian Religion* 3.1.1, vol. 1, Library of Christian Classics, ed. John T. McNeill (Philadelphia: Westminster Press, 1960), p. 537 [3.1.1].
[47]*Works*, 11:339-41.
[48]Ibid., 1:489.

spiritual union he adds this comment: "by virtue of this union, Christ suffereth in our afflictions; and we fill up in our bodies what remaineth as his."[49] This union is not merely abstract and legal, but relational, life giving and life sustaining: in sum, it is participatory. When we suffer, Christ suffers with us, and we carry forth the ministry of the ascended Christ as those united to him bear his continued marks of suffering for the sake of the gospel. In other words, the cross does not simply point to the past reality of the Savior's atoning work, but it continues to shape the present reality of his body, the church, which is united to him. Consequently, this side of the resurrection, those who have spiritual life will participate in the "remaining" afflictions, which Christ bears through his church. Here one might sense a startling similarity to the words of Dietrich Bonhoeffer in the twentieth century:

> His is the only suffering, which has redemptive efficacy. But the Church knows that the world is still seeking for someone to bear its sufferings, and so, as it follows Christ, suffering becomes the Church's lot too and bearing it, it is borne up by Christ.[50]

Christ, according to Owen, continues to show to the world the reality of God's holy love and sacrificial grace, and he does this through his church as his people bear his afflictions. Yet they bear them not on their own, but as those united to him by his Spirit, and thus they are supplied with continuous grace through such difficulties.

Not surprisingly, Owen draws the connection that the Spirit who unites the elect with God is also the same Spirit who unites believers together, making them one body.[51] The body of Christ is not individual, but is the reality of the communion of saints held together by the Spirit.[52]

Some fear, in a common misunderstanding, that union with Christ means loss of ourselves by absorption into God, and thus an oblitera-

---

[49]Ibid., 1:489 n. 2. Cf. Col 1:24.

[50]Dietrich Bonhoeffer, *The Cost of Discipleship*, 2nd rev. ed. (New York: Macmillan, 1959), pp. 81-82. Bonhoeffer takes this beyond Owen's intention, focusing not simply on the way the church images Christ to the world, but the way the church stands before God as its representative.

[51]*Works*, 11:338-39.

[52]Ibid., 3:465.

tion of the creature by the divine. Owen explicitly argues against the idea that union with Christ would "destroy" believers, as if they "lose their own personality—that is, cease to be men, or at least these or those individual men."[53] Union with Christ maintains the distinction between us and God, but unites us because the "self-same Spirit" is both ours and his.[54] God does not absorb us into the divine by this union, nor does he blend believers into an undifferentiated sameness with each other. The church is one body with many members, and union brings the differences into harmony under Christ Jesus as the head and held together by the Spirit. Counterintuitively, union with Christ glories in maintaining the Creator-creature distinction, as well as the endless differences that remain between people. The promise of union in Christ by the Spirit is not to overcome difference, but to overcome sin.

Evangelical Holiness Is Expressed Through Imitation of Jesus the Christ

According to Owen, we do not have to choose between having Christ by the Spirit as the source of our sanctification and having Christ as our example of holiness. Not everyone, however, combines the concepts as readily as Owen. In recent years, the various forms of the WWJD (What Would Jesus Do?) phenomena, represented by promise bracelets and trendy T-shirts, for which Jesus appears to serve merely as a model for being good, have created a backlash among some pastors and theologians, especially in the Reformed community. In what appears to me to be an overreaction, some seem to flirt with the idea that Jesus is actually not our example, arguing that since he alone was the atoning sacrifice, the high priest, the God-Man, the *imitatio Christi* does not properly apply to us today. John Schneider moves in that direction: "There is no doubt, I believe, that the tradition of *imitatio Christi*, admirable as it may be, undervalues the uniqueness of Christ's particular

---

[53]Ibid., 11:336.
[54]Ibid., 11:337. Cf. Calvin: "the Holy Spirit is the bond by which Christ effectually unites us to himself," *Institutes of the Christian Religion* 3.1.1, trans. F. L. Battles, ed. John T. McNeill (Philadelphia: Westminster, 1960), p. 538 [3.1.1].

experience and its sufferings."[55] In a thoughtful article, Jason Hood makes a disquieting observation about the conspicuous neglect of the imitation of Christ in recent New Testament literature, concluding that it is the "most neglected aspect of recent work on the NT message of the cross. This neglect is particularly acute among works produced in Reformed and evangelical circles."[56]

This should give us warning against reductionist conceptions of the gospel, to which all of us tend, especially in reaction to someone else's reductionism. Some focus on what we should believe, while others give almost exclusive attention to how Christians should act. This, according to Owen, splits in half what we should keep whole. Yes, of course, we must hold and savor the beauty of such doctrines as redemption, the atonement and our reconciliation with God in Christ. But Owen clearly states that believing these things is "not all that is required of us."[57] That is merely "half of it," with the other "half" coming in Christ's pattern of life and death. It is a "cursed imagination" to think that the whole purpose of the incarnation was to provide us merely with a blueprint for how to live, but similarly, "to neglect his so being our example, in considering him by faith . . . and laboring after conformity to him, is evil and pernicious."[58] Christians, because they embrace Jesus, cannot avoid looking at his example to follow what he did. Any attempt at spiritual life that omits either thoughtful doctrine or thoughtful imitation of Christ will find that it has cut off one of its necessary legs.

We are called not merely to imitate Jesus, nor simply to believe in him: we are called to follow Jesus, and that includes fully embracing by faith the reality of who he is and patterning our lives after him. Owen points his readers to Jesus the Messiah, who is "the exemplary cause of our holiness."[59] Elsewhere he states, "We are obliged to profess that the life of Christ is our example."[60]

---

[55]John R. Schneider, *The Good of Affluence: Seeking God in a Culture of Wealth* (Grand Rapids: Eerdmans, 2002), p. 149.
[56]Jason Hood, "The Cross and the New Testament: Two Theses in Conversation with Recent Literature (2000-2007)," *Westminster Theological Journal* 71 (2009): 281-95.
[57]*Works*, 3:513.
[58]Ibid.
[59]Ibid., 3:509.
[60]Ibid., 3:649.

Biographies often portray people at their best; sometimes the aim is to provide a prototype for others to emulate. Owen recognizes that in such biographies and historical retellings, "heroical virtue or stoical apathy which are boasted of among the heathens" inevitably hide the flaws and shortcomings of those they describe. But each "hero" has grave flaws, which is the point of Greek tragedies. Similarly, even when Christians choose their favorite saints who attempted to live faithfully, they inevitably prove to be somewhat problematic examples, for there are times when conforming to their lives will actually point in an ungodly direction. That is why, in the end, Christians are "followers" of Jesus Christ and none other than him.[61]

Part of the wonder of the incarnation is not merely to provide an atoning sacrifice, but that God might assume a genuine human nature, like us in all ways except sin. In this way Christ proves to be both the source and the model for the believer's renewal in the image of God. Denying the value of the *imitatio Christi* puts one in danger of creeping docetism. Beholding Christ in his glory includes beholding his human faithfulness, and in this process of beholding him saints find they are conformed to him.[62] This occurs as they share in his Spirit, the same Spirit that sanctified Jesus, preserving him from sin, growing him ever more in grace and truth.[63] That same Spirit who unites believers to the Son also remolds them in his image.[64]

Owen mentions in passing that sometimes the call to imitate Christ can become twisted if it reduces Christianity to simply following a great leader's example. Yet the sign that this has occurred is not that people try to imitate Christ, but that they despise the practices at the heart of his life. For example, Owen highlights the qualities of "meekness, patience, self-denial, quietness in bearing reproaches, contempt of the

---

[61]Ibid., 3:510.

[62]Ibid., 3:511-12.

[63]For more on this theme of the Spirit in the sanctification of Jesus, see Alan J. Spence, "Christ's Humanity and Ours: John Owen," in *Person's, Divine and Human*, ed. C. Schwöbel and Colin E. Gunton (Edinburgh: T & T Clark, 1991); Alan J. Spence, *Incarnation and Inspiration: John Owen and the Coherence of Christology* (London: T & T Clark, 2007); Kelly M. Kapic, "The Spirit as Gift: Explorations in John Owen's Pneumatology," paper presented at conference at Westminster College, Cambridge University, England, August 20, 2008.

[64]*Works*, 3:512.

world, zeal for the glory of God, compassion to the souls of men, con-descension to the weakness of all."[65] Owen's picture of imitating Christ includes his humiliation, so that when people use the incarnate Lord as a way to power rather than sacrificial service, they have misunderstood his example, and thus have distorted the faith.

Following Christ means following the path to the cross. The cross shapes Christian spirituality this side of heaven, showing us the depth of the triune God's love, freeing the saints from sin and making us alive to God by means of resurrection. The new life of believers, then, is pat-terned after the Savior and his cross, ever loving and willing to offer oneself for the sake of the other in the liberty of the gospel. God in Christ by the Spirit did not merely set people free from sin by the cross, but he set the church free to do good works, to offer itself up, to pour itself out, all in and through the grace of God. And, in doing that, the Christian is a true imitator of Christ.

HOLINESS: LIVING IN THE NOW AND NOT YET

Finally, Owen was well aware that the Scriptures show holiness to be both fully accomplished and yet also in progress. He holds together what is sometimes described as the definitive and progressive nature of sanctification.

> Every believer is truly and really sanctified at once, but none is perfectly sanctified at once. It is not, therefore, necessary unto union that we should be *completely* sanctified, though it is that we should be *truly* sanc-tified. Complete sanctification is a necessary effect of union in its proper time and season.[66]

Here he draws upon John 15:1-5 as a textual example of this twofold nature: believers are united to the vine, and this also means they will bear fruit. Such a harvest often comes as the vinedresser prunes the vine, which he does not to hurt the plant but to promote its health and growth.[67] All evangelical holiness, in terms of its "virtue, power, and

---

[65]Ibid., 3:513.
[66]Ibid., 3:465.
[67]The Puritan distinction between union and communion should be kept in mind. Whereas *union* highlights the unilateral nature of our renewed life secure in God, *communion* highlights

grace" is "derived immediately from Jesus Christ," and this through the union and relation to him supplied by the Spirit.[68]

Seventeenth century Reformed theologian William Twisse, in his *Catechetical Exposition of Christian Doctrine*, similarly tries to make sense of the complex nature of holiness. He explores the three properties of the true church: it is holy, catholic and a communion of saints.[69] When examining the attribute of holiness, he notes that the church's holiness has two sides: that of faith and that of life. Holiness by faith is our justification, whereas holiness of life is our sanctification. He considers holiness by faith to be perfect holiness, because the "object" here is Christ and his righteousness. Holiness of life is imperfect since it has two sides, the legal and the evangelical. Legal holiness of life is to be without sin by the law, but this is not the holiness required of God's church, presumably since Twisse believes it has been fulfilled in Christ. In contrast, "evangelical holiness" marks the true church, and this holiness occurs not in the absence of sin, but in confession and repentance, with the desire to have the saint's life amended.[70] Twisse here stresses the progressive nature of evangelical holiness.

While Owen understands holiness as a gift of God by the Son and Spirit, he, like Twisse, does not view it as at odds with genuine human agency.[71] Justified saints who have received the infusion of God's principle of life by the Spirit are still called to engage, respond and be full of activity. Those who neglect spiritual disciplines, and act as if human agency is irrelevant to holiness, misunderstand both God's creation and

---

the mutuality of this renewed relationship we are called into as we respond to God's love, returning our love to him. See Kapic, *Communion with God*, pp. 139-42, esp. pp. 152-55; Kapic, "Worshiping the Triune God," pp. 20-23.

[68]*Works*, 3:521, 523.

[69]This paragraph draws from William Twisse, *A Brief Catechetical Exposition of Christian Doctrine* (1632; reprint, London: Printed by I. Norton for Robert Bird, 1633), pp. 58-60.

[70]Cf. Thomas Goodwin, "A Discourse of Election," 9:398, 406. The early eighteenth-century brother-in-law of Jonathan Edwards, Samuel Hopkins (1721-1803), similarly uses "evangelical holiness" in Sermon XVI: "An Improvement of the Subject," in *Twenty-one Sermons, on a Variety of Interesting Subjects, Sentimental and Practical* (Salem, Mass.: Printed by Joshua Cushing, 1803), p. 271.

[71]Owen demonstrates his serious call to continuous human agency in the Christian life in his three memorable works on mortification, temptation and indwelling sin; found in *Works* 6:1-322, or in the newly edited John Owen, *Overcoming Sin and Temptation: Three Classic Works by John Owen*, ed. Kelly M. Kapic and Justin Taylor (Wheaton, Ill.: Crossway, 2006).

re-creation. If we do not participate through the "exercise of grace," then we risk finding ourselves "decaying." "Doth any man wonder to see a person formerly of a sound constitution grown weak and sickly, if he openly neglect all means of health, and contract all sorts of diseases by his intemperance?"[72] Similarly, if we neglect the means of grace and our agency, we will then find ourselves entangled in the web of sin. While holiness is eschatologically secure for believers, the Spirit normally grows this holiness through our "diligence." We follow the Spirit diligently in this work because sanctification is a "progressive work that hath many degrees."[73] Owen unabashedly affirms the true sovereignty of God and our radical dependence on the Holy Spirit's gifts of grace, and yet he never thinks this contradicts the biblical call for human participation.

> It is required of us that we give all diligence unto the increase of grace. . . . Whatever diligence you have used in the attaining or improving of holiness, abide in it unto the end, or we cast ourselves under decays and endanger our souls. If we slack or give over as to our duty, the work of sanctification will not be carried on in a way of grace. And this is required of us; this is expected from us, that our whole lives be spent in a course of diligent compliance with the progressive work of grace in us.[74]

CONCLUSION

Owen's concept of "evangelical holiness" as it relates to his understanding of spiritual formation provides a gold mine of wisdom and comfort for Christians today. It takes us beyond moral virtue and the fallible human will. It points us to the free gift of the gospel and our encounter with the triune God. Holiness is Christ-centered and Spirit-enabled, growing out of union with Christ, and it calls us to imitate Jesus in the freedom he gives as we are reshaped in his image. As we live in the beautiful and agonizing tension of the now and not yet, may God continue to shape and move our lives toward this wonderfully rich concept of evangelical holiness.

---

[72] *Works*, 3:405.
[73] Ibid., 3:464-65.
[74] Ibid., 3:405.

7 Seeking True Religion

Early Evangelical Devotion and Catholic Spirituality

D. BRUCE HINDMARSH

During the years that I was finishing high school and entering into my twenties, there was a growing interest on the part of many evangelical leaders in the ecumenical sources of Christian spirituality down through the centuries. Jim Houston's teaching career at Regent College shifted in the early eighties from environmental ethics to spiritual theology, and evangelical publishers began to augment their offerings on devotional topics with reprints of classic works of Christian spirituality. Richard Foster's *Celebration of Discipline* (1978) both stimulated and symbolized this movement, and it sold over one-and-a-half million copies in the two decades following its publication. The word *spirituality* itself entered evangelical discourse, and it supplanted phrases such as "personal devotional life." Through reading and retreats, through seminary courses and conferences, evangelicals were listening to new voices, such as the desert fathers of the fourth century, the Cistercian monks of the twelfth century or the Spanish mystics of the sixteenth century. As an exhausted staff worker at Youth for Christ in the 1980s, I myself remember how important it was for me to meet with my youth pastor once a week for breakfast and read together through spiritual classics such as Thomas à Kempis's *Imitation of Christ*, or to go on my first personal retreat and read Henri Nouwen's little book on the desert fathers, *The Way of the Heart*.

This evangelical *ressourcement* of classical Christian spirituality in my own lifetime has been fruitful and has provided a much needed recovery of depth and wisdom for Christian living. It has also, however, raised questions of what it means to be grounded in a stable, identity-giving evangelical tradition, and whether or not this is important. Is there a distinctive evangelical *paideia*, an ethos or culture, that forms Christian men and women in their life in Christ? If so, how does this evangelical tradition connect with the wider and longer Christian tradition of spirituality?

INTERPRETING THE RISE OF EVANGELICAL DEVOTION

In this essay, I want to address these questions by going right back to the roots of the evangelical tradition and offering an interpretation of the rise of evangelical devotion as a form of Christian life that takes shape distinctively in the seventeenth and eighteenth centuries and that has proliferated since. I will argue that early evangelical leaders drew on a common core of classical Christian spirituality and "naturalized" this within a Protestant and Reformed framework. Early evangelicalism is best interpreted therefore as a devotional movement in continuity with classical Christian spirituality, expressed under modern conditions and witnessing to a work of the Holy Spirit in the church. The concern of this movement was, above all, with "true religion."

Historians are agreed on the rise of evangelicalism as a significant new religious bloc in the modern world, whether in its Anglo-German beginnings in the 1670s or its Anglo-American origins in the 1730s.[1] Evangelicalism emerged on the cusp of the modern period as a trans-denominational spiritual movement. By the late 1730s and early 1740s contemporary observers across the North Atlantic world reported a general spiritual awakening, which they most often described as a "work" of God.[2] Thus John Wesley reported at the beginning of the

---

[1]See, e.g., Michael J. Crawford, *Seasons of Grace* (New York: Oxford University Press, 1991); W. R. Ward, *The Protestant Evangelical Awakening* (Cambridge: Cambridge University Press, 1992); Mark A. Noll, *The Rise of Evangelicalism* (Downers Grove, Ill.: InterVarsity Press, 2004); Thomas S. Kidd, *The Great Awakening* (New Haven: Yale University Press, 2007). These works correct any simple revisionist notion of the international evangelical awakening as an interpretive fiction, invention or myth. See further my review essay of Kidd's book in *The Evangelical Studies Bulletin* 68 (2008): 1-5.
[2]Crawford, *Seasons of Grace*, pp. 148-49; Bruce Hindmarsh, *The Evangelical Conversion Narra-*

year 1750, "Many sinners are saved from their sins at this day, in London . . . in many other parts of England; in Wales, in Ireland, in Scotland; upon the continent of Europe; in Asia and America. This I term a *great work of God*."[3] The notion of a new "work of God," which Wesley defended here against his critics, has its theological analogue in the affirmation of a "founding charism" for a religious order or new school of Christian devotion. Interpreting the movement in this way, evangelicalism appears less as a partisan alignment in Protestant Christianity than as a dynamic school of Christian spirituality something like a religious order in the Catholic church, a sodality or confraternity that arises at a particular time with a particular purpose within the wider church. Comparing early evangelicalism to a Roman Catholic religious order is not as far-fetched as it might at first seem. Thomas Babington Macaulay wrote that the Roman Church would have known exactly what to do with John Wesley and the Countess of Huntingdon and other early evangelicals. The Countess would have had her place in the calendar as St. Selina, and Wesley would have been made the first director general of a new religious society devoted to the needs and honour of the church.[4]

To put this another way, the early evangelical movement appears as a new school of spirituality within the church universal. The nineteenth-century historian John Henry Overton (1835-1903) often used the term *school* when he wrote about the evangelical revival. He wrote of "the Evangelical *school* in the last century" or "the earlier members of the Evangelical school" or "the practical and devotional works of the Evangelical school," and so on.[5] I do not think that Overton was par-

tive (Oxford: Oxford University Press, 2005), pp. 62-67.

[3]John Wesley, *A Letter to the Author of The Enthusiasm of Methodists and Papists Compar'd* (London: 1750), pp. 40-41; or, in the modern critical edition, John Wesley, *The Appeals to Men of Reason and Religion and Certain Related Open Letters*, ed. Gerald R. Cragg, in *The Works of John Wesley*, ed. Richard P. Heitzenrater and Frank Baker, 14 vols. (Nashville: Abingdon, 1989), 11:374.

[4]Lord Macaulay, *Selections from the Writings of Lord Macaulay*, ed. George Otto Trevelyan (London: Longman, Green, 1876), p. 246. Macaulay's speculation is mentioned in John Walsh, *John Wesley 1703-1791: A Bicentennial Tribute*, Friends of Dr. Williams's Library Forty-Eighth Lecture (London: Friends of Dr. Williams's Library, 1993).

[5]John Henry Overton, *The Evangelical Revival in the Eighteenth Century* (London: Longman, Green, 1886), pp. 78, 59, 101, 104 (emphasis added). Overton used this term chiefly to desig-

ticularly self-conscious in his use of the term *school* for the evangelical movement, though he may have been taking a cue from John Henry Newman who wrote in his *Apologia Pro Vita Sua* that "there are various schools of opinion allowed in the church."[6] This nomenclature has also appeared in the history of Christian spirituality, so that it is common to speak especially of Counter-Reformation movements as schools: the Spanish school after St. Teresa, the French school after Francis de Sales or the Italian school in the sixteenth century, and so on.[7] Raymond Deville provides an account of a school of spirituality:

> A spirituality or a spiritual tradition is a certain, symbolic way of hearing and living the Gospel. This "Way" is conditioned by a period, a "fertilized soil[,]" the particular influence of a specific milieu. It can be incarnated in a clearly identified group of human beings and can continue, historically, enriched or impoverished. . . . In this way, a "spiritual tradition" or a "school" of spirituality comes to be.[8]

The description of spirituality by Deville as a "way" recalls the ancient philosophical schools in Greece, where philosophy was likewise understood not as a subject but as a way. The early evangelicals also insisted that their first concern was with a "way" of life itself—true religion or real Christianity—more than with a system of ideas, and their concern was that women and men be formed or "schooled" within this way. I think this nomenclature of "school" may therefore be illuminating in considering the early evangelical movement as a devotional tradition.[9]

---

nate evangelicals in the established church, but he was well aware that the movement embraced Methodists and Dissenters.

[6]John Henry Newman, *Apologia Pro Vita Sua* (1864; reprint, London: Penguin, 1994), p. 247. Again, as Newman wrote later, "The freedom of the Schools, indeed, is one of those rights of reason, which the church is too wise really to interfere with" (ibid., p. 487). In other places, Newman could use the language of schools more pejoratively. Thus, the Protestant Reformers "have been founders of schools; St. Austin is a Father in the Holy Apostolic Church." John Henry Newman, *Lectures on Justification* (London, 1838), p. 65.

[7]See, e.g., Pierre Pouratt, *Christian Spirituality*, trans. W. H. Mitchell and S. P. Jacques (1927; reprint, London: Newman, 1953), 3:x-xii. See also Lawrence S. Cunningham and Keith J. Egan, *Christian Spirituality: Themes from the Tradition* (New York: Paulist, 1996), pp. 22-23.

[8]Raymond Deville, *The French School of Spirituality: An Introduction and Reader* (Pittsburgh: Duquesne University Press, 1994), pp. 153-54. See also Joseph de Guibert, *The Theology of the Spiritual Life*, trans. Paul Barrett (New York: Sheed and Ward, 1953), pp. 22-25.

[9]Cf. the discussion of schools of spirituality by Lawrence Cunningham in chapter five of this volume.

This use of the term *school* for devotional traditions has its parallel not only in ancient philosophy but also in art history, and for this usage, the eighteenth century itself was pivotal. It was in the eighteenth century that the artist and critic Joshua Reynolds, the first president of the Royal Academy in England, spoke often of his hope that "this nation should produce genius sufficient to acquire to us the honorable distinction of an English School."[10] Reynolds realized that such a school would have its own artistic originality, even while drawing deeply on the past masters' tradition. Thus, whether philosophical or artistic or devotional, the idea of a school suggests a unique genius and a distinctive ethos or *paideia* for the instruction and formation of its members, even if a school still exists as one among other schools and as a part of a larger tradition.

A TALE OF TWO BOOKS: CLASSICAL CHRISTIAN SOURCES FOR EARLY EVANGELICALISM

In order to argue that evangelicalism emerges as a devotional movement in continuity with older traditions Christian spirituality, I would like to look at some of the sources on which the movement depended. The reading lists of the early evangelicals show that they were in fact reading some of the very same sources that evangelicals seem to have rediscovered since the late 1970s. However, early evangelical leaders distinguished between what they read as authorities for doctrinal theology and what they read devotionally ("practical divinity"). The calf-bound folios tended to be broadly from the Reformed tradition, but the cheap octavo and duodecimo pocket books ranged much more widely in scope.[11] Still, there was a deep "experimental" tradition of classical

---

[10]Joshua Reynolds, *Discourses on Art*, ed. Robert Wark (San Marino, Calif.: Huntington Library, 1959), p. 248 (Discourse XIV). Reynolds's hopes were soon fulfilled, and it was not long until artists of his generation were widely spoken of as an English school. Holdger Hoock writes, "The concept of a 'school' of art changed from the early seventeenth-century notion of a studio with the assistants and pupils of a master, through vaguely evoking a body of art produced in a country, to connoting something like a national style around 1800. In eighteenth-century England these meanings were used alongside each other." Holdger Hoock, *The King's Artists: The Royal Academy of Arts and the Politics of British Culture, 1760-1840* (Oxford: Oxford University Press, 2003), p. 67.

[11]The important contemporary distinction between doctrinal and controversial theology, on the one hand, and practical divinity, on the other, is described by Isabel Rivers, "Dissenting

spirituality that nourished the early evangelical leaders. This was, as
C. S. Lewis famously wrote, "the great level viaduct which crosses the
ages," and the early evangelicals were in continuity with it.[12]

I have sought elsewhere, as have other historians, to point out the debt
of evangelicalism on both sides of the Atlantic to the old Puritan divinity.[13] Whether it was the colorful parson William Grimshaw in Haworth
in Yorkshire discovering a volume by John Owen on justification on the
shelf at a friend's house, opening the book and feeling a palpable flash of
heat, or whether it was the future Methodist preacher John Pawson from
near Leeds who found that several of John Bunyan's books and Joseph
Alleine's *Alarm to the Unconverted* "fell into his hands" while under the
travail of conversion, or whether it was the Anglican James Hervey getting his cloudy understanding of evangelical doctrine cleared up by reading Marshall's *Gospel Mystery of Sanctification*—by these direct means,
and by many other more indirect paths, Puritan teaching reached the
early evangelicals and stimulated their own movement.[14]

In what follows, however, let me illustrate the continuity of early
evangelicalism with earlier Catholic spirituality by telling the tale of
two books—one that points to the appropriation of the mystical tradition by early evangelicals, and another that points to their appropriation of the ascetical tradition.

HENRY SCOUGAL, *THE LIFE OF GOD IN THE SOUL OF MAN*

The Life of God in the Soul of Man was written by Henry Scougal (1650-
1678), a Scottish bishop who died young but who was most remembered for this book, published in 1677, the year before he died. He was
part of a circle of Scottish Episcopalians who gathered round Robert

and Methodist Books of Practical Divinity," in *Books and Their Readers in Eighteenth-Century England*, ed. Isabel Rivers (Leicester, U.K.: Leicester University Press, 1982), p. 127.
[12]C. S. Lewis, "On the Reading of Old Books," in *God in the Dock*, ed. Walter Hooper (Grand Rapids: Eerdmans, 1970), p. 204.
[13]See D. Bruce Hindmarsh, *John Newton and the English Evangelical Tradition* (Oxford: Claren-don, 1996), esp. pp. 49-82, 119-68; and the summary of Puritan antecedents in Noll, *Rise of Evangelicalism*, pp. 48-54.
[14]These and other examples are given in J. D. Walsh, "The Origins of the Evangelical Revival," in *Essays in Modern English Church History*, ed. G. V. Bennet and J. D. Walsh (Oxford: Oxford University Press, 1966), pp. 159-60.

Leighton and who were devotees of the Continental mystics in general, and Mme Guyon in particular. They have been described, not inappropriately, as "the mystics of the Northeast." Scougal was influenced by the Catholics Thomas à Kempis (c. 1380-1471), Teresa of Avila (1515-1582) and Gaston de Renty (1611-1649) as well as by several contemporary English writers, such as the Cambridge Platonist Henry More (1614-1687).[15] Scougal's spiritual doctrine was mystical, urging the reader to experience for herself, in reality and not in name only, the true bliss of union with God. His metaphors too were those of the mystics. The divine life in the human soul was, he said, "a real participation of his Nature, it is a beam of the Eternal Light, a drop of that Infinite Ocean of goodness."[16]

The Life of God in the Soul of Man was, originally, a letter of spiritual counsel Scougal wrote to a certain Lady Gilmour, but the published version makes this more universal, like the way Francis de Sales's counsel to Mme Charmoisy becomes generalized as advice to "Philothea" (a lover of God) in his *Introduction to the Devout Life*. Scougal's book was divided into three parts. Part one describes true religion as "an Union of the Soul with God, a real participation in the Divine Nature, the very Image of God drawn upon the Soul, or in the Apostle's phrase, *it is Christ formed within us*. Briefly," says Scougal, "I know not how the nature of Religion can be more fully expressed than by calling it a *Divine Life*."[17] Part two describes the excellencies of true religion, thus defined. Scougal seeks to draw out the reader's affections by sketching a compelling picture of the beauty and desirability of the divine life. It is what we have really been longing for all along. It is what shall restore the understanding, will and affections to wholeness. He asks, for example, "What is a little skin-deep Beauty, or some small Degrees of Goodness, to satisfy a Passion which was made for God?"[18] Finally, part three offers practical guidance in the duties and difficulties of this life, including instruction on meditation and prayer.

---

[15]D. G. Henderson, *Mystics of the North-East* (Aberdeen: Third Spalding Club, 1934), p. 13.
[16]Henry Scougal, *The Life of God in the Soul of Man, or, the Nature and Excellency of the Christian Religion with the Method of Attaining the Happiness It Proposes* (London, 1677), p. 12.
[17]Ibid., p. 5.
[18]Ibid., p. 18.

This book had a profound influence on John Wesley when he read it in Georgia in 1736, and Charles Wesley later gave a copy of his book to George Whitefield, who would write in his *Journal* that he never really knew what true religion was until he read this "excellent treatise." After reading Scougal on union with God and Christ formed within us, Whitefield said, "A Ray of Divine Light was instantaneously darted in upon my Soul, and from that Moment, but not till then, did I know that I must be a new Creature."[19] In 1739, when John Wesley described how he differed from the majority of the clergy, he quoted Scougal, saying that while they might see holiness as an outward thing, he believed it to be an inward thing, namely, "the life of God in the soul of man," and he continued, quoting Scougal almost verbatim.[20] This was also a book that Jonathan Edwards comments on twice in his catalogue of books.[21] Indeed, Isabel Rivers has recently traced just how widely Scougal was read and appropriated by a range of denominational leaders in the eighteenth and nineteenth centuries.[22]

How influential was this book beyond this circle of famous evangelical leaders? Consider for a moment a Methodist layman named John Lancaster who started a Sunday school in a cellar at the corner of Travis Street and London Road in Manchester in 1785.[23] The next year he had a printer bind several of his duodecimo Methodist tracts and pamphlets in one volume, and he signed his name on the inside of the front cover in a rough and uneven hand, with large round letters: John Lancaster, 1786. When I examined this bound volume for myself, I saw that the front and end papers were filled with his handwriting, mostly

---

[19]George Whitefield, *A Short Account of God's Dealings with the Reverend Mr. George Whitefield . . . from His Infancy, to the Time of His Entring into Holy Orders* (London, 1740), p. 28.

[20]John Wesley, September 13, 1739, *Journals and Diaries II (1738-1743)*, ed. W. Reginald Ward and Richard P. Heitzenrater, vol. 19 of *The Bicentennial Edition of the Works of John Wesley* (Nashville: Abingdon, 1976-), p. 97.

[21]Jonathan Edwards, *Catalogues of Books*, ed. Peter J. Thuesen, vol. 26 of *The Works of Jonathan Edwards* (New Haven: Yale University Press, 2008), pp. 219, 281.

[22]Isabel Rivers, "Henry Scougal's *The Life of God in the Soul of Man*: The Fortunes of a Book, 1676-1830," (paper presented at the monthly lecture program of the Bibliographical Society, November 20, 2007; electronic copy provided by the author).

[23]My identification of John Lancaster, whose marginalia appears in the Bodleian volume, is based on the reference in Luke Tyerman, *The Life and Times of the Rev. John Wesley*, 3rd ed. (London: James Sangster, 1876), 3:416n.

with the words of hymns he had copied out. There were other signs of heavy use throughout the volume. It was well worn and soiled, and it had nearly fallen apart from being lovingly read and reread. It brought to mind my grandfather's Bible, which I remember him reading hour by hour at his kitchen table, and which in the end had barely a sheet left stitched in place.

The first pamphlet in Lancaster's collection was a frayed copy of the fifth edition of John and Charles Wesley's *The Nature, Design, and General Rules, of the United Societies* (1747). This was an appropriate piece to give first place in his book, since it was a kind of constitutional document for early Wesleyan Methodism. It begins with a narrative written by John Wesley giving an account of how the movement began in 1739, as Wesley gave spiritual direction to eight or ten conscientious souls in London as a group. In Wesley's account, he explains that what emerged was "a Company of Men having the Form and seeking the Power of Godliness, united in order to pray together, to receive the Word of Exhortation, and to watch over one another in Love, that they may help each other to work out their Salvation."[24] As a lay Methodist in 1786, John Lancaster would have been under Methodist discipline in just such a society in Manchester, and no doubt he returned often to read and reread the directions in this pamphlet. And so he marked up several passages and underlined important sentences here and there.

I came across John Lancaster's volume by a kind of accident. I went to Oxford for most of one summer to work in the Bodleian Library, and several of the volumes I was reading happened to be from the eighteenth-century Godwyn pamphlets, many of which are in bound collections. I placed a stack request for a copy of John Wesley's edition of Henry Scougal's *Life of God in the Soul of Man*, published in 1744, and it appeared on my desk bound up with several other tracts as part of John Lancaster's volume. It was, in fact, the second piece in the volume, right after the *Nature, Design, and General Rules, of the United Societies*. Wesley's Scougal sold for four pence, and it was one of several spiritual classics that Wesley abridged in the 1740s as part of his program "to

---

[24]John Wesley and Charles Wesley, *The Nature, Design, and General Rules, of the United Societies, in London, Bristol, Kingswood, and Newcastle Upon Tyne*, 5th ed. (Bristol, 1747), p. 4.

furnish poor people with cheaper, shorter, and plainer books than any I had seen."[25] Wesley had a knack for condensing books, and he got Scougal's *Life of God* down to forty-eight pages duodecimo in his *ad populum* edition. But as I turned the pages of this devotional work in the Bodleian Library, I did so with a vivid sense of reading over the shoulder of John Lancaster in Manchester.

Given the importance of this volume in the spiritual biographies of John and Charles Wesley and George Whitefield, it is no wonder that John Lancaster would have valued this small book and had it stitched together with his other Methodists tracts in 1786. Perhaps he even read some passages to his Sunday school pupils in that cellar on London Road in Manchester, reminding them that the aim of true religion is not that we might appear godly, but that we might really become so.

John Lancaster's inscription on my reading copy of Wesley's Scougal is a nice little clue to how spiritual classics were read by the early evangelicals and how these classic works reached rank-and-file lay people. For John Lancaster the mystical doctrine of Scougal was literally contextualized, bookended and bracketed by the Wesleyan hymns he wrote out on the endpapers of the book, just as it was literally stitched to the rules of the Methodist societies, on one side, and a sermon by Wesley on the "Means of Grace," on the other. As literature, and in terms of practice and social location, Scougal's spiritual teaching was received and naturalized as evangelical Methodist spirituality. It was sandwiched, as it were, between "O For a Thousand Tongues to Sing" and "And Can It Be." This is a good example of how classical Christian spirituality could be transmitted from another time and place to nourish a new generation and stimulate a fresh experience of the word of God. Scougal's text transmitted the ideals of pure love and entire resignation to God as expressed in the Catholic continental tradition of Fénelon, Mme Guyon and Molinos, and these ideals in turn were taproots of evangelical spirituality. This reception

---

[25]John Wesley, Sermon 87, "On the Danger of Riches," §7, in *Sermons III*, ed. Albert C. Outler, vol. 3 of *The Bicentennial Edition of the Works of John Wesley* (Nashville: Abingdon, 1976-), p. 238.

history from Scougal to Wesley to the layman John Lancaster illustrates not only the continuity of early evangelical piety with one strand of continental mysticism but also the democratization and popularization of that tradition. At the very moment in history described as the crisis or twilight of mysticism for the Roman Catholic Church, elements of the mystical tradition surfaced in the popular piety of English-speaking Protestants.

One should not overstate the influence of the mystical tradition on early evangelicalism. One would look in vain for an appropriation of many sources in the Eastern Church beyond Pseudo-Macarius and Ephrem the Syrian, and there was likewise almost no appreciation for the long Pseudo-Dionysian tradition in the West or of the vernacular mystical tradition of the late middle ages. Wesley himself could be very critical of solitary religion, and he famously rejected mysticism as such in his narrative of his conversion at Aldersgate.[26] Nevertheless, the Wesleyan concern for assurance and for entire sanctification, like the Calvinist doctrine of contemplation and the ideal of entire resignation to the will of God, show the influence of Scougal and the ideals of writers such as Mme Guyon. But this does not mean that Wesley and other evangelicals appropriated continental spirituality uncritically. Wesley wrote a letter in November 1774 to Elizabeth Ritchie, in which he sounded ambivalent: "There are many excellent things in Madam Guion's Works; and there are many that are exceedingly *dangerous.* . . . And it is not easy, unless for those of much experience, to distinguish the one from the other."[27] In the end, the wry comment of Reginald Ward on John Wesley probably sums up well the influence of the mystical tradition on evangelicalism: "Mysticism . . . was pardonable provided the subject did not inhale."[28]

---

[26]Wesley famously wrote, "'Holy Solitaries' is a Phrase no more consistent with the Gospel than Holy Adulterers. The Gospel of CHRIST knows of no Religion, but Social; no Holiness but Social Holiness." John Wesley, Preface to *Hymns and Sacred Poems by John Wesley . . . and Charles Wesley* (London, 1739), p. viii. Again, in the narrative of his Aldersgate experience on May 24, 1738, he describes his brief encounter with, and subsequent rejection of, the mystical way. Wesley, May 24, 1738, *Journal and Diaries I (1735-1738)*, §§7-8, in *Works*, 18:245-46.

[27]*The Letters of the Rev. John Wesley*, ed. John Telford (London: Epworth, 1931), 6:125.

[28]W. R. Ward, *Early Evangelicalism: A Global Intellectual History, 1670-1789* (Cambridge: Cambridge University Press, 2006), p. 131.

THOMAS À KEMPIS, *THE IMITATION OF CHRIST*

In the front matter of Wesley's edition of Scougal, published in 1744, there is a two-page advertisement of books published by the Rev. Mr. John and Charles Wesley, and this includes forty-two items that were likewise offered in inexpensive editions, and many of these were, like the Scougal book, abridged reprints of spiritual classics. Wesley reprinted, for example, *A Serious Call to a Devout and Holy Life* by the high church Anglican devotee of inward religion, William Law (1686-1761); *Nicodemus, or, A Treatise on the Fear of Man* by the Hallesian Pietist, August Hermann Francke (1663-1727); *Pilgrim's Progress* by the Puritan John Bunyan (1628-1688); an extract of the *Discourses on the Redemption of Man by the Death of Christ* by the Moravian founder Count Nicolaus Ludwig von Zinzendorf (1700-1760); and *An Extract from Mr. Edward's* [sic] *Account of the late Work of God in New England* by Jonathan Edwards (1703-1758). Just from these few examples, reprinted early in the Evangelical Revival, before 1744, we see a wide number of spiritual traditions available to foster the piety of lay people such as John Lancaster. Wesley also reprinted Catholic writers with, for example, his *Extract of the Life of M. de Renty*.

However, the Catholic spiritual writer who most influenced Wesley and other early evangelicals was arguably Thomas à Kempis. In George Whitefield's conversion narrative, he described the period just prior to his breakthrough to faith, and mentions reading Thomas à Kempis, saying, it was "of great Help and Furtherance to me."[29] The Oxford Methodist and future Moravian evangelist Benjamin Ingham began reading Thomas à Kempis in 1733 at Oxford, and once he was finished himself, he began to read the book with a fellow student at Queen's College.[30] John Newton, the erstwhile slave trader and later hymn-writer and Anglican clergyman, also read Thomas à Kempis just before his conversion.[31] Clearly this was a book on the reading list of many of the early evangelicals.

---

[29]Whitefield, *A Short Account*, p. 45.
[30]Benjamin Ingham, *Diary of an Oxford Methodist, Benjamin Ingham, 1733-1734*, ed. Richard P. Heitzenrater (Durham, N.C.: Duke University Press, 1985), pp. 82, 87, 92.
[31]John Newton, *The Works of the Rev. John Newton* (London, 1808-1809), 1:56.

The Imitation of Christ, traditionally ascribed to Thomas à Kempis and completed about 1441, was collected in four books. Books one and two are thematically arranged counsels, directions and advice, but books three and four are given in the form of a dialogue between Christ and the believer. The first three books have often been taken as representing the threefold way of purgation, illumination and union.[32] Book one speaks of self-denial and turning away from the world, from vanity and temptation. Book two counsels the reader to turn inward, for the kingdom of God is within. Book three explores the union with Christ in secret, and book four continues this dialogue in the context of sacramental devotion. The treatise is fundamentally ascetical, and it presents a rigorous call to detachment, a *contemptus mundi* whose aim is that God would be one's supreme and final end. Deeply Augustinian, the *Imitation* often echoes passages in *On Christian Doctrine*.

The Imitation of Christ was yet another of the spiritual classics that came under John Wesley's editorial eye, to be reissued in abridged form or "extracts," as he typically called them. Wesley published two editions of the *Imitation*, one in 1735 and another in 1741.[33] Between the publication of his first and second edition, a lot happened for Wesley. In 1738 he experienced an evangelical conversion, his so-called Aldersgate experience. So the 1735 edition of the *Imitation* was produced in his more high-church period of "Oxford Methodism," a period he would later look back on as one when he was striving under the law but without real peace and joy in believing. But the 1741 edition was published at the height of the early evangelical revival, when Wesley was preaching salvation by faith alone. So in no way did he repudiate Thomas à Kempis after his evangelical conversion. Indeed, he carried a Latin copy around with him all his life, and as late as 1789, two years before his death, he was recommending the book to his nephew.[34] Moreover, Wesley required that every Methodist society be duly sup-

---

[32]See, e.g., Leo Sherley-Price, introduction to Thomas à Kempis, *The Imitation of Christ*, trans. Leo Sherley-Price (London: Penguin, 1952), pp. 14-16.

[33]Wesley also published just book IV of the *Imitation* as *A Companion for the Altar* in 1742 and a Latin edition of the whole text in 1748 for the scholars at Kingswood school.

[34]John Wesley, *The Letters of the Reverend John Wesley*, ed. John Telford (London: Epworth, 1931), 8:171.

plied with books, "particularly with 'Kempis.'"[35]

Wesley's 1735 edition of the *Imitation* was only the third book ever published by him, and it is a handsomely printed and bound octavo volume, with some red lettering and illustrated with five engravings. It is scholarly and contains a full preface by Wesley. Wesley lightly revises a translation by John Worthington made in 1677, chiefly to restore the starkness and directness of the original Latin text. But when you look at the volume, even just at its physical appearance as a material object, you can see that this was a volume for an educated person—a gentleman, an Oxford don or a parish priest.

The edition Wesley published in 1741 was very different. It was shorter (abridged), smaller and cheaper. He clearly had this volume in mind as one for the ordinary workingman or woman. This edition of the *Imitation* went through another eighteen reprintings during his lifetime. And these sold, like Wesley's Scougal, for probably four to six pence each. I examined a copy printed in 1791, the year Wesley died, and it was, like most of the other impressions, *tricesimo-secundo* or 32mo—very tiny, indeed—and it was shabby from use, the spine broken, the stitching unravelling and the pages heavily stained. What a contrast to some of the books I have read at the Bodleian, where I have had to slit the pages in order to read them, since the quires were unevenly sewn and the pages not trimmed properly after being folded and gathered. Clearly *those* pages had never been read until I did so. How different with the early evangelical texts. As I handled and read Wesley's edition of the *Imitation*, I found myself again thinking of earlier readers, working-class Methodist lay people, turning these pages with calloused hands and absorbing the piety of the fourteenth-century *devotio moderna* not within cloister walls, but as artisans, craftsmen and domestic servants in eighteenth-century Bristol or Norwich—or as Sunday school teachers in Manchester. These women and men, who read this volume before me, trusted these words because this small book was placed into their hands by a Methodist lay preacher or band leader or by John Wesley himself. Indeed, Wesley's four-page preface to this

---

[35]John Wesley, *The Works of the Reverend John Wesley*, ed. Thomas Jackson, 3rd ed., 14 vols. (London: Wesleyan-Methodist Book Room, 1872), 8:319.

book was a series of very precise instructions on spiritual reading (likewise abridged from an earlier source), a sort of *lectio divina* for the people, and he exhorted the reader to "read not cursorily and hastily; but leisurely, seriously, and with great attention."[36]

The miniature volume I handled would have fit nicely in a man's vest pocket or the pocket of a petticoat, and it would have been easy to take from one's bed chamber as a devotional companion or *vade mecum* to pull out during spare moments in the course of the day. On February 20, 1758, the lay preacher Thomas Walsh did exactly this, taking his copy of the *Imitation* with him in the coach on the way to Bristol. Though accompanied by three other travellers he was able to read undisturbed and find "great tranquility of mind."[37] And late in life he was still remembered for often quoting a dictum from this book as a reminder to him and to others of the absolute need for humility in all things.[38]

Some years ago I read dozens of manuscript autobiographies of early Methodist lay people, and I can easily imagine a barely literate Methodist sister such as, say, Elizabeth Hinsome, handling a book like this, reading from book one of *The Imitation of Christ*, as she walked to class meeting.[39] She might read the words in Thomas à Kempis that had meant so much to Wesley, "Do what lieth in thy power, and God will assist thy good-will," and receive these words as an exhortation to strive for holiness.[40] And in this way the *quod in se est* ("what in you lies") doctrine of the Brethren of the Common Life would be naturalized as basic Methodist spirituality (though Luther had earlier protested much against this very doctrine in the Heidelberg Disputation).[41] Again, she might read before meeting, "Love all for Jesus, but Jesus for himself," and find herself inspired, at several removes and all unwittingly, by the

---

[36]John Wesley, *An Extract from the Christian-pattern: or, a Treatise on the Imitation of Christ: Written in Latin by Thomas à Kempis*, ed. John Wesley (London: 1791), p. iv.

[37]Thomas Jackson, ed., *The Lives of Early Methodist Preachers*, 4th ed. (1871; reprinted in 3 vols., Stoke-on-Trent: Tentmaker, 1998), 2:192.

[38]Ibid., 2:154.

[39]See further Hindmarsh, *Evangelical Conversion*, pp. 133-35, 158-60.

[40]Thomas à Kempis, *Extract from the Christian Pattern*, ed. John Wesley (London: Printed by J. Paramore, at the Foundry, near Moorfields, 1780), p. 16.

[41]Wesley copied out these lines in the front of his diary in 1734, and he urged the same dictum on his wife, describing it as a "blessed rule." See Ingham, *Diary of an Oxford Methodist*, p. 35; Wesley, *Letters*, 3:213.

spiritual doctrine of Augustine in his teaching on use *(uti)* and enjoyment *(frui)* in *On Christian Doctrine*—that God is to be "enjoyed," loved for his own sake, and all else is to be "used" for the sake of God.[42] Just as Augustine had been an important spiritual guide for the *devotio moderna*, so this doctrine came via Thomas à Kempis to John Wesley, and was passed on again to Elizabeth Hinsome (as we might imagine) and the other members of her Methodist class meeting.

Here again we witness a transmission of classical Christian spirituality to the early evangelicals. If Scougal represented the transmission of a continental mystical tradition, then Thomas à Kempis certainly represented the transmission of a classical ascetical tradition. In eighteenth-century London, an Elizabeth Hinsome reads Thomas à Kempis and her Christian faith is enlivened as an earnest Methodist, just as John Lancaster reads Henry Scougal and likewise is inspired to seek after holiness. The reception and popularization of these texts bears witness to a literary culture that "schooled" the followers of Wesley in evangelical devotion.[43] These are but two examples of the way that the taproots of evangelical spirituality went down deep into various traditions of Christian spirituality, even as the evangelical recrudescence of Christian devotion appeared under new conditions in the eighteenth century and involved new forms and expressions.

THE RECEPTION OF CLASSICAL SPIRITUALITY BY THE EARLY EVANGELICALS

I have said of both of these texts that elements of Catholic spirituality were "naturalized" as these texts were read within the context of Methodism. "Naturalization" is the process by which a foreigner becomes a citizen of a new country, and just as there is adaptation for the immigrant, so also for immigrant texts. This was how the Anglican evangelical John Newton explained the process:

---

[42]Thomas à Kempis, *Extract from the Christian Pattern*, p. 68; cf. Augustine, *De Doctrina Christiana* (Oxford: Clarendon, 1995), 1.3-4.

[43]Vicki Tolar Burton, *Spiritual Literacy in John Wesley's Methodism: Reading, Writing & Speaking to Believe* (Waco, Tex.: Baylor University Press, 2008), demonstrates just how important the rhetorical practices and textual culture of early Methodism were for the spiritual formation of its members.

If such persons as De Fenelon, Paschall, Quenell, and Nicole (to mention no more), were not true Christians, where shall we find any who deserve the name? In the writings of these great men, notwithstanding incidental errors, I meet with such strains of experimental Godliness, such deep knowledge of the workings of the Spirit of God and the heart of man, and such masterly explications of many important passages of Scripture, as might do honor to the most enlightened Protestant.[44]

In this statement Newton grants honorary citizenship to Pascal, Fénelon and these others, among the host nation of "most enlightened Protestants," and he simply edits out their popish accents, which he glosses as "incidental errors." Not all Protestant evangelicals would have been even this generous, but I think that Newton captures almost exactly the process by which Wesley and many other contemporary evangelicals appropriated the insights of Catholic spiritual writers into their own devotion. It probably did not hurt, either, that the Vatican or the church hierarchy condemned most of the Catholic writers listed by Newton.

I am aware that we must be careful how far to generalize from the narrow reception histories of two books among John Wesley and his followers. But, as Reginald Ward has shown, there was a lively and eclectic interest in Christian devotional literature of all kinds on the part of several key Protestant figures in the late seventeenth and early eighteenth centuries, figures on the Continent such as Gerhard Tersteegen (1687-1769), Gottfried Arnold (1666-1714) and Pierre Poiret (1646-1719), who, like Wesley in England, republished exemplary biographies and spiritual handbooks from across a broad range of religious traditions as part of a broad-based movement for piety.[45] These figures each seemed to act as conduits for the spiritual literature of the past, gathering it up and passing it on for another generation. The result was a kind of spiritual equivalent of the "republic of letters" that would emerge among the educated members of society in the North Atlantic world.

A wider perspective on the taproots of evangelical spirituality may

[44]Newton, *Works*, 5:29.
[45]Ward, *Early Evangelicalism*, pp. 40-69.

be gained through an examination of bibliographies, reading lists, book inventories, text collections and church histories from the period.[46] For example, we get an appreciation for the spiritual literature that shaped early Methodism not only in some of these early pamphlets but also in the massive collection of texts Wesley edited in fifty volumes as *A Christian Library: Consisting of Extracts from the Abridgements of the Choicest Pieces of Practical Divinity, Which Have Been Publish'd in the English Tongue, in Fifty Volumes* (1749-1755). Wesley believed that the English language had been furnished with a virtually complete body of practical divinity in the variety of writings and translations that had been published over the previous hundred and fifty years, and certainly those who study the history of the book in Britain might agree with him. The problem, as it seemed to Wesley, was that if one had some fourscore years to read, one could hardly make a beginning on this literature. And among some, say, five hundred folios, where would one begin? Moreover, some of this literature was tedious in style, or contained a mixture of truth and error, or gave contradictory messages. "Now who will be at the pains to extract, the Gold out of these baser mixtures?" asked Wesley.[47] Having just identified this as a Herculean task that one could never accomplish in a lifetime, he went on to say that he was prepared to make an attempt. It took him six years, part time. As Richard Heitzenrater reminds us, he did all this while preaching more than seven hundred times per year, traveling four thousand miles by horse and continuing to publish his usual six or seven other titles per year, not to mention his continuing correspondence and oversight of the societies.[48]

In the end, Wesley abstracted seventy-one authors (and 123 titles), among whom were Anglicans of the Holy Living tradition, such as Jer-

---

[46]This literature is the subject of a major research project by Professor Isabel Rivers, "Vanity Fair and the Celestial City: Dissenting, Methodist and Evangelical Literary Culture in England, 1720-1800."

[47]John Wesley, *A Christian Library: Consisting of Extracts from the Abridgements of the Choicest Pieces of Practical Divinity, Which Have Been Publish'd in the English Tongue, in Fifty Volumes*, 50 vols. (Bristol: Farley, 1749-1755), 1:iv.

[48]Richard P. Heitzenrater, "John Wesley's *A Christian Library*, Then and Now," in *Summary of Proceedings: Fifty-fifth Annual Conference of the American Theological Library Association*, ed. Margret Tacke Collins (Chicago: ATLA, 2001).

emy Taylor, Puritans such as Richard Baxter and Continental writers (both Roman Catholic and Protestant) such as Johann Arndt, Blaise Pascal and Miguel de Molinos. Although he intended chiefly to include authors from the seventeenth and eighteenth centuries, he included some of the Apostolic Fathers and Pseudo-Macarius in the first volume. Again, a picture emerges of the importance of spiritual classics for the rise and progress of evangelical religion in the eighteenth century. Relatively, however, the influence of seventeenth-century authors predominated over earlier sources, and it is clear too that Wesley owed perhaps his largest debt to Puritan devotional writers.[49] These antecedent traditions came together or singly influenced various figures in the early eighteenth century. For all that Wesley read widely and deeply, he was not a serious patrologist like Lancelot Andrewes before him, or Jean Daniélou after. His *ressourcement* of earlier spiritual texts had its limits.

Other sources for the spiritual genealogy of the early evangelicals include reading lists for younger clergy, such as the Dissenter Philip Doddridge supplied to Wesley in 1746. Doddridge lists over forty authors to be consulted for "practical divinity," and these include Anglicans, Puritans and Dissenters from the seventeenth and eighteenth centuries.[50] Or, again, we can reconstruct partial reading lists or book inventories for several evangelical leaders, such as is possible now in the case of Jonathan Edwards with the final volume of the Yale critical edition that includes his "Catalogue of Reading." We also have evangelical church histories, such as, especially, Joseph Milner's five-volume *History of the Church of Christ* (1794-1809).[51] Milner's history was especially

---

[49]Mark Noll summarizes the main taproots for the evangelical awakening in three seventeenth-century movements that emphasized religious experience: English and American Puritanism, Continental Pietism and the Anglican High Church ascetical or Holy Living tradition. These traditions are what we see, above all, in Wesley's *Christian Library*. Mark A. Noll, *The Rise of Evangelicalism: The Age of Edwards, Whitefield and the Wesleys* (Downers Grove, Ill.: InterVarsity Press, 2004), pp. 48-63. Noll's account of these three seventeenth-century antecedents expands on the discussion in Walsh, "Origins of the Evangelical Revival," pp. 132-62.

[50]Philip Doddridge, *The Correspondence and Diary of Philip Doddridge, D.D., Illustrative of Various Particulars in His Life Hitherto Unknown, with Notices of Many of His Contemporaries, and a Sketch of the Ecclesiastical History of the Times in Which He Lived*, ed. John Doddridge Humphreys (London: H. Colburn and R. Bentley, 1829-1831), 4:484-95.

[51]See further J. D. Walsh, "Joseph Milner's Evangelical Church History," *Journal of Ecclesiastical History* 10 (1959): 174-87.

influential. Famously, John Henry Newman gained his love of the early church fathers through Milner. Milner's narrative was explicitly designed as what we might think of as a history of Christian spirituality from an evangelical perspective. In the early church he celebrated Cyprian, Ambrose and Augustine. In the early medieval period he eulogized Gregory the Great and traced the lives of several missionaries. Anselm and Bernard were the focus of the twelfth century (but Aquinas he passed over in the thirteenth as a semipelagian). The Cathari, Waldenses and Lollards helped preserve the doctrine of grace. A few other figures are notable for their only qualified approval (Wycliffe and Hus), or for their absence (Calvin). It was with Luther that the history ended (though John Scott later published a three-volume continuation). This was not a critical church history, and clearly the two heroes of his narrative were Augustine and Luther. Milner ended about where Wesley would begin his *Christian Library*, and by stitching the two together we can get the beginnings of an outline for a spiritual genealogy for early evangelicalism. More than inform evangelicals, Milner's history gave them a pedigree and helped to forge their identity. It was their issues, which he took with him back through the centuries, finding evangelicals in surprising places, and advancing an apology for distinctive tenets such as justification by faith and regeneration by the Holy Spirit. His church history was in essence an evangelical history of Christian spirituality.

What was the main concern of evangelical apologists as the movement coalesced in the eighteenth century? To what end did they seek out this spiritual literature from the past and appropriate its insights in the present? Joseph Milner said in the preface to his church history that he wanted to celebrate what he called "genuine piety," and this gets close to the heart of the matter.[52] Johann Arndt had earlier written a book that would be foundational for the movement for piety in Germany, and its title suggested the same theme: *True Christianity*. (Wesley abridged and republished this text also.) In the middle of the

---

[52]Joseph Milner, *The History of the Church of Christ* [with additions and corrections by Isaac Milner], new ed., 5 vols. (London: Printed by Luke Howard & Sons, for T. Cadell, in the Strand, 1827), 1:iv.

eighteenth century the Edwardsian Joseph Bellamy wrote *True Religion Delineated*, and at the close of the century William Wilberforce wrote his *Practical View of . . . Real Christianity.* "Genuine piety," "true Christianity," "true religion," "real Christianity"—all of these terms signal what was the central preoccupation of the leaders of the evangelical school, namely, that men and women who had a merely formal relationship with the church come to a real experience of Christian faith. The Cornish evangelical Anglican Samuel Walker published a popular sermon series in 1756 that was titled *The Christian*, in which he probed his hearers, saying, "I trust, you shall quickly find the Difference between *Formality* and *Christianity*, and wonder how you could have been so strangely deceived."[53] Another evangelical minister, Henry Venn, wrote a devotional manual, *The Complete Duty of Man*, in which he pled for the advantages of true faith, and called for prayer that all who hear the gospel would be "not almost, but altogether" Christians.[54] The biblical allusion here was to the words of King Agrippa after St. Paul had made his defense before him. Agrippa responded, "Almost thou persuadest me to be a Christian" (Acts 26:28 KJV). Both John Wesley and George Whitefield preached sermons on this text, and like Venn, they urged their hearers *not* to be like Agrippa, an "almost Christian," but to be "altogether" a Christian. The theme for all these early evangelicals was the same: *true religion.*

Christendom still cast its shadow over eighteenth-century society in such a way that most women and men regarded it as their duty (whether they fulfilled this duty or not) to "go to church and sacrament" and to "do no harm." Evangelicalism represented a protest against the idea that adhering to Christian civil society as a nominal Christian was sufficient for salvation.[55] Evangelicalism emerged precisely on the trailing

---

[53]Samuel Walker, *The Christian: Being a Course of Practical Sermons* (London: Printed for Edward Dilly at the Rofe and Crown in the Poultry, and Barnabas Thorn at Exeter, 1759), p. 281.

[54]Henry Venn, *The Complete Duty of Man: Or, a System of Doctrinal and Practical Christianity* (Bath, 1800), p. 326.

[55]Cf. Andrew Walls, "The Evangelical Revival, the Missionary Movement, and Africa," in *Evangelicalism*, ed. Mark Noll, David Bebbington and George Rawlyk (New York: Oxford University Press, 1994), pp. 310-30. Walls writes, for example, "The evangelicalism of the period takes its identity from protest, and in effect from nominal Christianity. Evangelical religion presupposes Christendom, Christian civil society" (p. 312).

edge of Christendom and the leading edge of modernity. Enough scope
had opened for individual agency that an appeal could be made to men
and women to respond knowingly and personally to the gospel message. No wonder so many regarded it as a message not heard before. As
George Whitefield exhorted his hearers in eighteenth-century Glasgow, when preaching on Saul's Damascus Road experience, "Ah my
dear Friends, this must be done to you as well as to *Saul*. . . . God must
speak to you by Name, God must reach your Heart in particular."[56]

This was, as Whitefield might have said, "the one thing needful."
The ancient trope of the contemplative life was the devout Mary, rather
than the busy Martha, in Luke 10. Mary had chosen the "one thing
needful." For evangelicals, who often preached motto sermons on this
text, Christ's words spoke not to a special calling to the religious life,
but to a universal call to devotion, or to "real religion."[57] In this enterprise of fostering "true religion" among lay people, evangelicals were
inspired by the examples of "real Christianity" in the past, and they
drew upon writers of any denomination past or present who seemed
able to communicate this message with power. Their overarching concern was that men and women be deeply formed in Christ.

In conclusion, then, the reception history among evangelicals of
Scougal's *Life of God in the Soul of Man* and Thomas à Kempis's *Imitation of Christ*, along with other indications of the reading of early evangelicals, confirms that the main spiritual influences for the early evangelicals were from the recent past in seventeenth-century Anglican,
Pietist and Puritan devotion, but for figures such as John Wesley and
Joseph Milner and John Newton, these influences were themselves
nested in a wider and longer tradition of "true religion" that was seen to
run from the earliest church right through to their own times, and
across the spectrum from Reformed to Catholic. Just as the painter Sir

---

[56]George Whitefield, *Saul's Conversion: A Lecture, Preached on . . . September 12th, 1741, in the
High-Church Yard of Glasgow* (Glasgow: Printed and sold in the Gallowgate printing-house,
and by Robert Smith, 1741), p. 14.
[57]See the sermon by Philip Doddridge, "On the Care of the Soul . . . One thing is needful" on
Luke 10:42, prefixed to *The Rise and Progress of Religion in the Soul* (Northampton, Mass.:
Printed by William Butler, for the Society for Propagating the Gospel Among the Indians and
Others in North America, 1804), pp. 9-28.

Joshua Reynolds obtained examples of past masters for the Royal Academy in London, even while hoping to establish a recognized English school of art, so also the early evangelical school of spirituality drew on a past masters' tradition, even as they innovated in other ways in light of the exigencies and opportunities of their own times.

Or to put this more personally, and to end where I began, when I started to read Thomas à Kempis for spiritual nourishment in my twenties while working for Youth for Christ, I was doing something very much in keeping with the earliest evangelical tradition. To be evangelical and to be catholic is not eccentric—these are affirmations that belong together in the quest for "true religion."

PART THREE
Spiritual Practices

8 Reading Christ into the Heart

The Theological Foundations of Lectio Divina

CHRISTOPHER A. HALL

Each morning and evening I, like many of you, spend time with the Scripture. I read it, ponder it, and often, thanks to encouraging technological advances, literally listen to it. Yes, through the wonder of iPod technology I am now listening to the Scripture on a regular basis. Sometimes as I listen I will simultaneously read the biblical text with my eyes, an ocular and auditory reading if you will, employing two senses rather than one.

But for the most part—at least as I engage with the Scripture through the use of my iPod—I simply listen to the text. For instance, over the last six months I've been listening to Jesus' Sermon on the Mount from Matthew's Gospel. I'll listen to the sermon in its entirety, click the return arrow on my iPod, and listen to it again. Occasionally I'll repeatedly listen to only part of the sermon—Matthew 5 or Matthew 6 or Matthew 7. I repeat the listening process again and again. As I do so, I'm sensing that Jesus' sermon is slowly seeping into me—a deep down inside kind of seeping, and as Jesus' words soak into me, so does the mind of Christ, a theological underpinning of *lectio divina* that we will investigate in some detail.

As I read and listen to the Sermon on the Mount the analytic side of my brain is surely at work. My mind is processing information, analyzing syntax, following arguments, thinking through metaphors and other illustrations and tracing key themes. After years of reading texts—Christian and otherwise—I can't prevent these ingrained reading habits from kicking in; they are key aspects of the discipline of study. Nor would I want to. When Jesus addresses issues concerning the fulfillment of the Law of Moses, murder, adultery, divorce, oaths, loving one's enemies and so on, the prudent reader will surely investigate how these issues were understood and interpreted in Israel, in Jesus' day and earlier. In fact, Matthew seems to take it for granted that his readers would understand the background to Jesus' statements; Matthew rarely provides contextual information for them because of his confidence that his readers already comprehend the context. Dale Allison reminds us that Matthew is a book "filled with holes," contextual gaps that Matthew is fully confident his readers will traverse readily—at least if they know their Bible well.[1] And so the spiritual discipline of study—a discipline more analytic than synthetic—safeguards and deepens my listening to Jesus' sermon.

Yet if I only employ the discipline of study in my reading of Scripture, a spiritual discipline that entails a purposeful distancing of the reader from the biblical text to facilitate an analysis of its content, my reading may well fall short of its ultimate goal—if the goal of my reading involves more than information gathering and analysis. If ever deepening transformation into the image of Christ is what I'm ultimately seeking in my reading, my study will have to be supplemented by another kind of reading, the spiritual or sacred reading known as *lectio divina*.

Let's return for a moment to my experience of listening to the Sermon on the Mount on my iPod. As I repeatedly listen to the text, I'm using my ears to "read" the text rather than my eyes. As I reflect on the dynamics of my listening, the verb "to seep" again comes to mind. Jesus' sermon is settling ever more deeply into me, filtering through my mind into my heart; his teaching is addressing both my intellect and my affections. Christ's words are percolating within me, much like the bubbling of hot water up through coffee grains. The water seeps through the grains,

---

[1]Allison's phrase comes from a lecture he delivered at the Billy Graham Center, Wheaton College, for the first annual meeting of the Society for the Study of Evangelicalism and Eastern Orthodoxy, September 28, 1991.

flows back to the bottom of the coffee pot, and then bubbles up through the grains again. The metaphor of percolation points to the rich soaking that occurs in *lectio divina*. Hence, as I listen to the text of Scripture I'm not simply gathering information for a future sermon or book. Rather, there is a watering, a soaking or immersion of my mind and heart that study helps to facilitate but is clearly different from study itself.

Most of this paper will focus on the theological foundations of *lectio divina* though a brief introduction to the discipline will help us to understand more fully its theological underpinnings. Eugene Peterson reminds us that reading the Bible can be downright dangerous. How so? Reading the Bible can be a perilous exercise—for ourselves and others—if we go about our reading the wrong way. "Reading the Bible," Peterson writes,

> if we do not do it rightly, can get us into a lot of trouble. The Christian community is as concerned with *how* we read the Bible as *that* we read it. It is not sufficient to place a Bible in a person's hands with the command, "Read it." That is quite as foolish as putting a set of car keys in an adolescent's hands, giving him a Honda, and saying, "Drive it." And just as dangerous.[2]

What kind of reading of Scripture would qualify as dangerous, at least from the perspective and practices *lectio divina* offers and develops? Dangerous reading occurs when we limit our reading of the text to analysis only. It occurs when we consciously or unconsciously distance ourselves from the text, making it a source of information and nothing more. It occurs when in our reading we attempt to control the text's access to us, rather than allowing the lively, active, inspired text of Scripture to address us directly, an address to which we must respond.

By way of contrast to a distanced, dangerous reading, *lectio divina* is, in Peterson's words, "a way of reading that refuses to be reduced to *just* reading but intends the living of the text, listening and responding to the voices of that 'so great a cloud of witnesses' [Heb 12:1] telling their stories, singing their songs, preaching their sermons, praying their

---

[2]Eugene H. Peterson, *Eat This Book: A Conversation in the Art of Spiritual Reading* (Grand Rapids: Eerdmans, 2006), p. 81.

prayers, asking their questions, having their children, burying their dead, following Jesus."[3]

Consider for a moment a cluster of participles that captures well the heart of *lectio divina:* pondering, ruminating, chewing, embracing, addressing, imitating, responding, following, repenting, eating, digesting, revering, meditating, praying, hearing, reflecting, considering, listening, remembering. All these participles connote a movement toward rather than away from the Scripture, a willingness to read slowly, hungrily, attentively, prayerfully, with the full expectation that there is a word in the text—an inspired word spoken by the eternal Word made flesh—that is to be believed, obeyed, hugged, devoured, as if all one's life depended on it. *Lectio divina* is a slow, paced, meditative reading of Scripture, a method of reading the text of the Bible—or other devotional material—in which the specific goal, as I mentioned earlier, is ever deeper transformation into the image of Christ.

Lectio divina concerns much more than the act of reading itself. Yes, in *lectio divina* we are reading a text, but we are reading in a manner and with a purpose that far surpasses the vocalization of written or printed words and their comprehension by the mind. We are reading to be changed, to be transformed, to be recreated, to be reshaped ever more fully into the image of the Word incarnate, Jesus Christ our Lord, sent by the Father to redeem and recreate.

Ignatius of Antioch loved to emphasize that we are all image-bearers.[4] Yet to employ a common phrase, we are "already but not yet." We still "live between the times," and the spiritual discipline of *lectio divina* is particularly concerned with the incompleteness, the imperfection, the "not yet-ness" of our present condition; we are created in and bear the image of God, but our image bearing is now cracked, skewed, distorted. The discipline of *lectio divina* works within us to straighten us out, to heal the spiritual genes that have mutated; indeed, it is a form of gene therapy.

---

[3]Ibid., p. 90.

[4]In every one of Ignatius's epistles he describes himself as "Ignatius the Image-bearer." Cf. The Letter of Ignatius to the Ephesians, Salutation, p. 183; The Letter of Ignatius to the Magnesians, Salutation, p. 203; The Letter of Ignatius to the Trallians, Salutation, p. 215 and so on. The page numbers are from *The Apostolic Fathers: Greek Texts and English Translations,* 3rd ed., ed. Michael W. Holmes (Grand Rapids: Baker, 2007).

The practice of *lectio divina* stretches back across the years to worthies such as Origen, Basil the Great, John Cassian, Gregory the Great and Benedict of Nursia. For instance, a fundamental aspect of Benedict's *Rule* concerns *lectio divina*. Almost all who joined Benedict's monastic community were expected to learn to read, a skill that would enable a more specific kind of reading that had as its ultimate objective the imprinting of what was read on the mind and heart, the intellect and the affections.

My modern iPod acoustic reading resembles somewhat the ancient Benedictine reading technique for spiritual transformation. Jean Leclercq explains that in Benedictine monasteries—and for Benedict himself—to read and to meditate entailed "the phenomenon of reminiscence." To facilitate reminiscence or remembrance, both the fathers of the church and medieval monastics read out loud.

> They read usually, not as today, principally with the eyes, but with the lips, pronouncing what they saw, and with the ears, listening to the words pronounced, hearing what is called "the voices of the pages." It [*lectio divina*] is a real acoustical reading; *legere* [to read] means at the same time *audire* [to hear].[5]

Benedict employed other words and phrases to describe the silent reading that marks how most moderns read texts: *tacite legere* (to read silently); *legere sibi* (to read to oneself); *legere in silentio* (to read in silence).[6] We will return to the importance of remembrance later in this essay.

Michael Casey helps to bring Benedictine reading practices to life:

> The monks tended to read slowly, probably vocalizing the words as they read. Often significant passages would be committed to memory; only a few scholars had the possibility of taking notes for permanent reference. With so few titles available, favorite works would be re-read many times. Because there were few reference books or commentaries, the monks had to learn to sit with difficulties and obscurities and try to puzzle out for themselves the meaning of the page before them. Reading became a dialogue with the text.[7]

---

[5]Jean Leclercq, *The Love of Learning and the Desire for God: A Study of Monastic Culture* (New York: Fordham University Press, 1961), p. 15.
[6]Ibid.
[7]Michael Casey, *Sacred Reading: The Ancient Art of Lectio Divina* (Liguori, Mo.: Triumph, 1995), p. 4.

Lectio divina is often described as including four key aspects or movements: *lectio, meditatio, oratio* and *contemplatio*. We will focus on the first two aspects in this paper. As we do so, I want to use each aspect to demonstrate or point to the theological foundations of *lectio divina* itself. That is to say, the theological foundations of the discipline support the rhyme and rhythm of spiritual reading, whether we are reading the biblical text or other devotional literature.

Lectio divina first involves *lectio*, the reading of the text, often out loud. Undergirding our reading of the text is a fundamental theological proposition that is deeply trinitarian: *the Eternal Word, sent by the Father, has become incarnate in Jesus Christ and continues to speak to us through the Holy Spirit.* The incarnate Word—Jesus of Nazareth—speaks and acts as an infinitely personal being; Christ is God the Son come to us in the flesh to save us from the havoc of sin and to restore us fully into his image. In and through the incarnate Christ's words and actions, then, we encounter and are called to embrace the redemption, restoration and recreation he offers us. As we embrace Christ in faith by listening deeply to his words and imitating his actions as his apprentices—transformation occurs. By faithfully allowing his words and deeds to sink down deep within us—a movement ignited and energized by the power of the Spirit—we are increasingly formed into Christ's image. In our embrace of his words through our intense listening to them, we are increasingly changed into what we were always meant to be, what I would call "real" human beings, recreated and reformed into the image of "the" human being, the incarnate Word.

Andy Crouch, in his book *Culture Making: Recovering Our Creative Calling*, draws our attention to the stories God gives us in the initial chapters of Genesis and reminds us that the first man and woman—Adam and Eve—found "themselves in the midst of a world," a story, if you will, that God was already telling. We, like that original couple, and like all human beings, "always and everywhere" find ourselves "in the midst of a story."[8] The problem is that our story—the story of the human race and our individuating of that story—has gone terribly bad.

---

[8]Andy Crouch, *Culture Making: Recovering Our Creative Calling* (Downers Grove, Ill.: InterVarsity Press, 2008), pp. 22-23.

We have attempted to rewrite God's original script, making ourselves both the authors and main characters—and in doing so have terribly skewed the story line. It is in *lectio divina* that we open ourselves "to a God who changes history." We "not only receive guidance and support," we "offer the opportunity to revolutionize the whole tenor of that segment of history that is my little life."[9]

Lectio divina, through its insistence that we relearn the story through our immersion in it, teaches us to tell and live the story right, reorienting and reforming us in the process. The goal of our reading is the reshaping of our thoughts and actions through an imitation of Christ grounded in an intense, responsive, receptive reading. As we read, our consciousness, as Michael Casey puts it, increasingly conforms to the mind of Christ.

> When our minds and hearts are formed according to Christ, then our actions can be vehicles of grace to others. The precondition is, however, that our consciousness is shaped to agree with that of Christ. And this is precisely the role of *lectio divina*. It is a school in which we learn Christ. . . . *Lectio divina* helps us to encounter Christ, it initiates us into the way of Christ.[10]

Or, in Eugene Peterson's words, *lectio divina* leads to the "fusion" of my story and Christ's story.[11]

To repeat, the theological foundation of *lectio divina* is the entrance into our history—personal and corporate—of the incarnate Word sent by the Father. Christ has spoken and continues to speak as the Holy Spirit enlivens the words of Scripture, applying them to our minds and hearts as we allow his divine speech to sink down within us, seeping into every crack and cranny.

One of the reasons why *lectio divina* is difficult is related to another theological foundation for its practice: in our sinful state we are deeply resistant to the truth about ourselves. We are split spiritually; as God's grace begins to penetrate our consciousness we both welcome it and resist it. We are spiritually schizophrenic, imagining

[9]Casey, *Sacred Reading*, p. 47.
[10]Ibid., p. 39.
[11]Peterson, *Eat This Book*, p. 90.

things that aren't true and blind to reality as it actually is.

The disciplined practice of *lectio divina* breaks into this spiritual blindness, penetrating darkness with light, falsehood with truth. A fundamental movement of the spiritual life is from self-deception to self-awareness, an awareness of the truth about the human condition and the state of our relationship with God that is initially horrifying as we acknowledge the true state of affairs. To acknowledge the truth terrifies and confuses us because we have believed a lie for so long; its falsehood is second nature to us. Over the years—indeed on a daily basis—our thoughts about ourselves and the world we live in have been deeply warped in a number of ways, a curving and cracking of our personalities related to a fundamental lie first stated in the Garden: we must be at the center of things; we must be the kings and queens of the universe. Thus, we are skewed, *incurvatus in se* (curved in on ourselves).

The symptoms of this inward turn—illustrated strikingly by Adam and Eve's fundamental sin—appear in a host of ways: the wounding of our DNA, the distortions and crippling manifest in our families, the disordered loves that mark our individual lives and our cultures. Our imaginations are misshapen, dwarfish, our memories distorted. We recall things we should forget and forget things we should remember.

Yet the incarnate Word—the embodiment of truth—insistently beckons to us. "I want to be in relationship with you," Christ says gently but firmly.

> And as I draw near, you will need to face the truth about me and about yourself. You have harmed yourself in a manner that you still do not recognize fully. You have lived with your spiritual cancer for so long that it seems like health. You are dying and yet you think that you live. And so I must reform you by my Spirit, the Spirit of truth. In this reforming I will ask you to trust me, to trust that I will not harm you, that I know what is best for you because I have created you in my image. As you learn to trust me, you must learn to distrust yourself. You must acknowledge what you have become. As you face and acknowledge the truth about yourself, I will be with you; I will offer you myself in place of your distorted self. For you were created to be what I am. As you listen to what I have said and continue to say, you will slowly become

what I have always desired for you to be. And the story I have always longed to tell you will enter your ears, inform your mind and descend into your heart. A new story, a recreation, will begin.

Lectio divina is a spiritual discipline—ordained and empowered by the Holy Spirit—that acknowledges these key theological foundations and is constructed upon them. If, for example, human beings flee from the truth, *lectio divina* will force them to face it. If sin has distorted the human imagination, *lectio divina* will heal it, often by employing the imagination in a new way, replacing old thought patterns with new ones. If human beings struggle to trust anyone but themselves, *lectio divina* will lead us away from ourselves, gently, slowly, insistently guiding us to the only one worthy of our trust, the one who has created us and made us for himself. Because the eternal Word is incarnated in Jesus Christ, *lectio divina* will employ words, his words, to form his mind in us. If we have parroted false speech, *lectio divina* will teach us to speak truthfully as it grounds us in incarnate truth. If we have imitated false teachers, *lectio divina* will beckon us to imitate the incarnate Word. Christ's words will slowly become our words, his actions our actions, as we apprentice ourselves to him. We will sit at his feet: reading, meditating, praying, contemplating and acting.

The first step, as we have seen, is reading. The theological foundations of *lectio divina* teach us, though, that our reading of a text cannot be a distanced, analytical perusal—one in which we keep the text at arm's length. This safe, calculated approach will simply not do, for the call of *lectio divina* is the call to change, to be formed into the image of the Son. *Lectio divina*, in Jean Leclercq's words, is a way of reading, "entirely oriented toward life, and not toward abstract knowledge."[12] Hence, as we move into the second step of *lectio divina*—*meditatio*—we will need to learn to read in a different fashion and with a different goal in mind.

Eugene Peterson employs a wonderfully evocative metaphor to describe the heart of *meditatio:*

Years ago I owned a dog who had a fondness for large bones. Fortu-

---

[12]Leclercq, *Love of Learning*, p. 17.

nately for him we lived in the forested foothills of Montana. In his forest rambles he often came across a carcass of a white-tailed deer that had been brought down by the coyotes. Later he would show up on our stone, lakeside patio carrying or dragging his trophy, usually a shank or a rib; he was a small dog and the bone was often nearly as large as he was. Anyone who has owned a dog knows the routine: he would prance and gambol playfully before us with his prize, wagging his tail, proud of his find, courting our approval. And of course, we approved. We lavished praise, telling him what a good dog he was. But after awhile, sated with our applause, he would drag the bone off twenty yards or so to a more private place, usually the shade of a large moss-covered boulder, and go to work on the bone. The social aspects of the bone were behind him; now the pleasure became solitary. He gnawed the bone, turned it over and around, licked it, worried it. Sometimes we could hear a low rumble or growl, what in a cat would be a purr. He was obviously enjoying himself and in no hurry. After a leisurely couple of hours he would bury it and return the next day to take it up again. An average bone lasted about a week . . . my dog [was] meditating his bone. There is a certain kind of writing that invites this kind of reading, soft purrs and low growls as we taste and savor, anticipate and take in the sweet and spicy, mouth-watering and soul-energizing morsel words—"O taste and see that the Lord is good" (Psalms 34:8).[13]

I don't know of a better metaphor describing *meditatio* than Peterson's description of his dog "meditating his bone." Abelard's image of *meditatio* as similar to a cow chewing his cud comes in a close second. You might also consider Baron von Hügel's comparison of *lectio divina* as "letting a very slowly dissolving lozenge melt imperceptibly in your mouth." Rainer Maria Rilke describes a reader who "does not always remain bent over his pages; he often leans back and closes his eyes over a line he has been reading again, and its meaning spreads through his blood," a description that applies well to the person practicing *lectio divina*.[14]

The metaphor of eating captures well the heart of *meditatio* and its theological foundations. If, for instance, we have been eating unhealthy

[13]Peterson, *Eat This Book*, pp. 1-2.
[14]The von Hügel and Rilke examples come from Peterson, *Eat This Book*, pp. 3-4.

food for the vast majority of our lifetime, should we be surprised that we need a change in diet? Christ describes himself as

> the bread of life . . . the bread that comes down from heaven, which a man may eat and not die. I am the living bread that came down from heaven. If anyone eats of this bread, he will live forever. This bread is my flesh, which I give for the life of the world. . . . I tell you the truth, unless you eat the flesh of the Son of Man and drink his blood, you have no life in you. Whoever eats my flesh and drinks my blood has eternal life, and I will raise him up at the last day. For my flesh is real food and my blood is real drink. (Jn 6:48-55)

While the church has often interpreted Jesus' words as supporting an elevated, realistic view of the Eucharist, these texts also provide the theological rationale for devouring the Scripture, for gnawing on it like a dog chewing on his bone. For the Scriptures speak of Christ, from beginning to end. Think of the experience of the disciples on the road to Emmaus. Jesus scolds them for failing to understand the Scripture and how the texts they had studied for much of their lives pointed to him. "'How foolish you are, and how slow of heart to believe all that the prophets have spoken! Did not the Christ have to suffer these things and then enter his glory?' And beginning with Moses and all the Prophets, he explained to them what was said in all the Scriptures concerning himself" (Lk 24:25-27). It is when Jesus breaks bread with these disciples that their eyes are opened (Lk 24:31). What had been their problem up to this point? They had been "slow of heart to believe" (Lk 24:25).

Jesus is insistent. He reiterates the point he made on the road to Emmaus when he appears to the disciples, perhaps within hours, again in a context of eating and fellowship: "They gave him a piece of broiled fish, and he took it and ate it in their presence. He said to them, 'This is what I told you while I was still with you: Everything must be fulfilled that is written about me in the Law of Moses, the Prophets and the Psalms'" (Lk 24:42-44).

To meditate upon the Scripture—a key aspect of *lectio divina*—involves more than simply reading it. *Meditatio* is a slow, paced, leisurely gnawing on the Scripture, a reading that breaks through the bone and sucks out the marrow, Christ himself. *Meditatio* is a christological munching, an eschatological feeding because the food offered to us is grown and harvested in the fields of the age to come. As we feed upon Christ in Scripture, we digest Christ, assimilating him, as Peterson puts it, metabolizing him in a concrete, earthy fashion so that he becomes what we are and in so doing changes us into himself.

To stay with the metaphor, we can see how this kind of eating will probably be a slow-paced, delight-filled affair. Cracking the bone will take some time. We will need to be patient, with the text and with ourselves. As far as the text is concerned, we all know that certain biblical texts are accessible, delightful and readily feed us. There is little bone to crack, for instance, in Psalm 23. Other texts are less accessible, bony, resistant to our gnawing, well nigh indigestible. "Why would the Holy Spirit want me to know this?" we ask. How, in any discernible way, is Christ present here?

We don't desert exegesis at this point, letting our imaginations run wild in a search for spiritual insight. Rather, exegesis helps us to crack open the text. Or, to develop the metaphor, solid exegesis is a textual nutcracker. Yet if we simply exegete the text—analyzing it in terms of its syntax, historical and cultural background, authorial intent, and so on—without feeding on the riches exegesis has revealed—we can starve spiritually. We have set the table and prepared the meal. In *meditatio* we enjoy the feast.

Solid exegesis prepares us for *meditatio*, setting our interpretive boundaries as it were, but the next step—founded on the theological principle of the incarnate Word—is to embrace Christ himself and in the embrace to be ever more deeply formed into his image. We increasingly experience his mind as our own as our awareness of reality—our consciousness, as Casey puts it—is transformed into Christ's. And the avenue for this expansion is the inspired words, phrases, narratives, poems, letters and wisdom of the Scripture. The Father, Son and Holy Spirit have inspired these particular sentences and stories; they have set them apart as utterly unique. In turn, the Trinity gracefully employs a spiritual discipline such as *lectio divina* to transfuse the marrow of the Bible into our spiritual blood stream.

Jean Leclercq earlier reminded us that reminiscence—a deepening of memory graced and empowered by the Holy Spirit—plays a crucial role in the forming of Christ's consciousness in us. Margaret Mitchell directs us to a "suggestive comment made by Libanios (Chrysostom's teacher) that through *paideia* [Greek education, tradition and culture] Greek gentlemen were taught to 'install Demosthenes in their souls.'" Chrysostom did much the same thing—substituting Paul and Christ for Demosthenes—during two years spent in solitude in a cave above Antioch. In Mitchell's words, "It would not be an exaggeration to say that Chrysostom saw himself as having installed Paul in his soul; during the two years he spent in the cave memorizing the New Testament, Chrysostom downloaded a great deal of Paul into his memory and consciousness."[15]

Though Chrysostom may not have understood his time in the cave as a period of extended *lectio divina*, his practices in the silence and solitude of the cave describe the discipline and its fruits well. Again, we turn to Mitchell:

> When he lived a solitary monastic life in a cave for two years, devoting most of that time to memorizing the New Testament, Chrysostom inscribed on his brain a lot of Paul, and, at that, a lot of Paul speaking in the first person, now vocalized through [Chrysostom's] own mouth. Not only did constant rereading and memorization of these texts serve to lay the foundation for a life of Scriptural exposition, but it also oriented Chrysostom's own consciousness in a Pauline direction, because of the domination of Paul in the New Testament canon.[16]

Consider Chrysostom's own description of the difference between the experienced and inexperienced reader. "The inexperienced reader when taking up a letter will consider it to be papyrus and ink; but the experienced reader will hear a voice, and converse with one, the one who is absent. . . . The things their writings said, they manifested to all

[15]Margaret Mitchell, *The Heavenly Trumpet: John Chrysostom and the Art of Pauline Interpretation* (Louisville: Westminster John Knox, 2002), p. 43.
[16]Ibid., p. 67.

in their actions. . . . You have a most excellent portrait. *Proportion your-self to it.*"[17]

In Chrysostom's thinking, to proportion oneself to Paul—through the use of a highly developed, engaged memory soaked in the Scrip-ture—is by definition to proportion one's mind and life to Christ. Paul and Christ are inseparable in Chrysostom's thinking. Chrysostom de-scribes Paul as "the teacher of the heavenly dogmas,"[18] "the one who preached that Christ was God,"[19] "the mouth of Christ,"[20] "the voice of the gospel proclamation,"[21] "the one on whose tongue Christ sat,"[22] "the tongue which shone forth above the sun,"[23] "the spiritual rhetor,"[24] "the heavenly trumpet,"[25] "the lyre of the Spirit."[26] "For it is not Paul who spoke, but Christ, who moved Paul's soul. So when you hear him shout and say: 'Behold, I, Paul, tell you' (Galatians 5:2), consider that only the shout is Paul's; the thought and the teaching are Christ's, who is speaking to Paul from within his heart."[27]

For John Chrysostom, to proportion oneself to another is to imitate or copy that person. Chrysostom acknowledges that the attempt to imitate Paul or Christ can be intimidating. Yet, Chrysostom writes, Paul encourages the Corinthian congregation to overcome its fears and doubts: "Now don't you tell me, 'I am not able to imitate you, because you are a teacher, and a great one at that.' However, there is not as great a distance between you and me as from Christ to me. But nevertheless, I imitated him."[28]

The dynamic of this Christological imitation illustrates well the rhyme and reason of *lectio divina*. For Chrysostom, even a brief title, such as "Paul, the apostle," demands that we prayerfully and imagina-

---

[17]Chrysostom quoted in Mitchell, *Heavenly Trumpet*, p. 50 (emphasis added).
[18]*Comm. in Galatians* 6.4, quoted in Mitchell, *Heavenly Trumpet*, p. 76.
[19]*Lazarus* 6.9, quoted in Mitchell, *Heavenly Trumpet*, p. 76.
[20]Ibid.
[21]*Hom. in Acts* 25.1, quoted in Mitchell, *Heavenly Trumpet*, p. 76.
[22]*Hom. in Romans* 32.2, quoted in Mitchell, *Heavenly Trumpet*, p. 76.
[23]*Hom. in Romans* Arg. 1, quoted in Mitchell, *Heavenly Trumpet*, p. 76.
[24]*Poenitencia* 2.5, quoted in Mitchell, *Heavenly Trumpet*, p. 76.
[25]*Hom. in 2 Corinthians* 11:1, quoted in Mitchell, *Heavenly Trumpet*, p. 76.
[26]*Lazarus* 6.9, quoted in Mitchell, *Heavenly Trumpet*, p. 76.
[27]*Judith* 2.1, quoted in Mitchell, *Heavenly Trumpet*, p. 77.
[28]Ibid.

tively shape our mind around it, forming "a mental image" so the reality of the title might sink into the memory and motivate holy action.

> For truly when I hear, "Paul the apostle," I have in my mind the one in afflictions, the one in tight straights, the one in blows, the one in prisons, the one who was night and day in the depth of the sea, the one snatched up into the third heaven, the one who heard inexpressible words in paradise, the vessel of election, the leader of the bridegroom of Christ, the one who prayed to be anathema from Christ for the sake of his brothers and sisters. Just like some golden cord, the chain of his good deeds comes into the head of those who attend with precision along with the remembrance of his name.[29]

Through the intense textual meditation ignited by memorization and skillful preaching, Chrysostom believes the soul becomes a canvas of sorts on which the Spirit paints Christologically. Preliminary cleansing is required.

> Consider the soul to be your portrait. So, before the true tempera of the Spirit comes, wipe away the habits which have been wrongly put into it . . . correct your habits, so that when the colors are laid upon it, no longer will you wipe things out again, and damage or scar the beauty which has been given to you by God.[30]

Chrysostom illustrates the link between imaginative meditation on texts, effective preaching and character change by exhorting his audience to imaginatively meditate on the suffering of the martyrs so that, in Mitchell's words, the "homiletical image becomes imprinted on the memory of the hearer" as the Spirit paints on the mind and soul of the auditor. As Chrysostom puts it,

> let us paint on the walls of our mind the punishments of the martyrs . . . it is sufficient to use willingness and genuine, sober-minded reasoning, and by this capacity, just as by some skilled hand, one can draw their punishments. Let us, then, paint on our souls those lying on frying pans, those extended over hot coals . . . so that, by furnishing our lovely house with the variety of this painting, we might make a suitable dwell-

---

[29]*Hom. in Acts* 9.1, 4.3, quoted in Mitchell, *Heavenly Trumpet*, p. 71.
[30]*Catech.* 2.3, quoted in Mitchell, *Heavenly Trumpet*, p. 60.

ing for the king of the heavens. For if he sees such paintings in our minds, he will come with the Father, and will make an abiding-place with us in the company of the Holy Spirit, and our mind will then be a royal house. No absurd thought will be able to come into it while the memory of the martyrs, like some bright-colored painting, is always stored up within us and releases a great shining splendor. And God, the king of all, dwells continually in us.[31]

Mitchell explains:

The paint of these portraits is words, the canvas upon which they are daubed and smoothed out is the memory of the individual auditor, who in the act of reception of the literary portrait recasts it . . . into a visual image upon his or her own heart or mind, where it lies in private exhibition for continual viewing.[32]

Here we have an imaginative, auditory reading available to all who have the opportunity to hear the text of Scripture read aloud—and hopefully explained. As we have seen, however, reading and explanation in the spiritual discipline of *lectio divina* are not for the amassing of information. We read with the intent of forming our human consciousness and character in Christ's image. Church fathers with a monastic background such as Chrysostom readily understood this powerful dynamic. Chrysostom drives his audience to form "an imaginative mental picture,"[33] precisely so that their conscience might be "pricked" and their character changed as they imitate the person of their focus. It is precisely this remembrance, focus and imitation that *lectio divina* facilitates.

The second movement of *lectio divina*—*meditatio*—the aspect we have largely focused on in this essay, indissolubly connects the theological and practical or ethical side of discipleship in Christ. "In secular usage," Leclercq observes,

meditari [to meditate] means, in a general way, to think, to reflect, as does *cogitare* or *considerare*; but, more than these, it often implies intent

---

[31]*Pan. Mart.* 3.3, quoted in Mitchell, *Heavenly Trumpet*, p. 61.
[32]Mitchell, *Heavenly Trumpet*, pp. 62-63.
[33]Chrysostom, *Pan Mart.* 1.2, quoted in Mitchell, *Heavenly Trumpet*, p. 62.

to do it; in other words, to prepare oneself for it, to prefigure it in the mind, to desire it, in a way, to do it in advance—briefly to practice it.[34]

Ponder Leclercq's explanation and Jesus' words in the Sermon on the Mount. The person who "hears" Jesus' words and "puts them into practice is like a wise man who built his house upon the rock" (Mt 7:24). The fool is the person who hears Jesus' teaching but fails to change in his behavior. Hearing, yes. Practice, no. *Meditatio* is specifically practiced to avoid this disjunction between what the ears hear and the arms and legs practice. In the secular world *meditari* was "applied to physical exercises and sports, to those of military life, of the school world, to rhetoric, poetry, music, and, finally, to moral practices. To practice a thing by thinking of it, is to fix it in the memory, to learn it."[35]

Meditatio also has a rich background in Jesus' Jewish heritage. It

> is used generally to translate the Hebrew *haga*, and like the latter it means, fundamentally, to learn the Torah and the words of the Sages, while pronouncing them usually in a low tone, in reciting them to oneself, in murmuring them with the mouth. This is what we call "learning by heart," what ought rather to be called, according to the ancients, "learning by mouth" since the mouth "meditates wisdom: *Os justi meditabitur sapientiam*."[36]

Hence,

> to pronounce the sacred words in order to retain them, both the audible reading and the exercise of memory and reflection, which it precedes, are involved. To speak, to think, to remember, are the three necessary phases of the same activity. To express what one is thinking and to repeat it enables one to imprint it on one's mind. In Christian as well as in rabbinical tradition, one cannot meditate anything else but a text, and since this text is the word of God, meditation is the necessary complement, almost the equivalent, of the *lectio divina*.[37]

To meditate upon a text, to chew on it like a dog chews on a bone, is

---

[34]Leclercq, *Love of Learning*, p. 16.
[35]Ibid.
[36]Ibid.
[37]Ibid., pp. 16-17.

to read a text and to learn it "by heart" in the fullest sense of this expression, that is, with one's whole being: with the body, since the mouth pronounced it, with the memory which fixes it, with the intelligence which understands its meaning, and with the will which desires to put it into practice.[38]

Or in Peterson's words:

Meditatio is the discipline we give to keeping the memory active in the act of reading. *Meditatio* moves from looking at the words of the text to entering the world of the text. As we take this text into ourselves, we find that the text is taking us into itself. For the world of the text is far larger and more real than our minds and experience.[39]

We return to the key theme of this essay, the theological foundations of *lectio divina*. *Lectio divina* is a spiritual discipline practiced with the specific goal of reading Christ into the heart, of proportioning our consciousness to Christ's mind, of shaping our thinking and behavior to the life of Christ—in his words and in his deeds. God, as the writer of the epistle to the Hebrews writes, "has spoken to us by his Son" (Heb 1:2). Thus, we need to learn to listen to him well.

The apostle John teaches that the eternal Word "became flesh and made his dwelling among us. We have seen his glory, the glory of the One and Only, who came from the Father, full of grace and truth" (Jn 1:14). John writes, "No one has ever seen God, but God the One and Only, who is at the Father's side, has made him known" (Jn 1:18). Jesus instructs the apostles: "It is for your good that I am going away. Unless I go away, the Counselor will not come to you; but if I go, I will send him to you," and when the Spirit "comes, he will guide you into all truth. He will not speak on his own; he will speak only what he hears, and he will tell you what is yet to come. He will bring glory to me by taking from what is mine and making it known to you" (Jn 16:7, 13-14).

We chew, digest and assimilate this rich revelatory meal served to us by the Trinity through the practice of *lectio divina*. As we do so, the

[38]Ibid., p. 17.
[39]Peterson, *Eat This Book*, p. 99.

possibility behind Paul's exhortation in his letter to the Philippians—
"Your attitude should be the same as that of Christ Jesus" (Phil
2:5)—increasingly becomes a reality within us. For, as Paul says to
the Corinthians, "we have the mind of Christ" (1 Cor 2:16).

And so, as the evening draws to a close and sleep approaches, I turn
on my iPod. I twirl the directional dial to Matthew 5 and once again I
am with Jesus on the mountain. I hear the now familiar cadences of the
beatitudes:

> Blessed are the poor in spirit, for theirs is the kingdom of heaven.
> Blessed are those who mourn, for they will be comforted. Blessed are
> the meek, for they will inherit the earth. Blessed are those who hunger
> and thirst for righteousness, for they will be filled. Blessed are the mer-
> ciful, for they will be shown mercy. Blessed are the pure in heart, for
> they will see God. Blessed are the peacemakers, for they will be called
> sons of God. Blessed are those who are persecuted because of righteous-
> ness, for theirs is the kingdom of heaven. (Mt 5:3-10)

I hit the pause button, rewind the dial and listen to the same words
again and again. They are forming me, shaping me, changing me, healing me. Christ's mind, slowly, ever so slowly and painfully, is gradually
becoming my own.

Metaphors to describe what is happening to me as I fiddle in the
dark with my iPod tumble together: I am gnawing on a bone; I am
listening to a symphony; I am eating a meal whose courses never end; I
am swimming in a river; I am drinking living water; I am silently listening, like a wolf in the mountains, with ears perched to pick up the
smallest hint of a sound that may lead me to my prey, my sustenance;
and occasionally, only occasionally, I let out a howl.

9 Spiritual Direction as a Navigational Aid in Sanctification

Susan S. Phillips

Some went down to the sea in ships. . . . they saw the deeds of the Lord, his wondrous works in the deep. . . . [H]e brought them to their desired haven.

Psalm 107:23-24, 30 (NRSV)

The words "uncharted territory" crop up repeatedly these days. People say the presidential election of Barack Obama signals a new era in American race relations, a venture into uncharted territory. The global economic crisis lands us in uncharted territory, and we are eager to find our bearings. In the world of theological education, we're exploring uncharted territory as the demand for and shape of seminary training changes. Throughout Scripture we see that the human condition entails entering uncharted territory and, at times, turbulent seas. And it is also true that God does "wondrous works in the deep," bringing those who call on him (in the Jerusalem Bible's words) "safe to the port they were bound for" (Ps 107:24, 30). The ancient Christian art of spiritual direction helps people navigate these realities.

Elsewhere I've written about spiritual direction from inside the practice.[1] This essay will address the subject from a wider perspective, in terms of how spiritual direction may offer navigational aid as we walk "according to the Spirit" (Rom 8:4) through our contemporary landscape. A century ago the early sociologist Max Weber wrote that the "disenchanted" world of Western modernity is one in which the earlier meaningful unity of life has been "split into rationalistic cognition and mastery of nature on the one hand, and 'mystic' experiences on the other."[2] These spheres are separated, obliterating any helpful navigational hermeneutic between them and privileging the legitimacy of the rational. Thus, the life of prayer and what passes for ordinary life are relegated to separate domains; or, as can be our experience, spiritual life is wholly private.

According to Weber, privatized "mystical" experience in our world "robbed of gods" is the result of the eclipse of a religious worldview, not a lingering remnant of or reaction against it. Religious faith in modern times thus becomes an inward, subjective—"mystical"—attempt at finding meaning that is distinct from that found through the overarching worldview of science and reason. Faith then is treasured in the solitary, at times lonely, haven of each person's heart, and "the individual can pursue his quest for salvation only as an individual."[3]

In this analysis, spiritual experience, while present, is separated from—uncharted by and uncharting of—reason and community. It is also extracted from its place among the traditional pillars of Christian discernment: Scripture and theology, church history and practice, and the community of believers. Private spiritual experience is not lost but, rather, sequestered. Spiritual directors witness this effect of modern life in those who seek their prayerful, spiritual accompaniment.

During the last thirty years in the United States, and elsewhere in

---

[1]See Susan S. Phillips, *Candlelight: Illuminating the Art of Spiritual Direction* (Harrisburg, Penn.: Morehouse, 2008).

[2]Max Weber, "The Social Psychology of World Religions," in *From Max Weber: Essays in Sociology*, ed. Hans Heinrich Gerth and C. Wright Mills (New York: Oxford University Press, 1946), p. 282. I am indebted to Jong-Tae Lee for his unpublished theological reflections on Weber's theory.

[3]Ibid.

the world, we have seen the proliferation of personal spiritualities unmoored from theological discourse and communities. People are, in the often-quoted expression, "spiritual but not religious." They meditate in the privacy of their own homes. The minivan and office cubicle become "monasteries," and people stitch together spiritual quilts composed of appealing pieces from the East, the West, the indigenous and the esoteric. Bookstore spirituality shelves carry titles proclaiming the acquisition of personal power through the appropriation of secrets. This bubbling up of the disenfranchised spiritual dimension of life into popular culture presents an opportunity for the Christian church. It's a privilege to participate alongside people bringing spirituality into substantive conversation with theology, historical Christian thought and practice, Scripture and the contemporary soul care arts.

Within evangelical Christianity, the "Call," issued in 2006 by Robert Webber and others, addressed the need to draw on the whole history of Christian thought and life, and "turn away from methods that separate theological reflection from the common traditions of the Church."[4] In hopes of revitalizing contemporary theology, pastoral ministry and Christian devotional life, some scholars have looked to the writings of the early church, not simply as historic records or repositories of doctrine, but as sources of spiritual guidance for the shaping of our sanctification.[5] Similarly, some evangelical Christians—in church communities and individually—are rediscovering the spiritually salutary possibilities of ancient spiritual disciplines, such as slowly praying biblical passages, taking occasional silent retreats, making pilgrimages and engaging in spiritual direction.

For discerning the helpfulness of spiritual writing and disciplines, Christian theology and Scripture set guidelines. We must ask of texts and disciplines if they help us better attend to the Holy Spirit. Do they help us pray, confess and repent? Do they enable us to follow Jesus in

---

[4]Robert Webber and Phil Kenyon, "A Call to an Ancient Evangelical Future" (Northern Seminary, Lombard, Illinois, May 2006), article 3. Cited at <www.tumi.org/migration/images/stories/pdf/calltofuture.pdf.>

[5]For an extended discussion of this subject, see the published papers from the 2007 Wheaton Theology Conference: Mark Husbands and Jeffrey P. Greenman, eds., *Ancient Faith for the Church's Future* (Downers Grove, Ill.: InterVarsity Press, 2008).

biblically informed discipleship, expressing God's love and truth in the world? Do they aid in the integration of our spiritual experience, intellectual understandings and moral comportment in the world? These questions help us chart our course by the One who established the moon and the stars in their courses, and they are questions on the minds of spiritual directors as they attend to those who seek their listening care.

SPIRITUAL DIRECTION AS SPIRITUAL DISCIPLINE

As a Christian spiritual director and sociologist, I care about these orienting theological and pastoral questions and how they help us—individually and corporately—follow Jesus. Our cultural situation, characterized by the polarization of spiritual experience and rational understanding, is also marked by the accelerated rationalization and work-domination of all spheres of life. If this culture is "disenchanted," it is also dehumanizing. We become isolated performers and spectators in all-encompassing socioeconomic dramas, and, sadly, this can be true in our churches.

Yet as the explosion of communication devices and websites shows us, we long for relationship. We crave connection. The relationship of spiritual direction extends a quiet space for listening to one's soul and reorienting toward God. Dietrich Bonhoeffer wrote, "The first service that one owes to others in the fellowship consists in listening to them. . . . But Christians have forgotten that the ministry of listening has been committed to them by Him who is Himself the great listener and whose work they should share."[6] All Christians are called to the ministry of listening. Spiritual directors see themselves as specially called to this ministry, by the grace of the One who is the true spiritual director. We listen for the Holy One in another's life as that person traverses uncharted territories.

In an attachment-disordered and attention-deficient culture that "tweets" and "friends," being listened to helps us hear God, ourselves and our neighbor. We live in postresurrection days, trusting that God is nearby, but not always noticing God. For us as for the pair traveling

---

[6]Dietrich Bonhoeffer, *Life Together*, trans. John W. Doberstein (1938; reprint, New York: Harper & Row, 1954), pp. 97-99.

to Emmaus, another's listening attention might help us stop on the road of life, experience our deepest sadness, hope, fear and faith, and then, perhaps, see God for a moment.

A story from spiritual direction illustrates this. Monthly for nearly ten years Jim has been seeing me for spiritual direction. With him as with all directees, I light the candle at the beginning of the session and say, "We light the candle as a reminder that God is with us." Jim regards the candle in silence, and then tells me about his life. During his first visits he told me about experiences he had of God that led him, in midlife, to pursue ordained ministry. He felt God called him clearly, but indirectly, in particular moments over a number of years. These experiences occurred while standing alone one day in a circle of trees; when seeing the eternal flame at a Holocaust museum; and when hearing Scripture read in a foreign language in a beleaguered church in Eastern Europe.

When Jim told me about the church experience, noticing what looked like God's grace, I said, "Tell me about being so moved in that church." And he did, seemingly re-experiencing grace as he spoke. Across from him as the candle flickered, I registered God's love for Jim, and Jim's for God.

Jim had cherished these experiences in his heart. Unspoken and unexamined though they were, the few quiet, ordinary experiences in a grove of trees, a museum and an old wooden church shaped his experience of God's call and charted his vocation, though they never seemed relevant to seminary conversations. They sustained him through years of theological study, a serious illness and complications in his work toward ordination. In spiritual direction Jim noticed what made his heart burn within him, assuring him that God was with him.

Jim told me: "Meeting with you helps me hold onto God's call, time and again, even when God seems silent. It helps me trust, confess and hope." Remembering the way God communicated to him reorients his attention to God. Spiritual direction has been one means of God's grace, enabling Jim to metabolize private spiritual experiences with the rest of life, including his understanding of faith, Scripture and ministry. Spiritual direction gives Jim the opportunity to speak about his most private spiritual experience, thus bringing it into the fellowship of believers, first with me, and then with others.

Spiritual direction is a spiritual discipline that trains attention toward God and bridges the gap between the spheres denoted by Weber. It gives voice to spiritual life and brings it into conscious dialogue with the rest of life, including religion and intellectual inquiry. This bridging work happening in individual lives needs to happen in the church as well, through bringing spiritual direction into corrective and illuminating conversation with theology and congregational life.

RECENT SHIFTS IN PRACTICES OF SOUL CARE

While the practice of spiritual direction is growing in the Christian church, so, too, the eruption of spirituality in the popular culture is altering the secular practices of soul care, with which spiritual direction has not yet become a full conversation partner.

For example, in February 2009 a San Francisco psychoanalytic institute sponsored a conference titled "Sitting on the Couch: Psychoanalysis Considers Spiritual Practice."[7] The stated aim of the conference was to address the question, "What happens when we open into modes of consciousness that go beyond the personal self?" The psychoanalysts attending the conference were interested in how their rational, scientific practices could be enhanced by "Buddhism and other meditative practices that have flowered in the West."[8] No attention was given to Christianity (which has also "flowered in the West") or its ancient practices of soul care. However, the secular professionals were attempting to move beyond the "disenchanted" incommensurables of private mystical experience, on the one hand, and rational cognition and mastery of human nature, on the other. Increasingly, psychotherapists are trying to understand and work with spiritual phenomena, for, contrary to the expectations of many who developed the theories and treatments of the mind, people don't inevitably turn away from religion as they mature; personal

---

[7]February 7, 2009, sponsored by the Psychoanalytic Institute of Northern California, including speakers A. Hameed Almaas, Diane Hamilton, Peter Carnochan, Charles Dithrich and Karen Peoples.
[8]Text from program flyer.

spiritual experience and desire haven't disappeared despite the efforts of many sciences of the mind; and religion hasn't ebbed in the face of greater civilization. People continue to sense they are part of something large and spiritual, something relational and meaningful. More and more psychotherapy is attending to that awareness.

The legitimation of spirituality by the social sciences has been slow in coming.[9] In naming his science of the mind, Freud chose a German word for "soul" *(Seele)* with all its complexity; however, his English translators substituted the more scientifically acceptable words "mind" and "mental apparatus" to represent the human faculty of focal concern for psychotherapeutic treatment.[10] In the United States the psychological arts were granted scientific status, and the contemporary professions of soul care—the various government-licensed psychotherapies—developed in sharp differentiation from religion.

Most early psychotherapeutic theorists viewed religious thinking as pathology, personal illusion or social brainwashing. Writing of the early psychoanalytic view of religion, one contemporary analyst claims religion "has been thought to keep us childish, looking for a divine mommy or daddy, and to leave us unable or unwilling to face the harshness of reality and the reality of the unconscious." Religion has also been seen "as the weapon of repression, authoritarianism, even of theological sadism, not to mention a great deal of fuzzy thinking."[11]

For decades in the mid-twentieth century, many Christians with firm biblical convictions were wary of psychotherapy as threatening to families, traditional morality and faith in God. Many viewed psychotherapy as creating a pseudoreligion of its own that relativized categories of good and evil and focused on personal satisfaction at the expense

---

[9]Recent years have seen tremendous growth in social scientific study of spiritual experience (such as the healing power of prayer) and concepts (for example, forgiveness, flourishing and gratitude).

[10]For a discussion of mistranslations of Freud's writings into English, see Bruno Bettelheim's *Freud and Man's Soul* (New York: Alfred A. Knopf, 1983). Bettelheim wrote: "St. Jerome remarked about some translations of the Bible that they are not versions, but, rather, perversions of the original. The same could be said of the way many psychoanalytic concepts have been translated into English" (p. 103).

[11]Ann Belford Ulanov, "Mending the Mind and Minding the Soul: Explorations Towards the Care of the Whole Person," in *Spiritual Aspects of Clinical Work* (Einsiedeln: Daimon Verlag, 2004), pp. 40-41.

of costly discipleship and knowing God.[12] They also felt psychotherapy misunderstood faith, at times even ridiculing or eroding it.[13] In sum and on average, until the late twentieth century many Christians saw psychotherapy as cultic, narcissistic and elitist, while many in the field of psychotherapy viewed much religion as repressive, delusional and infantilizing. This was the situation when, thiry years ago, on a National Institute of Mental Health fellowship, I wondered what the church did for the care of souls, and, then, discovered classical accounts and the surviving practice of spiritual direction.

Despite the early antagonism between psychotherapy and religion, the American church, evangelical and otherwise, has increasingly outsourced much of its care of souls to secular professionals. But during the initial period of estrangement, spiritual direction was rediscovered and adapted to contemporary needs, and it continues to thrive even with the growing rapprochement between psychotherapy and religion.[14] Pastoral counseling and Christian psychotherapy have also experienced growth, and more conversation is needed among the Christian practices of soul care.

Unlike psychotherapy, spiritual direction does not rest within a paradigm of treatment and cure. Rather, at its best, it helps people pay attention to God's presence and call in their everyday lives, and it rests in a paradigm of prayer and discernment. For more and more Christians in North America, the rediscovery of the art of spiritual direction offers hope of serious attention to prayer and spiritual formation. Younger evangelicals report they want to follow, not just know about, God, so they seek spiritual direction as a way of staying in touch with God in the midst of their busy, noisy lives.[15]

---

[12]See ibid., p. 41.

[13]See, for instance, Robert R. King Jr., "Evangelical Christians and Professional Counseling: A Conflict of Values?" *Journal of Psychology and Theology* 6, no. 4 (1978): 276-81.

[14]The collegial organization Spiritual Directors International began in 1989 with a few hundred members, and now has an international membership of nearly seven thousand. Still incipient and undeveloped are two needed conversations: (1) among mental health professionals and spiritual directors and (2) among Christian theologians and Christian soul care practitioners of all kinds.

[15]Robert E. Webber, *The Younger Evangelicals: Facing the Challenges of the New World* (Grand Rapids: Baker Books, 2002), p. 185.

Many of us engaged in the discipline of spiritual direction are convinced that the church needs to reclaim soul care (including, but not exclusively, spiritual direction), embed it in Christian community and discourse, and evaluate the common practice today of outsourcing character and psyche formation to secular professionals. In doing so the territory of personal spiritual experience will be informed by the guiding lights of Scripture, community and tradition, and the church as a whole will more fully benefit from people's awareness of the Holy Spirit's action in their lives.

Direction as Navigation

Christian spiritual directors rest in the assurance that we live and move and have our being in God (Acts 17:28), or as Dallas Willard phrased this affirmation, "this is a God-bathed and God-permeated world," even if it doesn't always feel like it.[16] Spiritual directors offer navigational accompaniment in this God-saturated world and part of what they attend to is our spiritually potent uses of metaphors and images. In Scripture metaphors collaborate to express the complex beauty of sanctification: We are born, mature, grow, journey and plant ourselves in Christ. Or not. At times we fail to run the race, walk the path, grow to maturity and sink our roots in good soil. Directors pay attention to images and metaphors as their directees strive to bridge the gap between the mysterious and the rational spheres of life that have been segregated in modernity.

Some are uncomfortable with the imagery evoked by the word *direction*, and prefer the more egalitarian terms spiritual (or soul) *friend* and *companion*. Classical and contemporary writers have attempted to clarify the concept of spiritual direction by analogies to the work of physicians, teachers, coaches, mentors, psychotherapists and sponsors. Other writers use metaphors based in socially organized practices, including those of hospitality, midwifery, spotting (as in weight-lifting) and gardening. But whence and wherefore "direction"? This is an important question, for, according to George Eliot, "we all of us, grave or light, get our thoughts

---

[16]Dallas Willard, *The Divine Conspiracy: Rediscovering Our Hidden Life in God* (San Francisco: HarperSanFrancisco, 1998), p. 61.

entangled in metaphors, and act fatally on the strength of them."[17] What strength lies in the metaphor embedded in the term *spiritual direction?*

The origins of the word *director* have been elusive, but it seems the first such use of the word that became "director" (with reference to spiritual direction) was in a treatise to "The Shepherd," a letter to spiritual directors appended to John Climacus's early seventh century *Ladder of Divine Ascent.*[18] He wrote, "A ship with a good navigator [or pilot] comes safely to port, God willing."[19] The Greek word is *kubernetes,* also used in the New Testament to refer to a ship's pilot (Acts 27:11; Rev 18:17), as well as to the spiritual gift of guidance or "administration" (see 1 Cor 12:28). John Climacus's word describing spiritual fathers or mothers, *kubernetes,* has been translated "pilot of a ship," "helmsman" and "guide," and from this ancient Greek word a number of English guidance-related words derive, including *gubernatorial* and *cybernetics.*[20]

Metaphors of soul navigation abound throughout history. Some fix it within the person. Socrates claimed that reason is the pilot of the soul.[21] "Let Your Soul Be Your Pilot," sang Sting in 1996, the popular YouTube music video showing him and others moving slowly toward the center of a leafy labyrinth, until he is left alone, spread-eagled like Leonardo's Vitruvian man. While his soul piloted him to a kind of Weberian mystical solitude, Sting sang of the failure of physicians, medication and counselors to offer guidance in our journey between hell and heaven, leaving us to our own navigational efforts.[22]

---

[17]From *Middlemarch,* quoted by Bonnie Howe in *Because You Bear This Name: Conceptual Metaphor and the Moral Meaning of 1 Peter* (Leiden: Brill, 2006), p. 1.

[18]Kallistos Ware, "Foreword: The Spiritual Father in Saint John Climacus and Saint Symeon the New Theologian," in Irenee Hausherr's *Spiritual Direction in the Early Christian East,* trans. Anthony P. Gythiel (Kalamazoo, Mich.: Cistercian, 1990), p. xxvii. *Kubernetes* was used as early as the fourth century to describe the individual Christian as like a pilot on the journey of faith.

[19]Kallistos Ware, "Introduction," in John Climacus, *The Ladder of Divine Ascent,* trans. Cilm Lubheid and Norman Russell (Mahwah, N.J.: Paulist, 1982), p. 37.

[20]The word also exists in academic life as the Kappa of the fraternal Phi Beta Kappa Society, a name that weaves together love of wisdom (Philosophy), style of life (Bios) and skill in navigation *(Kubernetes)* as the crowning glories of an aretegenic education. See James M. May, "Address to the Phi Beta Kappa Society of St. Olaf's College," April 24, 2003. Cited at <www .stolaf.edu/academic/pbk/speeches/jame_m_may.html.>

[21]See Plato (427-347 B.C.), *Phaedrus* (New York: Dover, 1993).

[22]Cited at <www.metrolyrics.com/let-your-soul-be-your-pilot-lyrics-sting.html> (accessed on February 2, 2009).

The work of today's maritime pilot is less romantic and solitary than that of Sting's soul, and more illuminating of the art of spiritual direction. The maritime pilot, heir to an ancient profession, is a senior advisor to the master of the ship. When a ship is in unfamiliar, dangerous, narrow or congested waters, a local pilot may be called on to direct the captain (who remains legally in command of the ship). The boat bringing the pilot to the ship matches the speed of the larger ship, and, when the two vessels are side-by-side, the pilot climbs aboard the larger, taller ship (up what's called a "Jacob's Ladder"). Then the pilot, attending to the salient realities of the situation, serves as a consultant to the captain, saying, perhaps, "Captain, I believe there's a submerged rock about two degrees off the starboard bow."

This piloting imagery expresses some core aspects of the experience of being a spiritual director. It is the other's life that is of focal concern, yet the director brings some knowledge about the Christian faith and life, as well as specialized training and experience. We accompany directees, by God's grace. The director does not see the whole of the other's journey or even the whole of the ship. The director does not override the other's agency or responsibility. Rather the spiritual director directs the other's attention to the presence and activity of God as God sets the directee's course. Sensing God piloting Jim's soul, I might say, "You seem to be moved now in the same way you were moved in that Eastern European church."

THE CALL TO SANCTIFICATION

Scripture tells us we are being "sanctified by the Spirit to be obedient to Jesus Christ" (1 Pet 1:2 NRSV), and spiritual direction may serve as a navigational aid in sanctification. Several of my evangelical directees have told me how disappointed they are to keep discovering they have much to learn and far to go in sanctification. Somehow we think we can achieve a static state of piety, though we also know we are enjoined to follow Christ (Jn 21:19), grow in grace (2 Pet 3:18) and become evermore rooted and grounded in love (Eph 3:17). According to Christian historian William Bouwsma, "the essential element in the Christian idea of adulthood is . . . the capacity for growth, which is assumed to be a potentiality of any age of life."[23] Elements of our culture as well as some faulty theology in our churches impede our growth and our vision for it.

Earlier this year while reflecting on thirty years of spiritual formation ministry, Richard Foster lamented that the "overall dysfunction in our culture is so pervasive that it is nearly impossible for us to have a clear vision of spiritual progress."[24] His observation, drawn from in-depth work across North America, is consonant with findings from a recent study of one of our country's largest churches. In 2007 Willow Creek Community Church's much-noted self-study revealed—to the church leadership's dismay—that "nearly one out of every four people at Willow Creek were stalled in their spiritual growth or dissatisfied with the church—and many were considering leaving."[25]

The Willow Creek congregants unhappiest with church and their own spiritual growth fell largely in the "Stalled" category, composed of people early in their spiritual lives without established spiritual practices (such as praying, confessing, Bible reading and listening to God), many of whom experience difficulties or personal weaknesses that interfere with their lives of faith. For them, the report recommends "spiritual friendships."[26]

Another segment of the church, those identified as the "Dissatisfied" segment, make up 10 percent of the congregation. Unlike the "Stalled" group, they are spiritually mature as measured by spiritual behaviors, such as tithing, evangelism and serving, and spiritual attitudes, such as love for God and people. The two measures of spiritual maturity, behaviors and attitudes, were expected to correlate (for example, more church activity being indicative of greater love of God and people), but did not. Though faithful to spiritual disciplines, these people feel they're missing what they hope for in a life of walking according

---

[23]William J. Bouwsma, "Christian Adulthood," in *Adulthood*, ed. Erik H. Erikson (New York: W. W. Norton, 1978), p. 85.

[24]"Spiritual Formation Agenda: Three Priorities for the Next 30 Years," cited at <www.christianitytoday.com/ct2009/january/26.29.html>.

[25]Greg L. Hawkins and Cally Parkinson, *Reveal: Where Are You?* (Barrington, Ill.: Willow Creek Resources, 2007), p. 4. Survey data from several other large U.S. churches was also included in the analysis.

[26]Ibid., p. 57.

to the Spirit. From their church they long for more spiritual challenge and depth, and they "also seem to want a personal growth coach or spiritual mentor."[27]

One-quarter of the people in this evangelical megachurch are stagnating in a kind of gap between belief and thriving. They want help to grow in sanctification and are not asking for psychological help or arcane spiritual practices. Theirs is a call for accompaniment and guidance in holy Christian living, and a response is needed from the church; from Christian theology, including its practical, spiritual and sapiential forms; and from those gifted and equipped in the care of souls.

In 1997 theologian Ellen Charry wrote that she was "persuaded that over the course of centuries of action and reaction to the ups and downs of theological practice, theology has lost its ability to address questions of happiness and perhaps even goodness."[28] She called on the church to reclaim the "aretegenic"—virtue or excellence-shaping—function of Scripture and theological doctrine. Embedded in Scripture and doctrine is God's divine teaching for the shaping of disciples, and the pastoral work of recovery is necessary to make it available for the nourishing of souls and communities. According to the Willow Creek study, evangelical Christians are eager for this, and are calling for spiritual companionship—friendship, direction and mentoring—that is spiritually fortifying. Spiritual directors hear and respond to this call.

This is illustrated by another story from my work as a spiritual director. This past February 13 I saw four well-educated men and women, unmarried professionals between the ages of thirty and forty-five. Each is part of a church as well as a small prayer and Bible study group, and each engages in private daily practices of prayer and Scripture study. Each has also benefited from psychotherapy. Valentine's Day was on their minds. They would like to be married.

One of them said to me, "I know that being married would help me be a better person. It would improve rather than interfere with my abil-

[27]Ibid., p. 53.
[28]Ellen Charry, *By the Renewing of Your Minds: The Pastoral Function of Christian Doctrine* (New York: Oxford University Press, 1997), pp. 17-18.

ity to love God. I feel as though who I am and can be is suffocated by my loneliness."

I listened as these good people cried out to God in frustration and sadness about the unmet desire for someone to love and marry. Unrequited hope for what seems good in a Christian life is deeply spiritual and theological. How do we trust and follow God when a core longing seems unheard? Where do we allocate blame for the suffering? Does one's heart need cleansing and correction? Is it acceptable to be angry with God? One directee quoted Proverbs 13:12: "'Hope deferred makes the heart sick, but a desire fulfilled is a tree of life.' Why is God letting me be a stunted, bitter tree?" she asked plaintively.

These cries of the heart are not easily spoken and addressed in church communities, or in the offices of therapists who are not conversant with faith matters. These cries call for the skilled listening of a person fluent in the language of faith and committed to this ministry. These directees are in the middle passage of spiritual direction, an opportunity to examine questions about suffering in the company of another who has seen and remembers their experiences of God's grace. Jim has similar questions about his own serious medical diagnosis, heartfelt questions allowed expression by trust in a loving God as well as by a spiritual discipline that allows honest reflection. Friends, pastors and loving members of the community can listen, too, but there is a special grace in the spiritual discipline of confidential, regular, holy listening.

Clergy and laity alike need safe, skillful people to listen to us, for, as Eugene Peterson wrote, we all seek accompaniment from one who can "guide the formation of a self-understanding that is biblically spiritual instead of merely psychological or sociological."[29] As that unmarried woman's spiritual director, I take particular interest in how her heart grows and the tree of her life flourishes.

Accompanying Others as They Are Sanctified by the Spirit

Some ask whether spiritual direction is necessary given that each soul and each community is the "temple" of God's Spirit (1 Cor 3:16; 6:19).

---

[29]Eugene Peterson, *Working the Angles: The Shape of Pastoral Integrity* (Grand Rapids: Eerdmans, 1987), p. 104.

Spiritual direction is one way of improving the acoustics of the temple, but this listening charism is far broader than our conventions of practice. For example, ancient Christians direct us through their writings, and so do our contemporaries. Some of them do it through letter writing, as, for example, C. S. Lewis did with many, and Bruce Hindmarsh recently wrote about being spiritually directed a dozen years ago through letters from James Houston.[30] The breadth of the gift called "spiritual direction" was elucidated by Henri Nouwen in 1982:

> The church itself is a spiritual director. It tries to connect your story with God's story. To be a true part of a church community means you are being directed, you are being guided, you are being asked to make connections. The Bible is a spiritual director. People must read Scripture as a word for themselves and ask where God speaks to them. Finally, individual Christians are also spiritual directors. The use of an individual person in spiritual direction has as many forms and styles as there are people. A spiritual director is a Christian man or woman who practices the disciplines of the church and of the Bible, and to whom you are willing to be accountable for your life in God. That guidance can happen once a week, once a month, or once a year. It can happen for ten minutes or ten hours. In times of loneliness or crisis, that person prays for you.[31]

We in the body of Christ, like Paul, are in labor for our brothers and sisters as Christ is formed in them (Gal 4:19). Spiritual directors also participate expectantly and, at times, laboriously in another's sanctification. The image of the spiritual director as midwife appears often in the literature, for we witness birth and growth as Christ is formed in the other.[32] Certain people experience God's particular call to engage in this ministry on a regular basis, just as some people experience the

---

[30]Bruce Hindmarsh, "Written on Tablets of Human Hearts," *The Regent World* 21, no. 1 (2009): 1.

[31]Cited at <www.christianitytoday.com/biblestudies/areas/biblestudies/articles/060621.html>. From a *Leadership* conversation with Richard Foster (later republished by *Christianity Today*).

[32]See Margaret Guenther, *Holy Listening: The Art of Spiritual Direction* (Cambridge: Cowley, 1992). Bruno Bettelheim writes of Freud's use of midwifery imagery with respect to psychoanalysis; see *Freud and Man's Soul* (New York: Alfred A. Knopf, 1982; reprint, New York: Vintage, 1984), p. 36.

call to serve as pastors. As our culture offers pastoral education, professional standards and systems of accountability, so too the ministry of spiritual direction now has access to similar safeguards that a community of practice offers. Some directors offer the service on a freestanding basis, some are employed by larger organizations to be spiritual directors, and others offer the service as one of a number of different ministries in which they engage. All are part of an unregulated, unlicensed caregiving practice, which has training, practice and ethical standards held by the larger community of spiritual directors.

The care of souls is foundational to our faith, with Jesus being the ultimate exemplar to our soul care practices. Caring for souls seems inherent in human life, and there are classical, informal ancestors to the contemporary psychotherapies. In ancient Greece, philosophy assumed responsibility for the moral direction of daily life, and philosophers were the *curatores animarum*, tending the divine element in human nature. The care of souls entailed right teaching, holding up a mirror to the self-examining soul, direction in right living and the formation of the soul toward good and away from evil. It was aretegenic. Philosophical communities of inquiry and examination developed, and today some philosophers are reclaiming this territory by offering "clinical" services for those wanting guidance in living.[33]

Aristophanes' play *The Clouds* offers a playful Socratic illustration of soul care:

Socrates:	Come, lie down here.
Strepsiades:	What for?
Socrates:	Ponder awhile over matters that interest you.
Strepsiades:	Oh, I pray not there.
Socrates:	Come, on the couch!
Strepsiades:	What a cruel fate.
Socrates:	Ponder and examine closely, gather your thoughts together,

---

[33]See, for example, the writings of Alain de Botton, Kiyokazu Washida and Antonio T. de Nicolas.

let your mind turn to every side of things. If you meet with
difficulty, spring quickly to some other idea; keep away
from sleep.[34]

Spiritual direction has a deep and broad root system. What distinguishes Christian spiritual direction from the secular listening arts is the centrality of prayer: We serve as under-pilots to the Pilot of our souls. We listen, with the other, for God.

In earlier times the Christian church embraced the cure of souls as part of its mission, and clergy in several Christian traditions have been called "curates." However, Christians other than clergy also undertook the cure of souls.[35] One historian of Christian spiritual direction writes, "Spiritual direction was never a clerical preserve, neither was it traditionally reserved for the especially advanced or gifted."[36] Today the cure of souls in the general secular culture, while professionalized, is practiced by a preponderance of what Freud termed "lay" practitioners—meaning nonphysicians. A similar flourishing of "lay" practice is evident in contemporary Christian spiritual direction, in this case meaning nonclergy.[37] More and more spiritual direction in the church is a ministry offered by people who are not trained as clergy or psychotherapists, who may be trained as spiritual directors, and who experience themselves as called to and guided in this ministry by the true Spiritual Director.[38]

---

[34]Aristophanes (463 B.C.), *The Clouds*, in *The Complete Plays of Aristophanes*, trans. and ed. Moses Hadas (New York: Bantam, 1962), p. 120.

[35]See John T. McNeill, *A History of the Cure of Souls* (New York: Harper & Row, 1951).

[36]Martin Thornton, *Spiritual Direction: A Practical Introduction* (London: SPCK, 1984), p. 19.

[37]Freud wrote presciently, "I want to entrust [analysis] to a profession that doesn't yet exist, a profession of secular ministers of souls, who don't have to be physicians and must not be priests." This quote is from Freud's article "The Question of 'Lay' Analysis" (1926) and quoted in Bettelheim, *Freud and Man's Soul*, p. 35.

[38]There are many books on the subject of contemporary Christian spiritual direction, including, in addition to references already cited, Tilden Edwards, *Spiritual Director, Spiritual Companion: Guide to Tending the Soul* (New York: Paulist, 2001); Gary W. Moon and David G. Benner, *Spiritual Direction and the Care of Souls: A Guide to Christian Approaches and Practices* (Downers Grove: Ill.: InterVarsity Press, 2004); Bruce Demarest, *Soulguide: Following Jesus as Spiritual Director* (Colorado Springs: NavPress, 2003); Janet Ruffing, *Spiritual Direction* (New York: Paulist, 2000); William A. Barry and William J. Connolly, *The Practice of Spiritual Direction* (San Francisco: HarperSanFrancisco, 1982); and Gerald May, *Care of Mind, Care of Spirit* (San Francisco: HarperSanFrancisco, 1992).

Spiritual Direction and the Contemporary American Evangelical Church

The past fifteen years of culture-changing spiritual expression have witnessed phenomenal growth in the practice of spiritual direction and formal training programs. These have also been significant years for American evangelicalism.

In 1994 historian Mark Noll published his assessment of American evangelicalism in *The Scandal of the Evangelical Mind*. Noll made a plea for evangelicals to exercise their minds for Christ in the world, the academy and the church, and that plea has been met with dramatic change toward greater intellectual engagement. At the end of that book, Noll wrote: "[I]f evangelicals are ever to have a mind, they must begin with the heart. . . . [T]he search for a mind that truly thinks like a Christian takes on ultimate significance, because the search for a Christian mind is not, in the end, a search for mind but a search for God."[39] It is an article of our faith that we search for the One who searches our hearts and renews our minds (1 Jn 4:19; Acts 1:24; 15:8; Rom 8:27; 12:2), and searched for us by sending "his only Son into the world so that we might live through him" (1 Jn 4:9 NRSV). Spiritual directors pay attention to hearts and minds as they shift, grow, search for God and experience being sought by God. A director might say, "It sounds as though your heart was burning that day in the church as you heard the words of Scripture."

During the fifteen years since Noll's book was published, I have directed New College Berkeley, an evangelical, ecumenical affiliate of Berkeley's Graduate Theological Union. Our mission has been the theological education of the Christian laity, yet by the end of the twentieth century, we, like other theological educators, more and more have heard people asking, "Teach us to pray."

Clergy, too, are seeking renewed minds and hearts. The Carnegie Foundation for the Advancement of Teaching's 2005 report on clergy education expressed concern about the number of seminary students who had not been involved in churches and, therefore, were "spiritually

---

[39]Mark A. Noll, *The Scandal of the Evangelical Mind* (Grand Rapids: Eerdmans, 1994), pp. 249, 254.

unformed" before arriving at seminary.[40] In response to this situation, American seminaries have been introducing courses and programs to cultivate spiritual formation; some are recommending that students work with spiritual directors or mentors; and some denominations are providing funds to enable those working toward ordination to meet with spiritual directors.

From the pews of Willow Creek to the halls of our nation's seminaries, we hear a growing call for attention to sanctification by the Spirit, a form of attention spiritual directors are trained to provide. People individually and corporately, in person and writing, across the centuries, may offer spiritual direction. All believers benefit from a place where they can explore their life and growth in faith. All benefit from a pilot who will board their boat for a bit of the journey and help them navigate rough waters, make needed course corrections, notice the flow of grace and move forward in the sanctifying current of the Holy Spirit.

Over the course of the ten years I've known him, Jim has navigated great personal suffering. The way to intimacy with God has required the courage to be honest in prayer. In the past few weeks he has learned his illness is no longer in remission. He tells me he loves his work of ministry, and the threat of debilitating illness casts a bright light on that love. He says, "I feel more alive than I've ever felt, even now as I face the possibility of death. I am grateful for that. Grateful . . . angry . . . bewildered. But I feel fully alive and in constant conversation with God."

I join Jim in prayer, trust and wonder. I recognize and remember his call to ministry, and with him face the reality of his life-threatening illness. As I accompany him, I see in his life "the deeds of the Lord, his wondrous works in the deep." Doing so is a sacred privilege, enlivening my own faith.

Christian soul navigation takes place in the domain of God's sovereign grace. Ordinary life and prayer join as we pay attention to how

---

[40]Charles Foster, Lisa Dahill, Larry Golemon and Barbara Wang Tolentino, *Educating Clergy: Teaching Practices and Pastoral Imagination* (San Francisco: Jossey-Bass, 2005). I have witnessed this change in seminary students at the schools where I teach regularly: Fuller Theological Seminary, Regent College, San Francisco Theological Seminary and New College Berkeley.

God guides us to the place he has prepared for us. Sometimes another helps us as we navigate uncharted territory and bring our spiritual experience into meaningful integration with our lives. That other might be a friend, a person across from us at the Lord's Table, or it might be a spiritual director.

The Communion liturgy of the Ethiopian Orthodox Church contains a prayer to Jesus Christ, addressing him as "Pilot of my soul." It's a song radically different from a paean to the sovereign, solitary soul of our "disenchanted" age. We can pray:

> Pilot of my soul,
> guide of the righteous and glory of the saints,
> grant us, O Lord, the eyes of knowledge ever to see thee,
> and ears also to hearken to thy words alone.
> When our souls have been fulfilled with thy grace,
> create in us pure hearts, O Lord,
> that we may ever understand.[41]

---

[41]"Part II—Commentary: The Anaphora III," in James Norman's *Handbook to the Christian Liturgy* (London: SPCK, 1944; ed. Paul Ingram for Katapi, 2003), cited at <www.katapi.org .uk/Liturgy/Content.html>.

10 Centering Prayer

JAMES C. WILHOIT

How can one make the riches of the contemplative tradition of the desert and monastery accessible to the contemporary spiritual seeker marked by a frenetic, individualistic, self-directed and materialist lifestyle? Thomas Keating wrestled with this issue forty years ago as he observed Christian young people turning to Eastern religions and cults that seemed to offer an inviting and accessible spirituality. He was convinced of the richness of his tradition, but he was also aware that Christian contemplative practices were perceived, for some good reasons, to be the domain of monks in monasteries. In the 1970s Cistercian monks from St. Joseph's Abbey in Spencer, Massachusetts, under Fr. Thomas's leadership, developed a simple form of contemplative prayer based on well-established Christian contemplative practices and updated for nonmonastic urbanites. Fr. William Menniger found a pattern of praying in the fourteenth-century work *The Cloud of Unknowing* that significantly shaped the practice of centering prayer. Fr. Basil Pennington also contributed to developing the psychological and theological foundations for this practice. This chapter focuses on the work of Fr. Thomas Keating, who has had a unique leadership role in this movement, but is the first to acknowledge that this practice grew out of the work of a community seeking to bring renewal to the spiritual life of Christians.

This prayer method has received a wide following in the United States and around the world. The organization Thomas Keating founded to support and disseminate this practice, Contemplative Out-

reach, has over 120 active contemplative chapters in thirty-nine countries, supports over eight hundred prayer groups and, through its semi-
nars, annually teaches over fifteen thousand people the practice of
centering prayer.[1] Centering prayer has gained some national prominence, having been reported on in major newspapers and periodicals
like the *New York Times* and *Newsweek*,[2] and its effectiveness in shaping
character has been the subject of recent empirical research.[3]

THE METHOD OF CENTERING PRAYER

Centering prayer is intended to be an individual prayer practice that is
best learned in a group setting and is/should be maintained through
periodic retreats where it is intensely practiced. While centering prayer
is rightly classified as a contemplative practice, Keating has tended to
portray it as preparation for contemplative prayer. This preparation
comes through facilitating "the development of contemplative prayer by
preparing our faculties to cooperate with this gift."[4] The emphasis is
that this prayer provides a method to respond to God's initiative and
gives a method of being present to God. Centering prayer is intended
to provide a context and perspective for one's prayer practice, not to
become the sole form of prayer.

The method of centering prayer is quite simple. In terms of technique, the pray-er is asked to sit in silence for an established period of
time, twenty minutes is suggested, with the intention of being present
before God. The intentionality to be present is a distinctive of Keating's
counsel. Often meditative and contemplative prayer becomes very technical and skill-oriented. Centering prayer is not an achievement, but
making and keeping an appointment with God.

---

[1]Contemplative Outreach, Ltd., <http://www.contemplativeoutreach.org>.

[2]Jerry Adler et al., "In Search of the Spiritual," *Newsweek*, August 29, 2005; Rich Barlow,
"Some Drawn to 'Centering' Prayer," *The Boston Globe*, September 21, 2002, p. 1; Peter Stein-
fels, "Ideas & Trends: Trying to Reconcile the Ways of the Vatican and the East," *New York
Times*, January 7, 1990, p. 1.

[3]Michael Spezio, "Mindfulness in the Brain: A Study of Contemplative Practice in Relation
to Neural Networks of Social Judgment and Meta-Awareness" (paper presented as part of the
USC Templeton Lecture Series, October 25, 2006).

[4]Thomas Keating, *The Method of Centering Prayer* (Butler, N.J.: Contemplative Outreach,
2006).

Because the practice of intentional and focused silence is a learned discipline there is significant teaching devoted to cultivating this practice. There is an assumption that *lectio divina* is the entry way into centering prayer. Keating writes, "Centering prayer is a method designed to deepen the relationship with Christ begun in *lectio divina*."[5] The person with a well-developed practice of *lectio divina* has learned some measure of stillness, an appreciation for contemplative prayer and a stance of quietly receiving from God. The commitment of the originators to *lectio divina* as preparation for centering prayer is often ignored when this method is presented on retreats or to youth groups.

The method employed by centering prayer has two dimensions. The first dimension is one's intention or consent whereby "we consent to God's presence and action within."[6] Many forms of contemplative prayer place great emphasis on attention, but for Keating the emphasis is on intention, that is, our desire to be with God. In contrast, a popular book on meditation by an American Buddhist indicates that "meditation takes gumption"[7] and the concentration needed for it is "developed by force, by sheer unremitting willpower."[8] Keating does not discount the effort involved in prayer, but he portrays centering prayer as a way of grace in which we "cooperate with the gift" of God's presence.[9] Our intention can be represented as hands open to receive. The second dimension is a strategy for respecting one's intention by remaining mentally engaged with the prayer practice. To a large degree this consists of strategies for dealing with distracting or wandering thoughts.

Keating suggests four guidelines to help us consent to God's presence and remain with this engagement. The first is "choose a sacred word as the symbol of your intention to consent to God's presence and action within."[10] The pray-er is to ask in prayer for a word from the Holy Spirit, which will uniquely help him or her to focus in prayer.

---

[5]Thomas Keating, *Foundations for Centering Prayer and the Christian Contemplative Life: Open Mind, Open Heart, Invitation to Love, the Mystery of Christ* (New York: Continuum, 2002), p. 118.
[6]Ibid.
[7]Henepola Gunaratana, *Mindfulness in Plain English* (Boston: Wisdom, 2002), p. 7.
[8]Ibid., p. 149.
[9]Keating, *Foundations*, p. 118.
[10]Keating, *Method*.

Keating advises one not to change this word during a prayer session, but does not indicate that one must keep this word for the indefinite future. It is also important to note that this word is not a classic mantra. The word is not viewed as powerful in and of itself, but merely serves as shorthand for one's consent. Instead of declaring, "I intend to place myself in the loving presence of God with open hands of receptivity," one merely repeats the prayer word as a summary of this intention.

The second guideline is "sitting comfortably and with eyes closed, settle briefly and silently introduce the sacred word as the symbol of your consent to God's presence and action within."[11] In centering prayer there is a sensitivity to embodied spirituality, but there is not the precise attention to posture and sitting that one finds in some approaches to meditation. There are just a few passing references to how to sit for prayer. The second step points to the essence of this prayer form, which is self-surrender.[12] This prayer word is to be used gently to recall one's intention and not as a club to beat away distractions or drown out mental noise. Keating asks the pray-er to "introduce the sacred word . . . as gently as laying a feather on a piece of absorbent cotton."[13]

His third guideline suggests, "When you become aware of thoughts, return ever-so-gently to the sacred word."[14] This advice shows his Benedictine commitment to Cassian and his concern about thoughts. His use of the term *thought* is carefully chosen, and he elects to avoid terms like *distractions*. Keating does not advocate an "emptying of the mind," but does favor a prayer posture similar to what is often described as "no-thought." Consequently, he does not encourage the use of mental images in centering prayer. The swirls of thoughts are not defeated by a direct frontal attack, but are allowed with the confidence that God, in his grace, will deal with them.

> As soon as a thought emerges, one returns "ever-so-gently" to the sacred word. The gentleness is important here. One invites God to do the

---

[11]Ibid.

[12]Cynthia Bourgeault, "Centering Prayer as Radical Consent," *Sewanee Theological Review* 40, no. 1 (1996): 52. See also Cynthia Bourgeault, *Centering Prayer and Inner Awakening* (Lanham, Md.: Cowley, 2004) for an extended discussion of Keating's emphasis on intention.

[13]Keating, *Method.*

[14]Ibid.

work. Grace moves one away from each and every distraction toward the silent presence of God within. The pray-er's role is to intend to return to God's presence through the use of the sacred word.[15]

Unlike some forms of meditation, centering prayer does not seek to suppress thoughts or "empty the mind," but exercises a "willingness to let go of thoughts as they arrive and return to the sacred word as a symbol of one's consent to rest in God."[16]

According to Keating's fourth guideline, one is to conclude the prayer by remaining "in silence with eyes closed for a couple of minutes."[17] It is suggested that this gentle ending be accompanied by a prayer such as the "Our Father" and a statement of gratitude to God.

THEOLOGICAL FOUNDATIONS

In Keating's writings both the theological and psychological foundations of this practice are evident. This may be no more than a slogan-like statement such as "silence is God's first language; everything else is a poor translation"[18] or "What is the essence of contemplative prayer? The way of pure faith. Nothing else. You do not have to feel it, but you have to practice it."[19] In his books and longer articles he always gives attention to the theological foundations.

Keating's writings are marked by a gentle certainty and clarity. He is content to posit his position, explain it and suggest applications, but seldom argues for or defends his position. He locates his work as standing squarely in the Christian contemplative tradition and credits *The Cloud of Unknowing* with suggesting this prayer practice: "It is an attempt to present the teaching of earlier times (e.g., The Cloud of Unknowing) in an updated form."[20] He sees his project as making accessible the riches of the contemplative tradition: "It is a way of bringing procedures to be found in the contemplative teachings of the spiritual

---

[15]Thomas Ward, "Centering Prayer: An Overview," *Sewanee Theological Review* 40, no. 1 (1996): 24.
[16]Bourgeault, "Centering Prayer," p. 48.
[17]Keating, *Method.*
[18]Thomas Keating, *Invitation to Love: The Way of Christian Contemplation* (New York: Continuum, 1999), p. 90.
[19]Keating, *Foundations*, p. 11.
[20]Ibid., p. 118.

masters of the Christian tradition out of the dusty pages of the past into the broad daylight of the present."[21]

The present indwelling of Christ in each believer is his theological touchstone. In what is essentially the official tract for centering prayer, written by Keating and widely distributed by Contemplative Outreach, he provides the following one-paragraph statement of "Theological Backgrounds":

> The source of Centering Prayer, as in all methods leading to Contemplative Prayer, is the indwelling Trinity: Father, Son, and Holy Spirit. The focus of Centering Prayer is the deepening of our relationship with the living Christ. It tends to build communities of faith and bond the members together in mutual friendship and love.[22]

The "indwelling Trinity" and "relationship with the living Christ" are constructs that appear throughout his writings. He is willing to push the envelope with his language on indwelling: "The risen Jesus is among us as the glorified Christ. Christ lives in each one of us as the Enlightened One, present everywhere and at all times."[23] The language he employs to describe this indwelling is more evocative than precise, and he seems bent on portraying this principle as utterly attractive. The primacy of this construct can be seen in a statement like, "Thus the fundamental principle of the spiritual journey is the Divine Indwelling," but despite its stated importance he does not nuance or develop this perspective.[24] His concern is to suggest ways for Christians to live and pray in light of this reality.

The main practice of the spiritual life, then, is to "be in" and participate in the indwelling Trinity through Christ. For Keating the origins of centering prayer are trinitarian, this union is not a direct communion of the soul with God, for this intimacy is always through Christ.[25] The language of intimacy in current spirituality often evokes

[21]Keating, *Foundations*, pp. 31-32.
[22]Keating, *Method.*
[23]Keating, *Foundations*, p. 117.
[24]Thomas Keating, *Fruits and Gifts of the Spirit* (New York: Lantern, 2007), p. 3.
[25]Gustave Reininger, "Centering Prayer and the Christian Contemplative Tradition," *Sewanee Theological Review* 40, no. 1 (1996): 34.

an image of interpersonal warmth, support, care and romance. For Keating, the intimacy emphasizes transparency, vulnerability, receiving care and participation. There is the "embrace element" in his intimacy, but he places more emphasis on a therapeutic intimacy. He writes, "As we sit in centering prayer, we identify with Christ on the cross and are healed of our emotional wounds."[26] Keating sees that centering prayer allows us to experience the reality that "perfect love casts out fear" (1 Jn 4:18 NRSV) and that our vulnerability, fostered by this unconditional love, allows "the fullness of grace to flow through us" healing "these wounds."[27]

> In contemplative prayer the Spirit places us in a position where we are at rest and disinclined to fight. By his secret anointings the Spirit heals the wounds of our fragile human nature at a level beyond our psychological perception, just as a person who is anesthetized has no idea of how the operation is going until after it is over.[28]

The solitude offered by centering prayer becomes a place of transformation. While it is a retreat from the world, it is not an escape. It is a time to do serious business with God. Keating's understanding echoes that of Nouwen: "Solitude is the furnace of transformation."[29] His language is never as raw as Merton, who describes meditation as being "brought naked and defenseless into the center of that dread where we stand alone before God in our nothingness."[30] He adopted the term 'centering prayer' from Merton as suggested by some retreatants and does portray it as both a comforting and challenging practice.

He also suggests that this prayer practice allows us to experience Scripture in a firsthand way. "We confidently identify with Peter, James, John, Mary of Bethany . . . [a]s we perceive our interior life described in those stories."[31] As a result of this prayer one finds that the horizons of Scripture merge, and one is ministered to directly by Christ as if you

---

[26]Thomas Keating, "The Theological Foundations of Contemplative Outreach: A Commentary by Thomas Keating," *Contemplative Outreach News* 15 (2001): 2.

[27]Keating, *Foundations*, p. 84.

[28]Ibid, p. 42.

[29]Henri Nouwen, *The Prayer of the Heart* (New York: Ballantine, 2003), p. 15.

[30]Thomas Merton, *Contemplative Prayer* (New York: Herder & Herder, 1969), p. 85.

[31]Keating, *Foundations*, p. 1.

were in first-century Palestine. Here we find a tension between the call to centering prayer, where we sit naked before God in vulnerability and the false self and other self-protective structures are stripped away, versus an outcome of this prayer that allows one to be ministered to directly by Jesus as one reads the Gospels, and here one seemingly encounters a Jesus who is playful, smart, wise, friendly and largely supportive.

Woven throughout Keating's presentation of centering prayer's theological foundations is a profound assumption of God's love. In speaking of this abiding love he uses relational images and describes the necessity of our responding to God's initiative. Deepening our relationship with God, through which we receive healing, membership in his community and giftings to serve, is the focus of this prayer. "When we say, 'Let us pray,' we mean . . . 'Let us deepen the relationship we have.'"[32] The call to this deeper intimacy and union is based on the certainty of God's trustworthiness.

Keating has drunk deeply at the wells of developmental psychology, and he often explains spiritual change using a developmental schema. He compares our relation to God to an ever-deepening human relationship, which Thomas Ward succinctly summarizes:

> He sees our relations to Christ going through four stages of increasing intimacy: acquaintanceship, friendliness, friendship, and union. We begin by meeting (acquaintanceship). If we sense an attraction and commonality, we might spend more time together (friendliness). Should we find a deeper pull, we might commit ourselves to a relation of fidelity over time (friendship). Then, if this commitment deepens, it might become the center of our world. Eventually, we might find ourselves at one with the other (union).[33]

Evangelicals are attracted to the warm relational language of Keating, but many will be bemused by the lack of grounding for his confidence in this relationality. He is content to posit this and obliquely tie it to Christ's redemptive work. The Christian's redemption is accessed in "baptism, the false self is ritually put to death, the new self is born,

[32]Ibid., p. 9.
[33]Ward, "Centering Prayer," p. 23.

and the victory over sin won by Jesus through his death and resurrection is placed at our disposal."[34] Evangelicals would prefer to see this identity tied to our regeneration, this position being classically stated by Lovelace, and would want to see union as both a fact established in redemption as well as a deepening experience.

> The Triple Way of classical mysticism, which moves from the stage of cleansing one's life through illumination toward union with God, seems to reverse the biblical order, which starts from union with Christ claimed by faith, leading to the illumination of the Holy Spirit and consequent cleansing through the process of sanctification.[35]

The emphasis in Keating's writing on centering prayer is that this is a means to deepen, not establish, a relationship with God. The deepening process comes through the pray-er taking seriously his sin and allowing God to lovingly cleanse and correct. Part of the appeal of Keating may be that he recognized the reality of human brokenness and has chosen to frame our sinfulness largely in psychological terms. He writes self-consciously to those who have not connected with traditional church teachings on sin. The following quotation illustrates his dismissal of some traditional understandings of sin.

> According to St. Augustine's theology, original sin has three consequences: (1) we don't know where happiness is to be found (ignorance); (2) we look for it in the wrong places (concupiscence); and (3) if we ever find out where it might be found, the will is too weak to pursue it anyway. That is the somewhat dismal view that Christianity has offered up to now.[36]

It is not clear that Keating offers a less dismal view of the human condition, but what he does offer is one that is thoroughly grounded in psychology and one that is compatible with centering prayer. In his writings he tends to focus on sin as "distortion of human nature" with its consequent blocking of our well-being and fostering of defeating

---

[34]Keating, *Foundations*, p. 109.
[35]Richard Lovelace, *Dynamics of Spiritual Life: An Evangelical Theology of Renewal* (Downers Grove, Ill.: InterVarsity Press, 1979), p. 19.
[36]Thomas Keating, *The Human Condition and Transformation*, Wit Lectures (New York: Paulist, 1999), pp. 11-12.

patterns of living.[37] Consequently, he sees Jesus' call to repentance as "calling them to change the direction in which they were looking for happiness. 'Repent' is an invitation to grow up and become a fully mature human being."[38] His writings find resonance with those who are seeking to live other-oriented lives based on a Christian ethic of love and find themselves frustrated by anger, self-protection and other defeating patterns. Keating sums up this reality by saying that humans are "programmed for human misery."[39]

In his writings on centering prayer he chiefly employs the construct of false self as his surrogate for sin. He defines the false self as

> the self developed in our own likeness rather than the likeness of God; the self-image developed to cope with the emotional trauma of early childhood. It seeks happiness in satisfying the instinctual needs of survival/security, affection/esteem, and power/control, and bases its self-worth on cultural or group identification.[40]

He views the false self "as deeply entrenched"[41] and resistant to our self-improvement strategies. Unless the false self is diminished it will accompany and dominate one through life changes like marriage, becoming more religious and charitable community involvement. It is only through conversion that we are able to get at "the heart of the problem."[42] Sin is universal and original in the sense that all of us suffer from self-defeating egoic patterns of thought, but sin is birthed in each person. "The tendency to sin is rooted in the energy centers that we create as infants and toddlers to deal with survival and security, affection and esteem, and power and control issues."[43]

Centering prayer becomes a means for the ongoing and inner conversion of the person. Through this prayer the unconscious is exposed, under the guidance of the Holy Spirit, and brought to the light in a way

---

[37]Ibid., p. 16.
[38]Ibid., p. 17.
[39]Ibid., p. 15.
[40]Thomas Keating, *Intimacy with God* (New York: Crossroad, 1994), p. 163.
[41]Keating, *Human Condition*, p. 17.
[42]Ibid., p. 18.
[43]Thomas Keating, *The Better Part: Stages of Contemplative Living* (New York: Continuum, 2000), p. 112.

that it can be constructively dealt with. He sees this as analogous to the process of psychotherapy and refers to centering prayer as "divine therapy."[44] This is accomplished ultimately by grace as the converted let "go of the false self, a humbling process, because it is the only self we know."[45] This process restores our true freedom, and we can then choose to live out the gospel virtues because the "inner tyranny" of the false self is replaced by "true freedom" whereby "we can *decide* what to do about particular events."[46] So instead of living out of our "habitual drives" we are able "to manifest God rather than the false self, with its emotional programs for happiness and attachment to various roles."[47] At times, Keating, with the fervor reminiscent of earlier meditation teachers, speaks of how centering prayer can be beneficial to all who responsibly engage in it.

Keating's view of sin is not atypical for persons working in the areas of practical theology. He does exceptionally well at showing the blinding effects of sin and its destructive effects on relationships. However, he seems to get one side of the equation really well—the loss of human flourishing—but does not emphasize the broken-heartedness of God over sin and its cosmic disruption.

His emphasis on the loss of flourishing does highlight dimensions of redemption that are often overlooked in strictly judicial depictions of the atonement. His analysis is similar to that of Ellens, who suggests that when we view salvation simply in legal terms, we often miss the deeply healing and restorative dimensions of salvation. Ellens contrasts two ways that people often think of salvation, and his second depiction is similar to Keating's but includes the forensic elements that are quite dim in Keating's writings. The first formulation is judicial and correct, as far as it goes. The second is more holistic and sees the end of salvation as not just "taking the punishment," but as a restoration of wholeness as well. The first he terms the "Blame-Justification Equation" where (anxiety/shame/guilt/blame) + (justice/penalty/punishment/ex-

[44]Keating, *Foundations*, p. 133.
[45]Keating, *Human Condition*, p. 20.
[46]Ibid., p. 32.
[47]Ibid., p. 44.

piation) = (justification/forgiveness/restoration/equilibrium); and the second he refers to as the "Grace-Wholeness Equation" in which (pain/shame/guilt/anxiety) + (passion/compassion/mercy/grace) = (forgiveness and other restorative actions/affirmation/healing/realizing potential).[48] Keating's grasp of human brokenness at the level of interpersonal estrangement and its impediment to full human flourishing and community is quite compelling, and he does well at selling spiritual seekers on the need to take their bentness seriously, but his conception of sin and redemption is quite anthropocentric.

UNIQUENESS OF CENTERING PRAYER

The writers on centering prayer tend to want to have it both ways when they appeal to history. On the one hand, they portray centering prayer as part of the long tradition of Christian contemplative prayer. And on the other hand, centering prayer is a new and distinct method. For this discussion I will grant both claims and am most interested in what might be unique about this method especially in terms of other contemporary approaches to Christian contemplative prayer. I see three unique emphases of centering prayer:

1. It places a unique emphasis on intentionality rather than on will power.

2. The movement has developed a clear and concrete method of prayer and a widespread and effective network of training.

3. Centering prayer locates one's prayer in a contemplative construal of the world.

Emphasis on intentionality. Keating makes it clear that the practice of centering prayer is enhanced by careful attention to practices like seated pose, posture, breathing and attention to the space in which you pray. However, he places his primary focus on having a proper intention as you go to prayer. Many forms of meditation and quiet prayer place a great emphasis on your attention. One can find instruction in atten-

---

[48]J. Harold Ellens, "Sin or Sickness: The Problem of Human Dysfunction," in *Seeking Understanding: The Stob Lectures, 1986-1988*, ed. The Stob Lecture Endowment of Calvin Theological Seminary (Grand Rapids: Eerdmans, 2001), p. 481.

tion-oriented meditation books on how to sit motionless for multiple hours. These methods emphasize locking one's mind to something as a primary focus.

Cynthia Bourgeault writes, "Centering Prayer works with an entirely different property—not attention, but *intention*."[49] During centering prayer the pray-er is invited to repeat a sacred word, but this is not to become the focus of one's thoughts; it is intended to be a "reminder of one's intent for the duration of the prayer period to relinquish attachment to one's surface flow of thoughts and associations, and to rest" in God's presence.[50] The contrast with methods that focus on attention can be seen in a story told by Keating. At a centering prayer training, a nun approached him to confess that her session had been an utter failure. "In twenty minutes," she says, "I must have had twenty thousand thoughts." Keating replied, "How wonderful! Twenty thousand opportunities to return to God."[51]

The emphasis on intentionality by Keating is a remarkable gift. A perusal of the current literature on forms of meditation and contemplative prayer, unless informed by centering prayer, shows that by and large meditation is portrayed as a human achievement obtained through increasing one's powers of focus and concentration. Keating's emphasis on intention allows for a gracious tenor to pervade this prayer practice. It is not a practice of human achievement, but one of intentionality and receptivity.

Method and training. One story of how centering prayer developed has Keating tasking his monks with finding a clear, simple and historically Christian method for introducing the practice of contemplative prayer. After various attempts Fr. William Menniger proposed a method he attributed to the popular medieval prayer book, *The Cloud of Unknowing*. Originally the prayer was called the "Cloud Prayer." This prayer was introduced to retreatants to St. Joseph's Abbey, and Keating constantly worked on ways of presenting it with clarity and focusing on its essentials. Through his retreats, writings, conferences

---

[49]Bourgeault, "Centering Prayer," p. 48.
[50]Ibid.
[51]Ibid.

and leadership, an effective network of supporters of centering prayer has developed around the world.

Centering prayer as a construal of the world. Keating sees centering prayer as more than a technique. A robust practice of centering prayer includes the cultivation of a particular way of viewing the world. Keating writes, "God's presence is available at every moment, but we have a giant obstacle in ourselves—our world view. It needs to be exchanged for the mind of Christ, for His world view."[52] This new perspective is both a disposition we cultivate and something we receive as a charism through centering prayer, "with the world view that Christ shares with you in deep silence. His view of things becomes more important to you than your own. Then he asks you to live that new life in the circumstances of everyday."[53] The importance of cultivating and receiving this new worldview can be seen in the amount of space Keating devotes to putting off the false self and its self-protective strategies and consciously putting on an ethic of love, a commitment to avoid the temptation to act out of anger, a stance of contemplative-action and living in the reality of God's presence. The vast majority of Keating's books focus not on the techniques of centering prayer, but on a construal of the world that is compatible with contemplative prayer.

CENTERING PRAYER AS A POSSIBLE EVANGELICAL PRACTICE

Centering prayer has enjoyed remarkable widespread support in its forty-year existence, but it is not without its critics. The criticisms are wide ranging. Some writers focus on concerns about the theological proclivities of the founders of the movement (Keating, Pennington and Menniger), but the most strident critiques locate centering prayer in what they see as a broad and pernicious movement of theological compromise in which orthodox Christianity is being supplanted by New Age mysticism. Centering prayer is also caught in the net of evangelical critiques that object to patterns of devotion that are not explicitly taught in Scripture because these writers see Scripture as the sole authority concerning faith and devotion. A wise and moderate advocate of this

[52]Keating, *Foundations*, p. 45.
[53]Ibid., p. 104.

position answered my query about centering prayer by saying, "I would think that the question of the sufficiency of Scripture 'for life and godliness' must be addressed. In my view, one would be hard-pressed to find centering prayer taught or modeled in Scripture as a method of prayer." To this author, centering prayer is ruled out as an evangelical practice because it is not explicitly practiced or advocated in the Bible. However, the confession of the Bible as our ultimate authority certainly does not mean that it is the sole authority or only source of knowledge on Christian spirituality. To the extent that Christian spirituality is the study of the lived reality of persons, why should we exclude insights from the empirical study of spiritual practices when setting forth principles of prayer?[54] More sympathetic critiques tend to focus on concerns about the centering prayer movement and some of its emphases (e.g., discouraging the use of mental images and heavy reliance on development psychology). And others raise concerns about the widespread use of centering prayer in some programs because they contend that Christian spirituality has seen contemplative prayer as something that one grows into and should not be presented as an attractive introduction to the life of prayer.

While these critiques raise a variety of concerns about centering prayer, I do not believe these disqualify centering prayer from being an appropriate evangelical practice. In speaking about an evangelical appropriation of centering prayer it is important to note that it is used in a both broad and narrow way. Those that use it in a broad way can be further divided between those who use it in passing as a descriptor of contemplative prayer and see it as essentially synonymous with terms like "prayer of the heart" or "interior prayer,"[55] and those who see it as an ancient prayer form that needs to be restored to contemporary evangelical devotional practice. In this vein Tony Campolo writes about his ex-

---

[54]J. P. Moreland, "How Evangelicals Became Over-Committed to the Bible and What Can Be Done About It" (paper presented at the annual meeting of the Evangelical Theological Society, San Diego, November 14-16, 2007).

[55]Ruth Barton, *Sacred Rhythms: Arranging Our Lives for Spiritual Transformation* (Downers Grove, Ill.: InterVarsity Press, 2006), p. 68; Adele Ahlberg Calhoun, *Spiritual Disciplines Handbook: Practices That Transform Us* (Downers Grove, Ill.: InterVarsity Press, 2005), p. 212; Richard J. Foster, *Celebration of Discipline: The Path to Spiritual Growth* (San Francisco: HarperSanFrancisco, 1998), p. 36.

perience with "what St. Ignatius called 'centering prayer'" and Tony
Jones writes that, "Like the Jesus Prayer, Centering Prayer grew out of
the reflections and writings of the Desert Fathers."[56] These authors tend
to advocate a method that has many of the features Keating suggested,
but without his fulsome foundations. Many of those critical of evangelical appropriations of centering prayer fail to note the vast difference
between someone like Ruth Barton[57] whose book contains one brief
reference to centering prayer and someone like Tony Campolo who
spends pages describing it and credits this practice with how he developed "intimacy with Christ."[58] A few evangelical authors use centering
prayer in the narrow sense of referencing Keating's prayer practice.[59]

However, I am cautious about introducing centering prayer into
evangelical churches and ministries. I must underscore that I see the
practice and underlying theology of centering prayer as bound together.
It seems naïve to speak of centering prayer as a theologically neutral
method, a mere spiritual technique. While the broad theological assumptions of centering prayer may be compatible with evangelical theology, they are not deeply evangelical in terms of emphases. For those
interested in introducing this practice to an evangelical context, I offer
the following suggestions:

1. Centering prayer should be presented as a complete package. Keating understood centering prayer as a practice grounded in a contemplative view of the world, and he suggests that the practice of *lectio
   divina* could serve as an appropriate introduction and context for
   centering prayer. His writings have something like a ratio of about
   five parts foundations (theology/psychology) to one-part method.
   The contemplative context is necessary for the practice to be done
   with a grace-oriented, receptive stance.

[56]Anthony Campolo, *Letters to a Young Evangelical* (New York: Basic Books, 2006), p. 179; Tony
Jones, *The Sacred Way: Spiritual Practices for Everyday Life* (Grand Rapids: Zondervan, 2005),
p. 69.
[57]Barton, *Sacred Rhythms.*
[58]Campolo, *Letters*, p. 26.
[59]J. David Muyskens, *Forty Days to a Closer Walk with God: The Practice of Centering Prayer*
(Nashville: Upper Room, 2006); Jan Harris, *Quiet in His Presence: Experiencing God's Love
Through Silent Prayer* (Grand Rapids: Baker, 2003); Bill Volkman, *Basking in His Presence: A
Call to the Prayer of Silence* (Glen Ellyn, Ill.: Union Life, 1996).

2. Centering prayer needs to be grounded in the gospel. In Keating's writings he grounds the Christian's assurance of God's love in creation and baptism. As evangelicals, we must ground our sense of intimacy with God in our union with Christ made available in our justification. In my perusal of several evangelical adaptations of centering prayer, I did not find a clear grounding for our courage to enter God's presence in the cross. Also, an evangelical will want to see that the tendency in centering prayer to privilege God's immanence is balanced by an appropriate emphasis on divine transcendence.

3. Centering prayer should be seen as an advanced form of prayer. I think evangelicals, with our radical democratic impulse, recoil at the idea of levels of prayer, but we need to respect the wisdom of the church that contemplative forms of prayer grow out of a well-developed practice of vocal prayer.

4. Centering prayer must be shown to be missional. In Keating's writings one cannot escape the call to use this prayer practice as a way of becoming a new person more deeply committed to loving others. However, it can be taught in a very narcissistic way with the aim of promoting personal peace and self-satisfaction. This distorts Keating's sense that the times of prayer are often terribly disquieting, as we come to see and experience our sins in new ways, and that it continually calls us away from our false self with its myriad of self-protective strategies.

Thomas Keating has certainly succeeded in his quest to make the riches of the contemplative tradition available to a wider audience. He has also accomplished his apologetic aim of showing young people that Christianity offers a rich contemplative tradition. He has shown the power of a clear technique coupled with compelling foundational teaching to provide a lifelong method of prayer. I think the most enduring legacy of Thomas Keating will be his emphasis on intention. In the past fifty years many writers have sought spiritual guidance on contemplation from Eastern religions, which place a great deal of emphasis on attention and concentration in prayer. In his quiet way Keating challenged this orientation by his gracious words; "Centering prayer is not so much an exercise of attention as intention . . . you intend to go to your inmost being, where . . . God dwells. You are opening to Him by pure faith."[60] His writings show contemplative prayer not as an achievement of human will, but the gracious gift of the God who loves his children and longs to embrace and heal them.

---

[60]Keating, *Foundations*, p. 36.

11

"Renewed in Knowledge in the Image of Our Creator" Through "Psalms, Hymns and Songs of the Spirit"

Cherith Fee Nordling

Singing the Spirit's Songs: Listening to the New Testament

"They sing," reported Pliny to Trajan, in a world in which psalms and cultic hymns were often sung to the emperor, among other deities. These Christians, he says, "sing hymns to Christ as though *he* were a God." And they did. In homes, in jail, in exile, even awaiting execution, sung worship to God and to his Christ was a constant sign of the life-giving Spirit among his people from the church's earliest days. And, the capacity to sing this knowledge of God, in wisdom and understanding of God's purposes in Christ, was only possible, according to Paul, by the Spirit of God, who knows the deep things of God. The Spirit led them into truth, as Jesus promised, and enabled a particular form of response: grace-filled song, to God, from the heart.

Embedded in the New Testament texts are echoes of some of these songs.[1] We hear Spirit-improvised riffs on prophetic themes, as new songs rising to Jesus of Nazareth, crucified Messiah, resurrected *Kurios*. There are long, sustained notes of former things being sung anew

---

[1]Gordon Fee, *God's Empowering Presence: The Holy Spirit in the Letters of Paul* (Peabody, Mass.: Hendrickson, 1994), p. 656.

(sort of like eschatological covers!). They spring forth out of God's much-anticipated, and yet wholly unexpected, new creation through his Son. Woven through church letters, or bursting through apocalyptic visions, we hear ancient psalms of ascent sung with a new cadence, as hymns of kingly ascension and glory, sung not only to the one who sits on the throne, but to the slain Lamb.

The young church apparently *did* let the message of Christ dwell in them richly. With the wisdom of the Spirit, they sang and made music in their hearts to the Lord. And occasionally it sounded something like this:

- "Wake up, sleeper, rise from the dead, and Christ will shine on you." (Eph 5:14)

- "Oh, the depth of the riches of the wisdom and knowledge of God! How unsearchable his judgments, and his paths beyond tracing out!" (Rom 11:33-34)

- The Father "has rescued us from the dominion of darkness and brought us into the kingdom of the Son he loves. . . . The Son is the image of the invisible God, the firstborn over all creation. For in him all things were created: things in heaven and on earth, visible and invisible, whether thrones or powers or rulers or authorities; all things have been created through him and for him. He is before all things, and in him all things hold together." (Col 1:13, 15-17 TNIV)

- "You are worthy, our Lord and God, to receive glory and honor and power, for you created all things" (Rev 4:11 TNIV). Worthy is the Lamb "who with [his] blood [has] purchased for God members of every tribe and language and people and nation." He has "made them to be a kingdom and priests to serve our God, and they will reign on the earth. . . . To him who sits on the throne and to the Lamb be praise and honor and glory and power, for ever and ever." (see Rev 5:9-10, 13 TNIV)

The crescendo of creaturely worship throughout the New Testament climaxes in John's eschatological vision. The Spirit shows him a picture of what is already going on, of reality as it has been eschatologically determined by the crucified, resurrected and ascended One, who is and forever will be truly human with us and for us. Our still incarnate High Priest, Jesus of Nazareth, son of Mary, divine Son of God, already reigns in the kingdom of his Father. Already, and again, they have poured out the Spirit, without measure. And in this vision, the Spirit gathers up the entire created order into worship of the Father and the Lamb. Their new song bears witness to what is true, to the One who *is* faithful and true (Rev 19:11). Every creature, in a united heaven and earth, gives glory, power, wealth, strength, praise and honor precisely where, and to whom, it is due—to the Creator of all things and progenitor of an entirely *new*, restored creation.

This song is a monumentally audacious thing for the church at this time—John's time—to sing, because on the ground, it looks like a completely different story. Amid bloodbaths of persecution and martyrdom, and imperial wealth and strength that oppress and destroy, other powers seem to be winning the day. Humans set themselves up as gods at the expense of all, while those who proclaim Jesus the God-man, die as ignominiously as he did, and worse.

This may be the case, the Spirit tells John, but this is not the end of the story, despite appearances to the contrary. It is certainly not the whole story, the real story, of God's "deeper magic," as it were. So, whoever has ears, let them hear what the Spirit says to the churches: *Charis* and *shalom*, "to you from him who is, and who was, and who is to come, and from the [seven-fold Spirit] before his throne, and from Jesus Christ, who is the faithful witness, the firstborn from the dead, and the ruler of the kings of the earth" (Rev 1:4-5 TNIV). "Do not weep," as if there is no hope (Rev 5:5 TNIV). They may kill you, but don't worry. God's bruised and battered King, glorious in his new body, has been raised, in every way. He has won everything back that was his, including you. Do not weep, for already the kingdom has come among you, already God the Spirit has taken up renewed residence in your midst, with all power and authority, with signs and wonders of new creation, and with strength to suffer for him, with him, and to die into resurrection. Sing this new song, live this story.

"The great heavenly scene of Revelation 4 and 5," says Tom Wright, "stands out as a moment when the church is gathering up the praises of all creation and presenting them before God's throne."

> How can God's purposes be fulfilled? How can the scroll of God's will be unrolled and read so that it comes to pass? The answer, through which the prayer and worship of the church and creation are taken through into a new dimension, is that the Lion who is also the Lamb has conquered, and through him God's purposes are going forward. And, with that, prayer and worship break out in a new way. Heaven and earth come together in a new way. In the death and resurrection of Jesus, the new creation has begun, and with it the new song, "Worthy is the Lamb," the song that lies at the heart of Christian adoration.[2]

"This is my story, this is my song." This is *our storied song*. Together we are new creation, shaped by the reality of the life, death and new life of *this* Lamb. We bear the image of the Son, in whom we see what God looks like, and thus what we are becoming, truly holy, truly human, to be joined in union with God and all that is his, forever. This is the song that frames all of our songs, by which the Spirit forms our lives into the true image of our Creator, and into his purposes. We are the bride, the New Jerusalem, or daughter Zion, adorned and awaiting our bridegroom. We sing on the way to our great wedding, echoing the songs of love sung in advance by our new Adam, who has already won the battle that secures our destiny.

> Sing, Daughter Zion;
> shout aloud, Israel!
> Be glad and rejoice with all your heart,
> Daughter Jerusalem!
> The LORD your God is with you,
> the Mighty Warrior who saves.
> He will take great delight in you;
> in his love he will no longer rebuke you;
> but will rejoice over you with singing. (Zeph 3:14, 17 TNIV)

So, when it comes to living and singing this reality, how are we doing?

---

[2]N. T. Wright, *Surprised by Hope* (New York: HarperOne, 2008), p. 279.

SINGING OUR CONTEMPORARY SONGS:
LISTENING TO TODAY'S WORSHIP

My father, Gordon Fee, has said on more than one occasion, "Let me
hear a congregation sing, and I will tell you their theology." To find out
what people really understand about God, and about whom they are as
God's people, listen to *what*, and *how*, they sing. The good news of
God in Jesus Christ has been sung through the centuries, through
every generation, and the church has been shaped by how the story is
sung. Stephen Pickard states that "given how much time and energy
goes into singing in Church, we should not doubt the power of song
and hymn to shape and inform Christian character."[3] Pickard, however,
makes this statement out of his concern for the current lack of theological grist, or clarity, in our sung worship. And I think he's right. It is
still possible to drink deeply from the well of the church's songs, old
and new, and in so doing, to be well taught and admonished. But the
longer I listen, I have come to believe that a good deal of our theological confusion, and lethargy, can be traced back not to a few bad sermons, or systematic classes; rather, they stem, at least in part, from
countless repetitions of anemic hymns and heretical choruses.[4]

You see, something deeply formative happens in the process of
singing "in Your presence, all my troubles disappear," or "Some fine
morning, when this life is over, I'll fly away." We end up worshiping
and glorifying "spiritual" experience rather than the Holy Spirit. Our
songs are often lifted up to a nonexistent Docetic or Apollinarian
Christ, who in his divinity shares hardly a trace of our tempted and
tried humanity. (Docetism holds that Jesus only seemed to have a real
human body; Apollinarianism holds that Christ has no human spirit.)
Such a Christ can tell us nothing about Jesus' truly human life lived
by the Spirit. And if Jesus' humanity doesn't ultimately matter, then
neither does ours. So we end up gnostically singing about bodiless
souls going to heaven, rather than permanent, resurrected human life,

---

[3]Stephen Pickard, "Hymns and Songs: Living on the Edge of Idolatry," *Market-Place* (November 2006): 11. This publication is an independent Anglican newspaper now published online at
<www.marketplaceonline.com.au>.
[4]Choosing any worship text for purposes of this paper risks causing offense, though it is not my
intent.

in a new heaven and earth, already begun in Christ by the Spirit.

Embedded in our lyrics are mixed messages about divine blessing and power. In our hymnals "God Bless America" sits alongside "For All the Saints." We sing about following "our God, the Servant King," from positions of privilege and power that cannot imagine it being truly costly and cruciform. We proclaim God's power in the world, but sing far less lustily, if at all, when the powers and authorities that God disarms include us. And we seldom celebrate the power of the Spirit to participate in Christ's suffering with and for his world.

We can overemphasize God's transcendence such that the "Immortal, Invisible God" only wise, is considered unknowable and disengaged from the plight of our broken world. Or, in reverse, when immanence is overemphasized, we cannot see the Lord of heaven and earth behind "Jesus, my best friend." Something particularly formative occurs when we sing "Jesus I am so in love with you," or "you took the fall, and thought of me above all." As we try to focus on Jesus, without missing a beat, *we* suddenly become the subject in worship. Our vision blurs, and rather than focusing on God, we're looking at our experience of God. And then, before we know it, our experience becomes the subject of worship. This is not to say that we cannot sing of our experience of God, or cry out in our brokenness and creaturely dependence. If so, we'd have to toss out the Old Testament Psalter. Nor can we help but sing of God's particular love for each of us, and rightly so.

Nevertheless, it is just here that we so desperately need the wise truth-telling understanding of the Spirit. For we have been weaned on a siren song so familiar that we don't even hear it. The narcissistic anthem of the dominion of darkness sings to us, calling us to fashion ourselves into an image placed at the center of everything. It leads, to use Pickard's words, to worship that is "turned in, self-referential and theologically vacuous":

> In a great deal of contemporary sacred song, the constant trap is that the song never rises above the human heart. The character of God vanishes; the worshipper is left locked in a self-referential loop. We may indeed repeatedly sing "It's all about you, Jesus" but in fact after a while the light may dawn that it is really all about me telling Jesus it's all about

him. *The true subject is the self and transformation becomes a fiction.* We have a choice, to live off milk and sweets or move on to a more substantive diet that enables . . . growth and maturity.[5]

At this point, Pickard sounds like the apostle Paul in his letter to the "holy ones" in Colossae. Here in prayer, exhortation, even song, Paul teaches and admonishes them so that they might continue to grow up into maturity in Christ. And he encourages them to do all these same things. Through their shared life in the Spirit, this congregation of slaves and free, men and women, Gentiles and Jews, all are to teach and admonish one another to be renewed in the image of the one who has given them their new humanity. And by what means does he specifically encourage them to do this? The answer is by singing psalms and hymns and songs of the Spirit.

WORSHIP AND THE NARRATIVE OF GOD'S STORY

Paul's letter to the church at Colossae provides a remarkable opportunity to see a lived, and sung, context for Christlike formation through the Spirit. The Father has brought these holy children into his kingdom of light to be inheritors of the all that belongs to his Son. This is possible because God the Holy Spirit has given himself to them, poured himself out in their midst.

As Paul addresses the new challenges facing them, he reminds them of the bigger story that they're in. And he anticipates their response, based on what the Spirit has already done among them, forming them through love. With the arrival of his letter, many eyes, both in and outside the church, are now on this community.[6] The reason is because Paul's letter to them is accompanied by another, also by Paul, and addressed both to Philemon and "to the church that meets in [his] home" (Philem 1-2 TNIV). And they are both being personally delivered by none other than Onesimus, Philemon's runaway slave, whom Paul now describes as his "son," his "heart," dear to him and them "both as a fel-

---

[5]Pickard, "Hymns and Songs," p. 11 (emphasis added).
[6]See Brian J. Walsh and Sylvia C. Keesmaat, *Colossians Remixed: Subverting the Empire* (Downers Grove, Ill.: InterVarsity Press, 2004), for a gripping description of what that anticipation, and the radical implications at stake, might have looked like (see esp. chap. 3, which offers the possible perspective of Nympha).

low man and as a brother in the Lord" (Philem 10, 12, 16 TNIV).

Among other things, both letters concern how the whole community, not just Philemon, will receive back Onesimus. Returning now as one born of the Spirit, he belongs to all of them, not just Philemon, and they to him, as "dear" brothers and sisters in the Lord Jesus. So, will they all look like Jesus, through the Spirit's power of reconciliation? Will they look like the One who loved them while they were against him, who exercised the power of the Spirit to forgive and to heal, with all authority given to him by the Father?

Paul's letter to the Colossians has hardly begun before he's praying; praying that the Spirit, given without measure, would empower them with wisdom and understanding to see what God is doing among them in and for his kingdom and to participate in it. Paul calls them to live lives worthy of the Lord, pleasing to him in every way, bearing fruit in every good work, growing in the knowledge of God and strengthened with power according to God's glorious might, to endure and suffer long, to continue in love—in short, to look like Jesus (Col 1:9-11). Paul's prayer is shaped by the story they all share, and it ends with an encouragement to give joyful thanks for that story. Seamlessly, he moves from prayer to song, weaving his prayerful longing into the context of the narrative of God's story among them. This story unfolds in the form of a joyous, awe-filled hymn.

> The Son is the image of the invisible God, the firstborn over all creation. For in him all things were created: things in heaven and on earth, visible and invisible, whether thrones or powers or rulers or authorities; all things have been created through him and for him. He is before all things, and in him all things hold together. And he is the head of the body, the church; he is the beginning and the firstborn from among the dead, so that in everything he might have the supremacy. For God was pleased to have all his fullness dwell in him, and through him to reconcile to himself all things, whether things on earth or things in heaven. . . . he has reconciled you by Christ's physical body through death to present you holy in his sight, without blemish and free from accusation. (Col 1:15-20, 22 TNIV)

Paul sings this gospel hymn in ways that echo his other moments of being caught up in the grand narrative. Texts such as Romans 8, 1 Corinthians 1 and 15, Galatians 4, and Ephesians 1 are narratives of the triune God in salvation history. In them God's particular way of being with and for his people, and perfecting their true humanity, has been reordered through the central reality of the incarnate Son.

From the beginning through the revelation of what is to come in Jesus Christ, Paul emphasizes that the origins, continuation and completion of this gift of holy love are particular to the person and work of God, the creating, transforming, perfecting Holy Spirit. God purposed before the creation of the world, from its genesis to its completion, that it would be thus: heaven and earth permanently united in creation finished and new, without blemish. And in Jesus, it has finally happened.[7]

No Docetic or Apollinarian Jesus here. In him, Creator and creature are united forever, in one person. The divine Son manifests the fullness of deity in bodily form. He is the incarnate, truly holy, human Son, in whom the Father is pleased to have his fullness dwell. He is Yahweh's "Israel," God's faithful embodiment of grace and truth, who wears his name and pleasure (see Mt 3:16-17). Amidst unrelenting opposition, he stands with the marginalized at the center of God's kingdom, entering the depths of depravity to reorder it toward life. God's faithful image-bearer, he withstands every human temptation to be otherwise, through the power, and presence, of the Holy Spirit (Lk 4:14-21; Heb 2:5-18).

There is no way to take our life in the Spirit seriously if we do not take Jesus' humanity seriously. Why? It is because there *is* no life in the Spirit that is not ultimately manifest by *Jesus' life in the Spirit.* From conception to resurrection, and with his Father's anointing, Jesus is and does everything by the Spirit. He is empowered, moment by moment, day in and day out, to choose to obey, over and over and over again. In ways mighty and mundane, his life realigns humanity back into shape, restoring the human image of Yahweh on the earth,

---

[7]"If we conceive of the church in the image of the humanity of Christ [which is the only image of God that we've been given], then: 'The gospel is that the Father interrelates with his world by means of the frail humanity of his Son, and by his Spirit enables anticipation in the present of the promised perfection of creation'" (Colin Gunton, *The Promise of Trinitarian Theology* [Edinburgh: T & T Clark, 1991], p. 73).

by the Spirit. By his Spirit-empowered obedience he became, in his physical body through death, God's reconciling gift, the gift of our new Spirit-filled life.[8]

WORSHIP AS SPIRITUAL FORMATION

> The Spirit is given so that we, ordinary mortals that we are, can ourselves be, in a measure, what Jesus himself was: part of God's future arriving in the present; a place where heaven and earth meet; the means of God's kingdom going forwards. The Spirit is given, in fact, so that the church can share in the life and continuing work of Jesus himself, now that he has gone into God's dimension, i.e., heaven. The Spirit is given to make God's future real in the present. . . . Just as the resurrection of Jesus opened up the unexpected world of God's new creation, so the Spirit comes to us from that new world, the world waiting to be born, the world in which, according to the old prophets, peace and justice will flourish.[9]

Since the baptizer in the Spirit has taken up residence in and among them, Paul urges them to live out their place in the gospel, conformed to the image of the Jesus in whom they also have been brought to fullness in the Spirit. They are embodied "brothers and sisters" "having the same Father," "born of the Spirit," "co-heirs with Christ," "new creation," who are being transformed into their immortal glory, in the image of the Son (Rom 8; Gal 4; 2 Cor 5; Philemon). And so, for and with each other, including Onesimus, they are to practice resurrection. "Since, then, you have been raised with Christ, set your hearts on things above, where Christ is seated at the right hand of God. Set your minds on things above, not on earthly things" (Col 3:1-2). In other words, pay attention to how the will of the Father is bringing the permanent kingdom of heaven to earth in your midst instead of things that will not last.

---

[8]See Gerald Hawthorne, *The Presence & the Power: The Significance of the Holy Spirit in the Life and Ministry of Jesus* (Dallas: Word, 1991); Gordon Fee, *Pauline Christology* (Peabody, Mass.: Hendrickson, 2007).

[9]N. T. Wright, "The Holy Spirit in the Church," Fulcrum Conference, Islington, 2005. See <www.fulcrum-anglican.org.uk/events/2005/inthechurch.cfm>.

For you died, and your life is now hidden with Christ in God. When Christ, who is your life, appears, then you also will appear with him in glory. . . . You have taken off your old self with its practices and have put on the new self, which is being renewed in knowledge in the image of its Creator.[10] Here there is no Gentile or Jew, circumcised or uncircumcised, barbarian, Scythian, slave or free, but Christ is all, and is in all. (Col 3:3-4, 9-11 TNIV)

"Putting off" and "putting on" is baptismal imagery, and so also imagery of the "renewing" work of the Spirit—those who are Christ's must bear his likeness in their behavior. The Colossians are to exhibit in their everyday lives the kind of behavior that is in keeping with the character of the One who created the new person in the first place. "As God's chosen people, holy and dearly loved, clothe yourselves" with the holy character of Yahweh. Be compassionate, gentle, humble, kind, patient. Love and forgive one another (including Onesimus!) as children of your heavenly Father, who loves and forgives you. Bear the fruit of the Spirit of God, without privileging your gendered, ethnic or cultural distinctions (see Col 3:12-14).

All of them—slaves, freeborn, Jews, Gentiles, women, men—they all are to admonish and teach one another by this word that dwells in their midst through the Spirit, forming them into who they really are, as a people. How, exactly, are they to do this? The same way Paul did: by singing their story, with psalms, hymns and spontaneous new songs given by the Spirit in the context of worship.[11] This requires "the Spirit's wisdom and understanding." They cannot speak or sing

---

[10]Fee renders this "for you have taken off the old humanity with its practices and have clothed yourself with the new, which is ever being made new until full knowledge after the fashion of him who created the new humanity" (Fee, *GEP*, pp. 646-47). Along with the baptismal imagery, which connotes the work of the Spirit for Paul, the appearance of the verb *anakaino* ("being made new") has in Paul the closest association with the Spirit (e.g., Rom 12:2; 2 Cor 4:16; Gal 5:13-26; Eph 3:16; Tit 3:5).

[11]"The first calling of God's holy people is praise and worship, which orients our way of being in the world," states Gunton. Worship becomes "the concrete means by which the church becomes an echo of the life of the Godhead," directing it from self-glorification to the source of its life in the creative and re-creative presence of God to the world." Worship also orients the church to the Word, "whose echo it is called to be, and to the communal love of God the Father towards his world as it is mediated by the Son and Spirit" (Colin Gunton, *The Christian Faith* [Grand Rapids: Eerdmans, 2003], p. 128; Gunton, *Promise of Trinitarian Theology*, p. 82).

truth *kata sarka*, from a "fallen" or "fleshly" point of view. Rather, the Spirit leads them into all truth, as Jesus promised, by allowing them to know the mind of the Lord together (Jn 14).[12] As Paul tells the church in Corinth:

> We declare God's wisdom, a mystery that has been hidden and that God destined for our glory before time began. None of the rulers of this age understood it, for if they had, they would not have crucified the Lord of glory . . . for God has revealed them to us by his Spirit. The Spirit searches all things, even the deep things of God. . . . We have not received the spirit of the world but the Spirit who is from God, that we may understand what God has freely given us. This is what we speak, not in words taught us by human wisdom but in words taught by the Spirit, explaining spiritual realities with Spirit-taught words . . . they are discerned only through the Spirit . . . [through whom] we have the mind of Christ. (1 Cor 2:7-8, 10, 12-14, 16 TNIV)

So too, the church at Colossae is led by the Spirit to Jesus Christ, crucified, resurrected and ascended, God's folly and mystery, and their hope of glory. In Christ, the mystery of God, says Paul, are hidden all the treasures of wisdom and knowledge (Col 1:27; 2:2-3). And it is this wisdom, knowledge and mystery that he "sings" in Colossians 1:15-20. The Colossians are to speak and sing the truth, with minds renewed and reconciled by the Spirit, joined to the "mind" of Christ. Transformation by the Spirit is that of conformity to Jesus Christ—still doing the will of the Father from his place of ascended rule—who has promised to be in their midst. Even as they participate in God's triune love and work among them, they begin to bear his resurrected likeness more and more, by the conforming presence of the Spirit. As Irenaeus affirms over a century later:

> At present we receive a part of His Spirit to perfect us and to prepare us for incorruptibility. In this way we become gradually accustomed to receiving and bearing God. The apostle calls this gift a "pledge" (cf. Ephesians 1:14), in other words, a part of the honor promised us by God. . . . This "pledge" here and now dwells in us and makes us spiri-

---

[12]Fee, *God's Empowering Presence*, pp. 642, 647.

tual. The mortal is swallowed up by immortality (cf. 2 Corinthians 5:4), for you are not in the flesh, but in the Spirit, "if the Spirit of God really dwells in you" (Romans 8:9). What is more, this is achieved not by casting off the flesh, but by communion with the Spirit; after all, the people to whom St. Paul was writing were not fleshless beings, but simply those who had received the Spirit of God, in whom we cry "Abba, Father" (cf. Romans 8:15). Therefore, if, even now, we have the "pledge" and cry "Abba, Father," how wonderful it will be when we rise again and behold Him face to face, when all the members burst forth into a hymn of exaltation, glorifying Him who raised them from the dead and gave them eternal life![13]

In the meantime, already in God's presence, the Colossians are to sing in exaltation of their promised resurrection and God's resurrection power among them, establishing new creation in and through them, even in worship. Corporately gathered, they hear God together and speak for God together, by means of each gift brought for the building up of God's people, including their songs. Worship becomes a central means in which, and by which, they become realigned to the truth—that to be for God is to be for the other.[14] As their love is multidirectional, directed both toward God and the gathered community, so too their hymns take on a multidimensional nature. This multidirectionality finds precedence in the Old Testament Psalter. Dozens of psalms address God in the second person, then move into the third person—extolling, reminding and declaring the faithfulness, greatness, sovereignty and power of God, precisely for the sake of those singing to him.

In the New Testament, hymns are mostly about, and for, Christ, as well as for the continuing instruction of his people. In 1 Corinthians 14 Paul states that praying and singing in the Spirit in the corporate assembly must be a multidirectional gift. As a gift from the Spirit, it becomes a gift again, to the community and to God, if it edifies the body and thus manifests the character of God—"so

---

[13]Ireneaus *Against Heresies* 5.8.1.
[14]Gordon D. Fee, *Paul, the Spirit and the People of God* (Peabody, Mass.: Hendrickson, 1996), pp. 153-61.

when you come with a hymn, a word of instruction, a revelation, tongue or interpretation, all must be done to build up the people of God."[15] This allows for a communal "amen," having heard the Spirit together, and a corresponding behavior in alignment to God and one another.

Ultimately, it is in worship that we know, and are known, by God and by one another, that we are reminded that we are for God and one another, precisely through God and one another. We enact our truth-telling identity, in several directions at once. The Spirit and the Son, with and through whom we pray, join us in *koinonia* to their shared life with the Father, whose kingdom is coming on earth, as it is in heaven. Our orientation toward that future reality already defines our present as "children of the resurrection." As holy, dearly loved children adopted through the Spirit, we sing the faithfulness of our Father, who has done what he said he would do through his Son, through whom he will bring all things to completion. Christ has taken what is ours, and given us what is his, in his physical body through death and into new life, so that we can be like him, truly human, holy and wholly embodied, image-bearing children of God.

Whether we are recapitulating the songs of the first exodus, singing of the invitation of the Spirit and the Bride who invite us into Christ's final exodus, or singing brand new songs, we get to hear, and echo, God by his Spirit. It takes God the Spirit, to hear the Word of the Father, says Paul; the inconceivably wonderful, ridiculous word that is Christ crucified and resurrected. "The Spirit searches all things, even the deep things of God" (1 Cor 2:10). And then he lets us indwell them, by indwelling us.

As the Spirit realigns us to God's story, and thus to our own, we become more and more who we are, converted, conformed into the image of the Son. This is the permanent formation project of the Spirit, who is God, who guarantees the outcome by his conforming, empowering presence and his power to raise us, like Jesus, into new, completed humanity. So let us sing, having first listened well. As we

---

[15]Ibid., p. 161.

"antiphonally" respond to Christ in us, to the Spirit who indwells us and speaks to and through us, we will be formed and reformed in the process. "Come, thou almighty King, help us thy name to sing; help us to praise. To thee, great One in Three, eternal praises be hence evermore!"

12

Spiritual Formation and the
Sanctity of Life

David P. Gushee

Introduction

The purpose of this chapter is to reflect on the relationship between
spiritual formation and Christian ethics. I want to address the connection between spirituality and the suffering world that exists outside of
the self-God relationship.

That there is a relationship between Christian spiritual formation
and moral engagement with our suffering world is to me so indisput-
able as to be beyond discussion. A socially disengaged spirituality or
Christianity is inconceivable and inexcusable. Just me and Jesus, growing closer all the time, while the world suffers outside of my field of
vision, is a way of being Christian that can flow only from cloistered
privilege—or perhaps in some cases from such extraordinary personal
misery that an inward spiritual retreat is the only path to emotional
survival. I fear that in evangelical Christianity these two paths to mere
inwardness sometimes converge—the cloistered privileged ones welcome the personally miserable ones and together they (we) escape the
world in the name of Jesus. But to escape the world is simply to reinforce the realities of the world as it is. This is not good enough. But
all too often it is what happens in our churches.

I believe in a Christian spirituality rooted in two core convictions
and obedient to two core commands. The first of these convictions
is that God is the majestic, holy, just and loving God who created

and rules the universe. The second is that the human being, created, sustained and redeemed by God in Christ, is infinitely sacred in God's sight.

As for the commands, they go like this: "'You shall love the Lord your God with all your heart, and with all your soul, and with all your mind.' This is the greatest and first commandment. And a second is like it: 'You shall love your neighbor as yourself.' On these two commandments hang all the law and the prophets" (Mt 22:37-40 NRSV). You shall love that majestic, holy, just and loving God with every fiber of your being. You shall love that infinitely sacred neighbor as yourself. Everything hangs on the quality of these two loves.

Jesus' teaching in the Great Judgment parable, in Matthew 25, closes the loop between these convictions and commands. He says that as we treat our fellow human beings, especially our most wretched, vulnerable and needy neighbors, so we treat the Son of Man, Jesus. In that terrifying parable, eternal judgment is depicted as hinging on whether we love our suffering neighbor and thereby love Christ himself.

THE SANCTITY OF LIFE AS FIXED ETHICAL STANDARD

My comments are especially affected by the deeply controversial fight against U.S.–sponsored torture, which I have been involved in over the last three years. That we have been fighting *torture*, not "enhanced interrogation techniques," has been confirmed by, among others, the International Committee of the Red Cross, which in a recently released 2007 report called U.S. conduct "torture," and documented acts that included repeatedly slamming prisoners against walls, partial suffocation by water, prolonged nudity, kicking and beating, continuous solitary confinement, shackling prisoners for days by their hands from the ceiling and holding them in small boxes and in frigid cells.[1] I have become only more deeply committed to the conviction that evangelical Christians must join Roman Catholics in establishing the sanctity of

---

[1]International Committee of the Red Cross, "ICRC Report on the Treatment of Fourteen 'High Value Detainees' in CIA Custody," February 2007. This report was leaked to the press; it can be accessed at <www.nybooks.com/icrc-report.pdf>. The fact that some evangelical Christians continue to defend these policies is appalling and scandalous.

human life as our utterly fixed, unshakeable and immovable moral standard. This is the plumbline against which we should measure our personal lives, our internal church behaviors, our relations to our near and far neighbors, and our engagement with every dimension of American public policy.

Christian spiritual formation must yield Christian disciples who are absolutely and stubbornly impervious to any temptation or enticement to sacrifice the sacredness of any group of neighbors for any private or public purpose, however compelling it may seem at the time. If truly governed by the sanctity of human life in this comprehensive sense, Christians will be both more faithful Christians and more profound contributors to American society. We will also be completely incomprehensible to the majority of our neighbors—for our society is essentially utilitarian, and at best the regnant moral-political visions honor the sacredness of life only in the most fragmentary ways.

Elsewhere I have established a working definition of the sanctity of human life that goes like this.[2]

> The sanctity of life is the conviction that all human beings, at any and every stage of life, in any and every state of consciousness or self-awareness, of any and every race, color, ethnicity, level of intelligence, religion, language, nationality, gender, character, behavior, physical ability/disability, potential, class, social status, etc., of any and every particular quality of relationship to the viewing subject, are to be perceived as sacred, as persons of equal and immeasurable worth and of inviolable dignity. Therefore they must be treated with the reverence and respect commensurate with this elevated moral status, beginning with a commitment to the preservation, protection and flourishing of their lives.

Let me try to unpack this definition.

The sanctity of life is a belief statement, truth-claim or expression of Christian theological-ethical conviction. The core conviction is that (each and every) human life is precious, of elevated worth and inestimable value—that it is sacred. I will spend the remainder of this essay

---

[2]David P. Gushee, *Sanctifying Human Life* (Grand Rapids: Eerdmans, forthcoming 2011). Considerable portions of the rest of this essay are drawn from draft chapters of this work.

showing why I believe this is a clear teaching of both Scripture and Christian tradition.

The sanctity of life is a conviction and claim about the *moral status* of human beings. Simultaneously, it is a claim about how human beings are to be treated by other human beings. One might put these together to say that the sanctity of life is a normative statement about moral *perception* and moral *behavior*. It includes implicit or explicit claims about how people should be both viewed and treated. Moral *conviction* (human life is sacred) leads to *perception* (humans should be seen as people of equal and immeasurable worth and inviolable dignity) and flows into *behavior* (humans should be treated with reverence and respect).

This conviction about life's sanctity is defined by its *comprehensiveness* and *universality*. It applies to the whole of humanity and to every individual human being. Some sanctity definitions are quite explicit about particular categories of people who must be included. I notice that definitions of politically or theologically conservative provenance tend to emphasize the unborn and the aged, and a correlative rejection of abortion and euthanasia. Definitions of more politically progressive provenance tend to focus on race, sex, sexual orientation, class and nationality, suggesting a correlative commitment to the inclusion of previously marginalized individuals and groups. Often the strongest adherents of each view have little interest in the sanctity of the lives not covered in their approach. Both are truncated. Both have become politicized and are linked to the Republican and Democratic parties. Those Christians who venture into political engagement are often swept up into one or the other approach.

But the true logic of life's sanctity must include all of these categories and others besides, and the more one sees this, the more one is inclined toward what has been called in Roman Catholicism the *consistent ethic of life*.[3] The sanctity of life is among the broadest and most inclusive understandings possible of our moral obligations to other human beings. All human beings are included (*each and every* human being), at all stages of existence, with every quality of experience, reflecting every

---

[3]Joseph Cardinal Bernardin, *The Consistent Ethic of Life* (Kansas City: Sheed & Ward, 1988).

type of human diversity, and encompassing every possible quality of relationship to the person who does the perceiving. (This latter category is especially important when dealing with the sacred lives of those who are enemies and strangers to us.) What they are included in is a vision of their immeasurable worth and inviolable dignity and the moral norms that correspond appropriately to that worth and dignity.

We might call this latter category "treatment norms." They include reverence and respect, but these are quite vague and abstract, so I added a statement specifying a moral obligation to the preservation, protection and flourishing of human lives. Some definitions go much further than this, for example, offering a specific ban on the deliberate and direct taking of innocent human life, then specifying examples of acts that qualify as prohibited. This is more common in Catholic statements than in others.[4] Sometimes discussion of these treatment norms is offered in "rights categories" and assumes the legitimacy of rights talk.[5] Other times the formulations do not use rights language. It is not hard to see that the more specific and detailed are the rights enumerated or the acts commended (or banned), the more disagreement there will be about either the sanctity-of-life norm or this or that specific application of it. Then we get into the thicket of moral theory. But in this chapter there is no need to pursue our subject any further into that thicket.

As I look back on the various subjects I have written about and causes I have embraced over the course of my career, it is clear to me that somehow this consistent ethic of life has never drifted far from my vision. Perhaps it is my Catholic DNA—I grew up a Vatican II–era Roman Catholic, leaving that tradition just before the wonderful papacy of John Paul II, whose work I have read and deeply appreciated for decades. Or perhaps it is evangelical statesman Ron Sider, for whom I worked from 1990 to 1993, and who introduced me to his evangelical appropriation of a consistent ethic of life at a pivotal stage in my early journey.[6] Or maybe it was my discovery of Christian rescuers of Jews during the Holocaust,

---

[4]Cf. *Catechism of the Catholic Church*, 2nd ed. (New York: Doubleday, 1997), p. 602, par. 2258.
[5]Cf. James F. Childress and John Macquarrie, eds., *The Westminster Dictionary of Christian Ethics* (Philadelphia: Westminster Press, 1986), p. 353.
[6]Ronald J. Sider, *Completely Pro-Life* (Downers Grove, Ill.: InterVarsity Press, 1987).

who embodied and sometimes articulated the conviction that every life—even hated and hunted Jewish life in Nazi Europe—is immeasurably sacred, worth paying any price to save from murder.[7]

But wherever it came from, it has become for me that fixed, unshakeable and immovable standard for Christian ethics.

- It has governed my opposition to abortion on demand, a policy based on making an exception to the sanctity of life in that vulnerable stage where, sheltered in the womb, a child is faceless and nameless to us.

- It has governed my opposition to the manufacture and exploitation of embryos for their stem cells, a most unfashionable position among the scientific and medical and academic elites.

- It has governed my opposition to the extraordinary coarseness of our media, where a major form of entertainment is to watch maniacs disembowel innocent people on screen or torture people on *24*, or, alternatively, humiliate and destroy each other in reality or talk TV shows.

- It has governed my opposition to assisted suicide and euthanasia, as well as to our grossly inadequate health care delivery system that leaves millions without adequate care.

- It has governed my opposition to the routine resort to war as an instrument of American foreign policy as well as to the continued complacent acceptance of nuclear weapons (at least, when we and our friends have them).

- It has governed my opposition not just to terrorism but also to U.S.-sponsored torture of suspected terrorists.

- It has governed my opposition to human-induced climate change and inadequate U.S. policies to address a problem that will affect most of us but especially the poorest.

- It has governed my opposition to the death penalty, both in itself and in the grotesque arbitrariness of its application—as well as much

---

[7]David P. Gushee, *The Righteous Gentiles of the Holocaust* (Minneapolis: Fortress, 1993).

that goes on in our criminal justice system and in our prisons.

- It has governed my opposition to Christian demonization of gays and lesbians and the way some of us have set our face against these neighbors as a central purpose of our Christian lives.

- And it has governed my opposition to the frequent internal viciousness of Christian culture, especially the way we deal so harshly with those with whom we disagree, either within the church or outside.

ONLY GOD IS STRONG ENOUGH TO GROUND THE SANCTITY OF HUMAN LIFE

I believe that only God is strong enough to ground that immovable commitment to the sanctity of human life as I have sought to articulate it here. By that I mean two things: only an *unbending theological-ethical commitment* to certain scriptural beliefs about God and God's relationship to the world is sufficient; and secondly, only a *totally committed Christian spirituality* that continually draws on the wellsprings of the Spirit of God at work in the lives of Christ-followers can provide an adequate foundation.

Many well-intentioned human rights and justice activists work vigorously for their causes apart from any obvious theological conviction. I have met and worked with some of them. They are highly impressive people. Their lived commitment to justice for the least of these is an inspiration to me. But in the end, reviewing the long trajectory of Western history in which the theological basis of many core ethical convictions has been abandoned (though some of those convictions have survived), I am convinced that we need a robust recovery of the deepest theological reasons for those moral beliefs that lead us to defend the dignity of our suffering neighbors. And that kind of work can only begin in the church.

Elsewhere I have established a starting definition of the theological foundations of belief in life's sanctity, which works like this:

> The belief that human life is sacred flows from biblical faith. In particular, life is sacred because, according to Scripture, God created humans in his image, declared them precious, ascribed to them a unique

status in creation, blessed them with unique, god-like capacities, made them for eternal life, governs them under his sovereign lordship, commands in his moral law that they be treated with reverence and respect— and forever elevates their dignity by his decision to take human form in Jesus Christ and to give up that human life at the Cross.[8]

Limits of space do not allow me to unpack all these claims. Here I want to linger briefly over the ethical implications of belief in Christ incarnate, crucified and resurrected, the central narrative of the Christian story. It is almost impossible to overstate the significance of Christ's incarnation, crucifixion and resurrection for belief in the sanctity of human life. And yet the connections are not often drawn.

"The Word became flesh and lived among us" (Jn 1:14 NRSV). The Word, which in the beginning was "with God," and "was God" (Jn 1:1), became human in Jesus the Christ. The eternal gulf between divinity and humanity was bridged in the God-man, Jesus. The New Testament writers consistently marvel at the divine condescension in which God stooped low to take on our frail, humble, sinful flesh, carry our nature, suffer humiliation and death at our hands and bear our sins as our suffering servant (Phil 2:1-11; cf. Is 53). The paradox of the incarnation is that when divinity stooped low and took on humanity, humanity revealed its vicious lowliness and yet was elevated through God's mercy. And it was elevated forever, for this moment in the career of God marked an irreversible change in God's relation to humanity and the world. After the incarnation, God has always been the One who became a human to save us in Jesus Christ.

The Old Testament teaches us to see the depth of God's loving and valuing of his human creatures and especially his people Israel. But the incarnation sees this loving and valuing incarnated in the person of Jesus Christ. When God becomes man, when divine nature and human nature join in Jesus Christ, God's sanctity touches humanity and is transferred through Christ to humanity in an unprecedented way. We are no longer "just" made in God's image, cared for in creation, delivered from our distress, protected by God's laws and promised eschato-

---

[8]Gushee, *Sanctifying Human Life.*

logical shalom; now God becomes one of us. In Christ, God embodies divine-to-human care, deliverance, protection and shalom.

If God became man, no human being can be seen as worthless. No human life can be treated cruelly or destroyed capriciously. Human dignity can never again be rejected or confined to only a few groups or individuals. God's incarnation in Jesus Christ elevates the human worth and dignity not just of the one man, Jesus of Nazareth; not just of the woman who carried him, Mary, or the followers who believe in him, the church, but every human being everywhere on the planet at any time in human history. The incarnation elevates human dignity both retrospectively and prospectively. It elevates the dignity of every human being at every stage of existence, in part because the arc of Jesus' own life included every stage of existence, from conception to death and even resurrection, which is our own destiny in Christ. If, as Karl Barth says, "Jesus Christ is *the* man, and the measure, the determination and limitation of all human being," and if he is "the decision as to what God's purpose and what God's goal is, not just for Him but for every man,"[9] then our understanding of humanity itself must be fundamentally transfigured and permanently elevated through its association with the God-man Jesus Christ.

I have already pointed to one particular teaching of Jesus that has proven hugely influential in linking incarnation to human life's sanctity. It is the eschatological judgment parable from Matthew 25:31-46.

In a profoundly important twist on the theme of incarnation, Jesus here suggests that God came to dwell not just in one man, but through the incarnation dwells in all people. Jesus teaches us to see in and through the face of every person his own face. This judgment parable (if it is a parable!) particularly instructs us to see Jesus Christ in and through the face of every *suffering person*, everyone who counts as among "the least of these," enumerated here as the hungry, thirsty, stranger, naked, sick and imprisoned. The Catholic servant-saint Mother Teresa of Calcutta saw this with perhaps more clarity than any known Christian leader. She was driven/called by this vision into a ministry with the

---

[9]Karl Barth, *Dogmatics in Outline* (New York: Harper & Row, 1959), p. 89.

lepers and dying of Calcutta. There she was sure she encountered Jesus Christ himself.[10] Her ministry incarnated the insight offered by Karl Barth when he wrote: "There is a general connexion of all men with Christ, and every man is his brother. . . . It is the most important basis, and the only one which touches everything, for what we call humanity. He who has once realized the fact that God was made man cannot speak and act inhumanly."[11] Why? It is because in every human being we encounter the person of Jesus Christ. Barth spoke these words amidst the ruins of a German university one year after the Nazi era was brought to its bloody close. He knew something about inhumanity.

Jesus came as a human being, and thus he came in a body, which was fully capable of hunger, thirst, suffering and death, and he experienced all of these to the uttermost. Because most religious traditions, including Judaism and Christianity, identify God as a Spirit (cf. Jn 4:24), it has been all too easy for adherents sometimes to denigrate the significance or dignity of human bodily existence. Heretical movements within Christianity have always struggled to accept the full bodily humanity of Jesus, perhaps out of an enduring human embarrassment at such humble functions as eating, drinking and dying.

But the incarnation forever elevates human bodiliness. What happens to human bodies (not just minds and spirits and souls, and not just the bodies of our friends but also our enemies) matters to God and must matter to us. One way we know this is because Jesus Christ came in a body; he was embodied, as a baby, a child, a teenager and a man. He enjoyed the proper functioning of his body. He also suffered grievously in his body. What happens to people's bodies must matter to us because God came in a body in Jesus Christ. This reality is a powerfully important contributor to Christian sanctity-of-life commitments as these relate to the preserving, protecting and flourishing of human life, which is always and irrevocably bodily life.

The body of Jesus Christ was nailed to a cross. On that cruel Roman cross Jesus suffered and died. There is no more central image in the

---

[10]See, for example, Mother Teresa, *The Joy in Loving* (New York: Penguin Compass, 1996), p. 344.
[11]Barth, *Dogmatics*, p. 138.

iconography, piety and theology of Christian faith than the suffering Christ on the cross.

The implications of the cross for the sanctity of life are abundant. One place to begin is with Christian grief over Christ's grief, Christian anguish over Christ's anguish. This grief and this anguish are central to Christian piety in many traditions and tend to overflow during the annual Lenten season. It is right that Christians should grieve Christ's grief and anguish over Christ's anguish—especially if that grief and anguish come to extend to all who suffer bodily humiliation, suffering, torture and death. The cross serves as a resource for life's sanctity when it functions to ground and motivate compassionate concern and intervention on behalf of all those who suffer. That concern can be sharpened and extended in appropriate ways if it is taken to focus on those whose victimization occurs at the hands of the state, who are victims of unjust legal processes and suffer humiliation, abuse and torture or death. In other words, Christ's innocent suffering and death leads to concern about the violation of life's sanctity by those who hold political power and use it to oppress and abuse and degrade. This is a major field of struggle in defense of life's sanctity, though obviously not the only one.

Jesus' death is always portrayed as an evil. It is *not good* that he was abused and killed. This is a reminder that it is not good that anyone is ever abused or killed. And yet, of course, the Bible teaches that this particular death brought the salvation of the world. "With his stripes we are healed" (Is 53:5 KJV). The precise theological formulation of the salvific meaning of Christ's death varies in the New Testament and has varied throughout Christian history. We need not settle on one single interpretation in the church. But what all such interpretations have in common is the basic claim that *Jesus died for us*. "God so loved the world, that he gave his only begotten Son" (Jn 3:16)—and that giving culminated at the cross.

God not only took flesh in Jesus Christ, God sacrificed that flesh at Golgotha, for our salvation. This staggering New Testament claim only deepens belief in the extent of God's love and care for humanity. God stopped at nothing to reach out to us. God-in-Christ suffered and bled and died for us. What more can anyone—what more could the divine One—do to demonstrate his love for the world? Belief in the sanctity of life is deepened considerably by reflection on the ultimate nature of the price God paid at the cross to demonstrate how valuable human life actually is to God.

New Testament teaching and later Christian thought include some related beliefs that are also highly significant for a consideration of life's sanctity. One is that "all have sinned and fall short of the glory of God" (Rom 3:23). This means a primal kind of human equality before God in terms of our shared, desperate need for divine rescue at the cross. A key part of our working definition of life's sanctity is its equalizing force—all human life counts the same, all human life is sacred, in the most significant sense all stands equal in value, and all must be viewed that way (Gal 3:26-28). If "all have sinned," this means that in this very significant fact about humanity there is indeed an irreducible equality. Everyone stands equal in our need for the sacrificial rescue that Jesus offered at the cross.

The New Testament also teaches that Jesus died for "the world," that is, everyone, people in all states, conditions, nations and orientations toward God and neighbor. Paul reminds us that Christ laid down his life not just for friends but also for enemies (Rom 5:10). The trajectory of the New Testament chronicles the ever-unfolding universality of those sought and reached by the good news of God's love in Christ. A movement that began as a Jewish splinter group spread geographically, linguistically, culturally and ethnically. Once again the universality of life's sanctity is affirmed. Paul's formulation becomes highly influential here: Who am I to harm one "for whom Christ died" (Rom 14:15). If the population of those "for whom Christ died" includes every human being in the entire world, those who believe and those who have yet to believe but might still believe, the moral implications are clear. Everyone must matter to us, because everyone matters to God, who sent Christ, who died for all.

And then Christ rose again. Entire theologies have been built on the significance of Christ's resurrection. There is no need to recapitulate them. But a few comments germane to our exploration here should be made.

First, it is significant that Christ rose in a body. It was a new, different kind of body. But it was still a body (cf. 1 Cor 15). This was a body that could be seen and touched. In this body Jesus ate and drank. Paul concludes from Christ's bodily resurrection that we too shall have bodies at our own resurrection. Human life never ceases to be bodily, even at the resurrection. Once again, human bodiliness gains powerful affirmation.

The resurrection of Christ also signifies the victory of God over evil, including the evil that took Jesus to the cross. In the resurrection, God triumphs, and God signals that in the end he will triumph over Satan and all forces that bring suffering and death; even death itself is destroyed (1 Cor 15:25-26).

The resurrection marks the triumph of life. The Gospel of John declares, "all things came into being through him [the Word], and without him not one thing came into being. What has come into being in him was life" (Jn 1:3-4 NRSV). In the incarnation, the One through whom all things were made, the one who sustains and holds together the creation itself (Col 1:1-18), became flesh, took on human life. At the cross this human being suffered and lost his life. But in the resurrection, Jesus lives again. Life wins, and therefore God wins. We are reminded that the triumph of life is indeed the triumph of God. God is for life.[12] All that wars against life is enemy to God, and God has defeated it proleptically at the cross. This demands that God's people participate in combating and sometimes defeating that which wars against life until Christ comes again.

Karl Barth reminds us that the confession of the church is not just that Jesus rose from the dead, but that he ascended to heaven, where he now sits at the right hand of the Father, and from which he shall come to judge the living and the dead (cf. Phil 2:5-11; Nicene Creed). Remembering that the Jesus who rose from the dead was fully God and fully human, this means, as Barth puts it: "The real mystery of Easter is not that God is glorified in it, but that man is exalted, raised to the right hand of God and permitted to triumph over sin, death and the

---

[12]A theme beautifully developed by John Paul II in his *Evangelium Vitae* [The Gospel of Life] (New York: Times, 1995).

devil."[13] God stoops low so that humanity can be exalted even to the right hand of God. And because Jesus goes ahead of humanity as trailblazer, where he has gone those who belong to him shall one day go as well. Human beings must be viewed and treated as those whose divinely intended destiny is to dwell eternally along with Jesus the Son in the presence of God the Father. That is how we should view everyone we encounter—as sacred human beings with an eternal destiny.

Conclusion

In the end, an unshakeable commitment to the majestic worth of the human person is grounded in the majesty and love of God—a God we love, not just a God we believe in or have read about, and not just a God concerned only with our spiritual well-being or personal growth. Indeed, we can make the argument more strongly to say that to recover the true roots of the sanctity of human life in God is at least as much a spiritual experience as it is a theological or ethical move. Those who tremble in loving awe before the God of all creation are the best prepared to, in turn, love all of God's creatures, especially human beings made in God's image and sacred in God's sight. Worship of God is the ultimate origin of a true appreciation for life's sanctity—if we remember what kind of God it is we truly worship. Remember the great line from *Les Miserables:* "To love another person is to see the face of God." Add to it this corollary: To hate, or degrade, or demean, or torture, or murder or ignore the suffering of another person is to spit in the face of God.

As we fall on our knees before God, as we fall more deeply in love with Christ incarnate, Christ crucified and Christ resurrected, may we likewise learn to love our neighbors as God loves them. This is the connection between spiritual formation and the sanctity of human life.

---

[13]Barth, *Dogmatics*, p. 115.

EPILOGUE

Theology, Spiritual Formation
and Theological Education
Reflections Toward Application

LINDA M. CANNELL

At the beginning of the Wheaton Theology conference that gave rise
to this volume, Jeff Greenman called for an understanding of theology
as formation. In the final address of the conference, Dallas Willard asserted that organizations do not have spiritual formation as their central focus—they are "doing something else." He proposed, "The future
of vital Christian life lies in the hands of the pastors and others who
teach for Christ—especially including those who teach pastors." How
this future will be realized in theological institutions remains a matter
of serious concern.

We are long past the day when theological institutions could do all
that's expected of them. Though it is too soon to offer a clear picture of
what they will be like in the next five to ten years, indications are that
the schools that survive will be deeply concerned about theological
education in relation to a biblical ecclesiology, committed to service
within society, increasingly decentralized in structure and affiliations,
and will have created *mutual* partnerships domestically and interna-
tionally. It is possible that only the smaller and larger schools will survive—the mid-size school being both too large and too small to maintain with a shrinking income.[1]

---

[1]Significantly, in 2006, Dan Aleshire, executive director of the Association of Theological

A THREAT MATRIX

The saga of efforts to reform higher education often seems like a Russian novel: long, tedious, and everyone dies in the end.
—MARK YUDOF, CHANCELLOR OF UNIVERSITY OF TEXAS SYSTEM

For the most part, the literature since the 1980s critiqued theological schooling in relation to one dominant factor, or in relation to two or three factors *treated separately* (e.g., lack of relevance to the church, lack of cohesion in the curriculum, inadequate spiritual formation, poor educational design, and so on).[2] This chapter proposes a matrix of four factors, potentially a threat matrix, that *taken together* profoundly affect the seminary and the church, and suggests possibilities for the future.

Factor 1: The rise of institutions. Educational institutions emerged over a long history. Dallas Willard once said that because the knowledge project is so vast and cannot be completed in one lifetime, it inevitably generates institutions. Where knowledge is understood as a body of content, educational institutions take on a form that seems to fit what people believe about how that knowledge is kept, enlarged on and communicated. Scholars and researchers brought together to fulfill these tasks are supported by increasingly complex institutional structures. Institutions seen as successful tend to take on a life of their own and persist from generation to generation.

Where the church is defined by its institutional expression, leadership will be defined in relation to the skills required to make the institution successful. Inevitably, the educational processes needed to serve the institutional church will be defined and circumscribed by what goes on in schools, whether in church-based or academic arrangements. The threat is that

---

Schools, in his report to the executive board, "Theological Education: The State of the Enterprise" stated, "While schools show strength and capacity to find ways to 'make do' financially, the current financial structure of theological education is likely not sustainable. We've been in financial straits before, but this time it might not be possible to support the proliferation of schools and the expanse of their programs and facilities. We may actually be in the end times for more theological schools than we realize." Used with permission.

[2]Material in this section and through the "four factors" that, taken together, create a "threat matrix" that affects the future of theological education is derived from Linda Cannell, *Theological Education Matters: Leadership Education for the Church* (Chicago: MorgenBooks, 2006).

academic institutions too easily fail in their most important tasks: coming to terms with the meaning of knowledge, how best to foster its development in communities of learning and how to stimulate responsible action, character development and spiritual values that permeate all of life.

Institutionalism and the nature of knowledge. The character and structure of academic institutions tend to shape faculty and administrators' understanding of the nature of knowledge just as much as their convictions about the nature of knowledge shape the character and structure of the institutions. Education and learning are often held hostage in this interplay.

Without question, most faculty take seriously their work as mediators of learning and development. However, curriculum design and opportunities to explore perceptions of the nature of knowledge and implications of those perceptions for learning and development in many institutions remain frustrating exercises. The assumption that the (only) way to do theological education is to build a school is a seriously limiting assumption. Just as education does not equal public school, theological education does not equal theological school. A theological institution is one expression of theological education; a number of decisions in the past 150 years or so have made it what it is today. It is conceivable that the purpose of theological education could be more properly understood and effectively designed if we were willing to entertain different decisions at this point in history.

Factor 2: The rise of academic theology and academic rationalism. Until the present era, the institutionalized structures of the university have tended to reinforce a *dominating* rationalistic orientation to knowledge with distinct disciplines. Studies within these disciplines are now at best parallel to, and at worst isolated from, studies in other disciplines. Academic theology emerged among these specializations.

Ellen Charry observes that academic theology viewed as "the theory of Christian belief" to a certain extent fostered the corollary assumption that theology "is to be understood, internalized, and acted upon in a purely cognitive procedure of assent and decision-making."[3] Unfortu-

---

[3]Ellen Charry, *By the Renewing of Your Minds: The Pastoral Function of Christian Doctrine* (Oxford: Oxford University Press, 1997), p. 240.

nately, when theology is approached as a process of disciplined, analytic rationality, that is, as an exercise of mind and language, the less precise understanding of theology as that which is derived from the desire to know God and the need to relate faith to all of life retreats to the margins of the academy. Interestingly, Charry, commenting on the purpose of her book, writes, "Although I started this project as an exercise in historical theology, a constructive thesis emerged: when Christian doctrines assert truth about God, the world, and ourselves, it is a truth that seeks to influence us. As I worked through the texts, the divisions of the modern theological curriculum began making less and less sense to me."[4]

In search of a role for academic theology. In the nineteenth century, in order to make theology a university-acceptable discipline, Schleiermacher recast it as a "positive science" related to the development of the church's leadership. By the late nineteenth century, theology had become an encyclopedia of several disciplines with tenuous linkages to certain practical fields. As the disciplines of academic theology were consolidated, theological specialists trained in the academy tended to be less equipped to relate theology to pressing issues in congregations and society.[5]

More recently, renewed concern for the spiritual, virtue-shaping function of theology and the role of theology in the transformation of the church and society is gradually refocusing attention on the relationship of theology to the historic and essential practices of congregations.[6] Nicholas Wolterstorff defines theology as sustained reflection about God in response to questions felt by the community of faith. More controversially, he asserts that the travail of theology in the academy is to be found in the expressed concern that theology "displays less and less the stamp of Christian conviction, and proves less and less useful

[4]Ibid., p. viii.
[5]For a theologian's perspective on this matter, see Miroslav Volf, "Theology, Meaning, and Power," in *The Future of Theology: Essays in Honor of Jürgen Moltmann*, ed. Miroslav Volf, Carmen Krieg and Thomas Kucharz (Grand Rapids: Eerdmans, 1996), p. 98.
[6]See the growing literature on "congregational practices," e.g., Craig Dykstra, *Growing in the Life of Faith: Education and Christian Practices*, 2nd ed. (Louisville, Ky.: Westminster John Knox, 2005); Miroslav Volf and Dorothy Bass, eds., *Practicing Theology: Beliefs and Practices in Christian Life* (Grand Rapids: Eerdmans, 2002).

for the life of the church."[7] Wolterstorff maintains that it was precisely the attempt to make theology university-acceptable that stripped it of its uniqueness and meaning.[8] Therefore, he asserts that academic theology shows little evidence of Christian conviction and is currently of little use to the church![9]

Nicholas Wolterstorff, Stephen Toulmin,[10] Miroslav Volf and George Marsden[11] are among a number of contemporary university-based historians, philosophers and theologians who propose that there is a growing and healthy shift from philosophical and theological rationalism to a concern for the role of theology in human experience and in the midst of the congregation. But, largely because of the forces of institutionalism and a dominating rationalism (and, subsequently, professionalism), congregations and theological schools have difficulty finding common ground.

Factor 3: The rise of professionalism in higher education. One of the most persistent criticisms of contemporary theological schools is that the curriculum is organized around specializations intended to serve the profession of ministry. Paralleling a similar trend in the universities, in the early to mid-twentieth century seminaries began to incorporate increasing numbers of specialized, professional degree programs. Because the nature of professional education is uniquely different from what is typical of the conventional theological curriculum, the church has not been well served in the effort to develop or improve leader capacity through this simple addition of courses and programs. Professional education presumes that intentionally planned and ongoing development of professional capacity extends over several years—it doesn't end once a degree is in hand. This presumption typically does not drive

---

[7]Nicholas Wolterstorff, "The Travail of Theology in the Modern Academy," in Volf et al., *The Future of Theology*, p. 37.

[8]Ibid., p. 40.

[9]See also a collection of Wolterstorff's work that continues his reflection on concerns cited in this section: Clarence W. Joldersma and Gloria Goris Stronks, eds., *Educating for Shalom: Essays on Christian Higher Education* (Grand Rapids: Eerdmans, 2004).

[10]See Stephen Toulmin, "Theology in the Context of the University," *Theological Education* 26, no. 2 (1990): 5-65.

[11]See George Marsden, *The Outrageous Idea of Christian Scholarship* (Oxford: Oxford University Press, 1997).

educational strategy in ministerial education. In reality, the theological curriculum is already hopelessly overcrowded with courses and programs. To what extent might the church be better served by some productive relationship, a synergy if you will, among academies, institutes and learning modes better suited for professional development, and venues where the spirituality can be fostered?

The seminary and professional education. The first seminary in North America (Andover) was established in the early 1800s.[12] Since that time, seminary development has been affected by the complex interplay of the demands of established churches for an educated clergy, the lingering effects of Colonial-era college ideals, the growth of the universities and their increasing distance from church concerns, professionalism, the Industrial Revolution, and the influence of graduates from German universities. Early in the nineteenth century, theological schools were still concerned to prepare people for a revivalist ministry. By the last half of the nineteenth century, many graduates of German universities returned to America and took teaching positions in the new seminaries, bringing the "new learning" to these schools. Research and scientific professionalism butted up against the ideal (at least) of pious learning oriented to character formation and service to society, and introduced into nineteenth-century Protestant theological schooling an element of confusion that continues to the present.

There was little resistance to the professionalization of the curriculum from the churches that were themselves, by the early twentieth century, becoming complex specialized organizations. It was inevitable that the schools (university divinity schools and then the new seminaries) would be called on to prepare ministry specialists for these churches. Once churches felt the need for professionally trained leadership, courses were added to the curriculum to address this felt need—most often without attention to the nature of the church as an organizational *and* theological entity or, for that matter, without attention to overall educa-

---

[12]For a history of the development and influence of the divinity schools and the subsequent emergence of the seminary, see Conrad Cherry, *Hurrying Toward Zion: Universities, Divinity Schools, and American Protantism* (Bloomington: Indiana University Press, 1995), p. 295.

tional strategy. For example, though the M.Div. is classified as a professional degree, in many seminaries it is treated as if it were an academic degree. Assessment standards are not consistent with those expected of a program with both academic and professional elements, admission requirements seldom assess the suitability of the applicant for lifelong development and practice in the ministry "profession," and systematic accountability of the graduate-cum-ministry leader is seldom linked to career-long, mandatory continuing education. The schizophrenic nature of the degree continues to trouble ministerial development. The increase of specialized "professional" degrees to compensate for the limitations of the M.Div. has not solved the problem.

Professionalism: Definition and critique. Critics of professional education and the ensuing professional associations asserted that the curriculum of universities and professional schools developed competencies more appropriate for a former era and with standards insufficient to ensure that women and men could function effectively.[13] Graduates of the professional schools were unable to learn adequately from one another, lacked the necessary skills for reflection on practice that could lead to productive change, communicated inexpertly with their clients, and tended to turn to how-to manuals when faced with a problem rather than reflecting on practice and interacting with their community.[14] The criticism that the professional's work can be accomplished through the application of professional technique tends to parallel concern about clerical functionalism in theological schools—the tendency to believe that one can fix the church, or grow the church, through the application of professional technique.

David Kelsey's observation that the use of the term *professional* is

---

[13]Arthur Wilson, "Professionalization: A Politics of Identity," *New Directions for Adult and Continuing Education* 91 (2001): 73-83. See also the historical background of critique leading to change in medical education in Abraham Flexner, *Medical Education in the United States and Canada: A Report to the Carnegie Foundation for the Advancement of Teaching*, Bulletin no. 4 (Boston: D. B. Updike, Merrymount, 1910).

[14]See also William Sullivan, *Work and Integrity: The Crisis and Promise of Professionalism in America* (San Francisco: Jossey-Bass, 2005). While he describes professional schools as the bridge between the academy and real-world practice, concern that professional education is faltering has prompted the Carnegie Foundation for the Advancement of Teaching to begin a study of professional programs including those designed to develop clergy, engineers, lawyers, nurses and physicians.

problematic for churches adds a further dimension to how seminaries and churches envision leadership education. Having traced common elements in the definition of *profession*, Kelsey proposes that church leadership is not consistent with many of the sociological characteristics of a profession. One of his more significant objections is consistent with a congregationally based understanding of leadership: "Theologically, it is important to stress that it is the *entire congregation* that engages in ministry in the public worship of God. Persons *who stand in parity with everybody else so far as their shared ministry is concerned* exercise various kinds of leadership in regard to that ministry. Hence a profession's stress on 'autonomy' and its view of those served as 'clients' are both inappropriate in congregational leadership."[15] Laity could also carry out many, if not most, professional activities of clergy. One could argue, then, that the appropriate "professional" responsibility of a leader is to assist congregations to understand and to live out their identity and purpose as the people of God. In this regard, theological education, in its broadest definition, must engage a biblical ecclesiology. To what extent have criteria from operational notions of professional behavior been adopted uncritically in theological schools—and churches? How did the apostle Paul credential leaders in the church? What indicators satisfied Jesus that his disciples were becoming leaders?

Factor 4: How the church and academy have understood and fostered the desire to know God. Discussions of the loss of a suitable understanding of theology in relation to theological schooling, or the loss of what it means to know God, typically reference Edward Farley's *Theologia*.[16] He positions the meaning of *theologia* within three major historical periods: From the patristic era through most of the medieval period *theologia* was understood as the knowledge of God—that is, a divine illumination of the intellect. From the twelfth to seventeenth centuries, *theologia* became a cognitively oriented "state and

---

[15]David Kelsey, *To Understand God Truly: What's Theological About a Theological School?* (Louisville, Ky.: Westminster John Knox, 1992), p. 247. Emphasis added.

[16]Edward Farley, *Theologia: The Fragmentation and Unity of Theological Education* (Philadelphia: Fortress, 1983).

disposition of the soul which has the character of knowledge." Finally, from the Enlightenment to the present, *theologia* is seen as "the practical know-how necessary to ministerial work." Theology in this period became "one technical and specialized scholarly undertaking among others; in other words, as systematic theology."[17] He asserts that the meaning of *theologia* found in the first two periods has largely disappeared in the academy, and clearly identifies the Enlightenment understanding as the source of most of the current problems in theological education. He argues, "in this period the two genres of theology continue but undergo such radical transformation that the original senses of theology as knowledge (wisdom) and as discipline [not in the sense of structured academic specialization] virtually disappear from theological schools."[18]

Farley favors a notion of *theologia* informed by the mysticism of the patristic era but shaped ultimately by the later medieval period through the Renaissance. The important distinction he makes between the patristic era and the later period is that, though the notion of divine illumination persisted, it was conceived in the later period as related to the emerging universities and was regarded as a habit—a *habitus*. That is, it could be "promoted, deepened, and extended by human study and argument."[19] Based on his interpretation of patterns in history, Farley concludes that *theologia* is best understood as the ecclesial counterpart of *paideia*.[20] The loss of this understanding in the current era, he asserts, has made theological schooling the "grasping of the *methods* and *contents* of a plurality of regions of scholarship."[21] For Farley, *theologia* is best depicted as a mode of understanding—a process—rather than as a science; and like *paideia*, it is a preparation for life. Properly understood *theologia* cannot be taught, but it can be the unifying principle for theological study and the orienting philosophy of the curriculum.

---

[17]Ibid., pp. 35, 39.
[18]Ibid., p. 39.
[19]Ibid., p. 36.
[20]Farley defines *paideia* in relation to one aspect of the Greeks' view of the purpose of education: culturing a human being in virtue. Farley, *Theologia*, pp. 152-53.
[21]Ibid., p. 153. Emphasis added.

In favoring the understanding of *theologia* that emerged in the twelfth to seventeenth centuries, Farley may not have taken enough account of the deep complexities and mysteries that bound theology and spirituality together from the patristic era to the seventeenth century. Theology and spirituality, now seen as two distinct areas of knowledge and practice, were, for most of history, one unified essence—holding *reason* and ineffable *mysteries* in tension. As institutionalism, academic rationalism and professionalism proceeded, this essence fractured. Clearly, spirituality without reason is untenable. However, reason too easily assumes the prominent, almost exclusive position of arbiter of the meaning of theology.

The search for a theology and spirituality for theological education. Efforts to recover a theology suitable for theological education, broadly understood, must address the fundamental issue: humanity is not brought into right relationship with God and empowered for service through doctrine, or experience, alone. Farley articulates the dilemma: Allowing that clergy education is necessary, he maintains that theology cannot be "restricted to clergy education and its array of scholarly endeavors. . . . Because theology arises as an adjunct to the life of faith itself, *the inquiries and instructions of degree-granting schools are always derivative and secondary.*"[22]

Perspectives on the nature of theology and spirituality. Is it necessary that the desire to know God results in the separation of theology and spirituality, reason and piety, service and virtue? Can the "path of reason" and the "path of love" be reconciled within a theological vision that is relevant for contemporary theological education for the whole people of God? Charry weaves together from the history of Christian doctrine a defensible thesis that character formation, trust, love of God and virtuous acts were once integral to theology and vital to knowing God. Her account seeks to recover the holism of Christian theology: the notion that integration of mind, emotions and behavior, within the context of a faithful community, is essential to the formation of Christian identity. "Communal practices such as participation in prayer, lit-

---

[22]Edward Farley, *Practicing Gospel: Unconventional Thoughts on the Church's Ministry* (Louisville, Ky.: Westminster John Knox, 2003), p. 36. Emphasis added.

urgy, sacraments, works of charity, and study all strengthen Christian identity. That is one reason why Christian communities have been fussy about ordering these communal tasks."[23]

Since the late Middle Ages, it seems, Western Christians have found it difficult to hold intellect and piety in constructive tension.[24] Without intellectual rigor and the intent to inquire into God's revelation, spirituality tends to be shaped by personal experience, opinion or the latest media personality. Without the desire to know God through the mysterious activity of the Spirit, intellectual inquiry and memorization of propositions tend to become meaningless activities of an empty soul. In light of this difficulty, Mark McIntosh worries, "What kind of god does theology divorced from spirituality end up describing?"[25] Any future for theological education that includes theology must also accept that intellectual justification for faith is in itself inadequate. The inevitable criticism that this perspective undercuts serious learning about theology ought to be rejected. Of course, much that has been gained over the centuries of the Christian church would be lost if learning were despised. Surely we have learned this lesson from history. However, once again, in this generation, a view of spirituality that is grounded in experience is in tension with a view of spirituality grounded in reason. Clearly, a theology that is simply a quest for experiences that will prove God's presence is not sufficient. However, a theology that is merely a transmission of propositions is similarly insufficient. Only a theology that allows reason and piety, virtue and service to stand together will be convincing in the context of theological education for the whole people of God.

---

[23]Charry, *By the Renewing*, p. 27.
[24]Mark McIntosh follows Bernard McGinn and Jean Leclercq in describing the historical practice of theology as making it possible for *all* Christians to partake of the divine nature. Mark McIntosh, *Mystical Theology* (Oxford: Blackwell, 1998), p. 40; Bernard McGinn and John Meyendorf, eds., *Christian Spirituality: Origins to the Twelfth Century* (New York: Crossroad, 1985); Bernard McGinn, *The Presence of God: A History of Western Christian Mysticism*, vol. 1, *The Foundations of Mysticism* (New York: Crossroad, 1991); Bernard McGinn, *The Presence of God: A History of Western Christian Mysticism*, vol. 2, *The Growth of Mysticism* (New York: Crossroad, 1994); Jean LeClercq, *The Love of Learning and the Desire for God: A Study of Monastic Culture* (New York: Fordham University Press, 1982).
[25]McIntosh, *Mystical Theology*, p. 15.

BEYOND THE THREAT MATRIX

I skate where the puck will be, not where it is.
—WAYNE GRETZKY

The familiar twentieth-century forms of North American higher education emerged as the four factors described above intersected with events in the seventeenth through nineteenth centuries. The English college model, imported in the seventeenth century, encountered the German research university model imported in the nineteenth and early twentieth centuries. In the nineteenth century both models suddenly had to cope with the Industrial Revolution and the rise of the professions. Then, the seminary, born in the early nineteenth century out of ideological conflict with the university, retained university-style structures and curricular patterns. For this reason, the same confluence of seventeenth through nineteenth century influences has shaped the conventional theological curriculum.

To complicate matters further, the Industrial Revolution provided nineteenth-century educational administrators with a way to manage large numbers of students. Processes not unlike the assembly-line procedures of factories were adapted to higher education to move students through various programs with minimum disruption and maximum efficiency. As the professions took root in America, functional forms of education were valued. Because the professions emerged during one of the most pragmatic eras of North American history, the models of education in professional schools and professional departments of universities quickly developed a practical cast as the demand for skilled professionals increased, even in churches. Efforts to classify, organize and systematize knowledge further defined institutional structures and reinforced a dominating rationalism that ultimately separated spirituality from the disciplines of knowledge and shifted it away from the center of discourse to the margins.

Movies set in the era when the horse and buggy were giving way to the automobile often show these modes of transportation coexisting. For a time, the symbols of two different eras traveled together on the same roads—not without mutual annoyance. It seems we are in another time of transition, in which the educational forms of one era coexist with initiatives that forecast the new. Schools are one expression of theological education; professional education need not be merely functional; academic learning need not be exclusively a rational enterprise. The face of higher education in the West is changing; and this change is accelerating as current economic realities threaten institutional survival. Educational leaders in other countries, aware that the forms they inherited from the West are not necessarily suited to their particular contexts, are becoming more intentional about seeking fresh and more effective ways to serve their churches and societies through education. International collaboration can help shape what theological education becomes in the next decade.

As difficult as it is, the processes that have shaped theological schools must be seen as a whole—a matrix. A matrix is an environment or source from which something else originates, develops or takes form. Men and women in churches, schools and other faith-based organizations are actively searching for that "something else." In recent decades, participants in numerous consultations have talked and written about the problems confronting theological schools; but these discussions have not yet produced consensus around clear action. Because it is too soon for that one perfect solution, church communities, individual donors and foundations are slowly beginning to commit significant resources to experimentation and innovation in theological education.

Developing academic capability: Challenging the institutionalized silos of theological schools. In one sense, the decision at some point in history to create disciplines of knowledge could be seen as a beneficial development that served to strengthen scholarship and understanding. But it is not necessary to structure departments and organize faculty around disciplines of knowledge. Disciplinary boundaries (or academic silos) make little sense when a student graduates and endeavors to minister in the world. In many cases, curriculum and educational practices tend to remain relatively fixed while the conditions in church and society change. Though the point is not disputed here that, at its best, academic institutions provide time, a context and expertise for men and women caught in the whirl of change and forces them to encounter ideas, think together and reflect on issues that affect church and society, but it is not necessary to create disciplinary silos, to separate faculty from one another, to organize course schedules that hinder integration, to fix a curriculum for years, to accept a particular architecture or to presume that only certain forms of instruction and assessment are of value. Knowledge management is too complex, and the problems of society and church are too urgent to permit the assumption that students learn to think productively and develop informed wisdom and practice as they march in orderly columns through classes selected from a potpourri of departments, accumulating enough credit hours and "seat time" to a secure a degree.

Winston Churchill once observed that we shape our cities and then they shape us. Institutional structures that resemble a series of loosely connected boxes of administrative functions and specialized disciplines have shaped the way we think about theological schooling for generations. The satisfaction level for this way of doing theological education has diminished significantly. Conceivably, renewed efforts to enhance instruction and to improve assessment, increased diversity and the emergence of other providers (i.e., church-based and other nonformal education initiatives) will significantly alter the landscape of theological education in the twenty-first century. Increasingly, faculty, students and other entrepreneurs are creating institutes, centers, consultations and interdisciplinary conversations to influence church and society, and to work on real tasks. Perhaps these ventures at the fringes of theological education are, in fact, the shape of the future.

Developing ministry capability: Discerning what is suitable for professional development. Thomas Edison left school in frustration and began inventing. The questions and problems he encountered while inventing drove him back to books and other sources of knowledge. Edison's experience is not uncommon. He demonstrated that the desire to learn is often stimulated when one encounters problems, challenges or anomalies. If we assume that the best professional development occurs as men and women are involved with real situations, a more dynamic curriculum is possible. Today, most professions make use of problem-based learning (PBL) and other curricular approaches that, when well designed, obligate learners to deal with real issues and interact with faculty and other resource people from diverse disciplines as they seek knowledge and strategies to address problems and questions.[26]

Joseph Hough and John Cobb suggest, "the current problem for the theological school is *not* that it is a 'professional' school, dominated by the 'clerical paradigm.' Rather it is that the church has become uncertain and confused as to what constitutes appropriate professionalism. There can be no clear ecology of theological education until there is clarity about the nature of professional leadership within the church."[27] For Hough and Cobb, the seminary can be a professional school—if professional education is understood as an opportunity for reflective practitioners to operate out of the church's ecclesial memory, fashioning questions that stimulate reflection on how God worked in the past, how God is working in the present and seeking to discern how God intends to work in the future. Thus trained, Hough and Cobb assert that the practical theologian then helps the whole congregation to understand its identity and purpose in the world.

Nurturing spiritual capacity: Theological learning for informed wisdom. If it is true that theological education is ultimately for the whole people of God, then the historic practices of the Christian church are central to educational planning. These practices are fundamentally related to the nurture of the soul and growth toward wisdom. While Gregory Jones proposes three intersecting communal settings as critical to the development of the minister—congregational life, formal education and social settings that require engagement—he stresses that the education of the minister requires that members of congregations participate in the process. Each of these settings contributes one or

---

[26]Hans Madueme and Linda Cannell, "Problem-Based Learning and the Master of Divinity Program," *Theological Education* 43, no. 1 (2007): 47-60. The article traces dynamics in the seminary that contribute to academic versus professional tensions in the M.Div. program and suggests that problem-based learning could be employed as a way to develop skills such as critical thinking, research, substantive dialogue and clear writing, as well as a way to equip men and women for their roles as ministry professionals. The authors provide suggestions for implementation and raise questions and cautions for further research.

[27]Joseph Hough and John Cobb, *Christian Identity and Theological Education* (Atlanta: Scholars Press, 1985), p. 5.

more elements: "catechesis, critical reflection, and faithful living in the world."[28] The congregation is a setting where desire for God is shaped by instruction, prayer, worship and authentic social engagement. The awareness and practices of leaders-believers will, in turn, be informed by habits of inquiry and self-reflection shaped in the academy. Finally, "faithful living in the [social settings] draws Christians into contexts in which the distorting and sinful desires, practices, and structures of our world ought to be challenged by the light of the gospel."[29] The interplay of the three settings and overlapping experiences in each informs, shapes and tests emergent beliefs and practices.

WHEN THE FUTURE ASKS OUR NAME

More than at any time in recent history, theological schools are confronting the need to make new decisions about purpose, structure and relationships; or to revise long-standing practices derived from old decisions. We cite the names of those from the past whose decisions have affected our present reality. Our names will likely be attached to decisions made in the present that will affect theological education in the future. Some of these decisions will be in areas such as the following:

1. *How we gather to engage issues that affect matters such as curriculum, faculty hiring and organizational change.* Unfortunately for organizational development, habits formed in much Ph.D.-level study—such as arguing for one's position *against* others, focusing on a narrow field and so on—do not transfer well to meetings where collaboration and broadly based thinking are essential. The ways in which we have defined teaching in the academy, and the ways in which meetings of academic guilds tend to be conducted, do not lead naturally to organizational process where framing *questions* is often more important than the answer, where relationship across difference is vital, ambiguity is common and where participants must listen to other points of view without immediately dismissing the other. Recent de-

---

[28]Gregory Jones, "Beliefs, Desires, Practices, and the Ends of Theological Education," in *Practicing Theology: Beliefs and Practices in Christian Life*, ed. Miroslav Volf and Dorothy Bass (Grand Rapids: Eerdmans, 2002), p. 188.

[29]Ibid.

scriptions of what are proving to be more productive ways to bring people together for conversation and decision-making offer a way forward. Peter Block, and Juanita Brown and David Isaacs[30] suggest collaborative approaches built on values that Christian communities would affirm. Joseph Bessler, Peter Cha, Mary Hess and Timothy Tennent propose more effective, collaborative models for theological faculties.[31] David Cooperrider and Diana Whitney, and Whitney and Amanda Trosten-Bloom suggest that human systems grow in the direction of that about which they persistently ask questions.[32] William Bergquist and Kenneth Pawlak describe six cultures of the academy and how to cope with them.[33]

2. How the twenty-first-century theological curriculum will integrate disciplines, consolidate and build knowledge, accommodate ethnic and cultural diversity, engage real world issues, reach across the life and career span and be driven by holistic outcomes.[34] Richard Rorty observed that the prob-

---

[30]Peter Block, *Community, the Structure of Belonging* (San Francisco: Berrett-Koehler, 2008). Note particularly his description of what many organizations have found to be a more effective process for meetings in chapters 10-14. See also Juanita Brown with David Isaacs, *The World Café: Shaping our Futures Through Conversations That Matter* (San Francisco: Berrett-Koehler, 2005). The World Café process depends on (1) diversity in culture, experience and perspective in order to gain insight into today's complex problems and circumstances and (2) questions that we care about and are driven to answer. They note that throughout history, one can find examples of small gatherings for conversations that matter: the Salon Movement prior to the French Revolution; sewing circles preceding the American Revolution; Wesley's class meetings; study circles in Scandinavia; and the workers' movements in various countries. Brown observes that there is a difference between "divider-cultures" and "connector-cultures." Where the divider-culture creates and maintains boundaries between people, the connector-culture, which characterizes the Café experience, encourages participants "to offer their diverse contributions while simultaneously increasing the density of connections among people and ideas" (p. 104).

[31]Joseph Bessler, Peter Cha, Mary Hess and Timothy Tennent, under the auspices of the Lilly-funded Lexington Seminar, worked together for at least three years in an innovative mentor project for academic leadership. The result of their work is recorded in Malcolm Warford, ed., *Revitalizing Practice: Collaborative Models for Theological Faculties* (New York: Peter Lang, 2008).

[32]See David Cooperrider and Diana Whitney, *Appreciative Inquiry: A Positive Revolution in Change* (San Francisco: Berrett-Koehler, 2005); and Diana Whitney and Amanda Trosten-Bloom, *The Power of Appreciative Inquiry: A Practical Guide to Positive Change* (San Francisco: Berrett-Koehler, 2003).

[33]William Bergquist and Kenneth Pawlak, *Engaging the Six Cultures of the Academy* (San Francisco: Jossey-Bass, 2008).

[34]Many hundreds of titles are available related to decisions we will make related to curriculum. Some useful reading includes Mary Hess and Stephen Brookfield, eds., *Teaching Reflectively*

lems of society are not contained in discipline-shaped blocks. The disciplines are frameworks developed by people in time, to deal with questions in time, and typically reflect a particular cultural and ethnic orientation. Imagine a different future: varied groupings of scholars in newly constituted disciplinary structures enable communities of scholars to work together across cultural and disciplinary boundaries in relation to real world tasks; an "ecology" of agencies serves the purposes of theological education for the whole people of God; curricular overcrowding is being dealt with by moving some courses and learning experiences from time-bounded degree programs—where they are often not offered at the point of student readiness—to a lifelong learning mode; in less crowded curriculum designs, space and time are available for reflection, critical thinking, mentoring, relationship, dialogue, spiritual practices, exploration of other cultures and international venues; graduate theological schools are less about "preparation" and more about the *continuing development* of adult learners; in the next evolution of twenty-first-century online learning, existing course management systems have been replaced by effective use of social networking systems—where all participants at a distance from one another are intentional about contextualization.

3. *How to create an ecology of theological education that serves the whole people of God.* Multinational, intercultural partnerships among churches, schools, mission enterprises and development work are emerging and stimulating decisions about what we include in curriculum and how we provide international experience for faculty and students. For theologi-

---

in Theological Contexts (Malabar, Fla.: Krieger, 2008); George Walker, Chris Golde, Laura Jones, Andrea Conklin Bueschel and Pat Hutchings, *The Formation of Scholars: Rethinking Doctoral Education in the 21st Century* (San Francisco: Jossey-Bass, 2008); Francis Ward, *Lifelong Learning: Theological Education and Supervision* (London: SCM Press, 2005); Craig Dykstra, "For the Love of God, for the Love of God's People," *Colloquy* 17, no. 1 (2008): 11-13; Charles Foster, Lisa Dahill, Lawrence Golemon and Barbara Wang Tolentino, *Educating Clergy: Teaching Practices and Pastoral Imagination* (San Francisco: Jossey-Bass, 2006); Michael Eraut, *Developing Professional Knowledge and Competence* (New York: RoutledgeFarmer, 1994); Oon-Seng Tan, *Problem-Based Learning Innovation: Using Problems to Power Learning in the 21st Century* (Singapore: Thomson, 2003); Sharan Merriam, Bradley Courtenay and Ronald Cevero, *Global Issues and Adult Education* (San Francisco: Jossey-Bass, 2006); Sharon Parks, *Leadership Can Be Taught: A Bold Approach for a Complex World* (Boston: Harvard Business School Press, 2005).

cal education, the church is a vital part of an emerging ecology.[35] James Hopewell,[36] and Joseph Hough and Barbara Wheeler[37] have proposed that a congregational paradigm replace the current paradigm of theological education. Their proposal allows for a community of scholars but shifts the focus of educational efforts from the cognitive and character development of the student to the cognitive and character development *of the church*. The congregation conceived as the organizing principle for the curriculum[38] would necessitate new decisions with regard to educational strategy. Daniel Schipani uses the term "ecclesial paradigm" to describe theological education that is "focused on the church's identity, nature and purpose, namely its very life and its ministry." Theological education then "will take place within contexts of authentic evangelical piety and spirituality, genuine Christian ethics and moral behavior, and an epistemology . . . governed by the very Spirit of God."[39] The theological curriculum is shaped around the text of the Bible, the life and story of the ecclesial community past and present, and cultural and intercultural circumstances. Learning processes are "communal, dialogical, collaborative, and discipleship/ministry-oriented."[40]

4. *How we evaluate what we do, in order to improve what we do.* Assessment for learning is part of curriculum design and educational strategy. John Harris, a noted specialist in educational assessment, avers that higher education assessment is conducted in ways that are not optimal for learning.[41] For example, the further away assessment is

---

[35]See Timothy Weber, "The Seminaries and the Churches: Looking for New Relationships," *Theological Education* 44, no. 1 (2008): 65-91.

[36]James Hopewell, "A Congregational Paradigm for Theological Education," *Theological Education* 21 (1984): 60-70.

[37]Joseph Hough and Barbara Wheeler, eds., *Beyond Clericalism: The Congregation as a Focus for Theological Education* (Atlanta: Scholars Press, 1998).

[38]To test his vision, James Hopewell initiated a program at Candler Seminary that brought together a pastor, a professor, twelve laypeople and twelve senior students to work on a problem of congregational significance for a term.

[39]Daniel Schipani, "The Church and Its Theological Education: A Vision," in *Theological Education on Five Continents: Anabaptist Perspectives*, ed. Nancy Heisey and Daniel Schipani (Strasbourg, France: Mennonite World Conference, 1997), pp. 22-24.

[40]Ibid., p. 30.

[41]John Harris, "Assessment of Ministry Preparation to Increase Understanding," *Theological Education* 39, no. 2 (2003): 117-36. See also <www.ats.edu/Accrediting/Documents/Handbook/HandbookSection8.pdf>.

from the settings where learning is to be applied, the less acceptable or reliable it is. He suggests that grades seldom correlate with much of anything except other grades. Further, standardized tests have low validity in terms of what they purport to measure. Knowing that a student can answer a question or perform an action is not sufficient. The more important issue is the extent to which a student can select and apply knowledge when faced with a new situation. It has been observed that the question now being asked of theological schools (Are you accomplishing educationally what you purport to accomplish?) was never asked before the 1980s. We rightly resist assessment that consists of simple measures of information acquisition or quantification of the obvious. Yet, to assess what the ATS accrediting standards require of theological schools—the development of theological reflection, the development of wisdom, spiritual awareness, moral sensibility and character, understanding of a tradition of a faith community and ministry capacities[42]—will require decisions related to how we foster academic, spiritual and ministry capacity, interact effectively with our students, stay with our graduates over the long term and plan for the holistic development of women and men.[43]

5. *How we envision the ethos of theological schooling.* What constitutes the "culture" of a theological school? The late Henri Nouwen once observed that the culture of the academy tends upward, toward pride, arrogance and elitism, whereas the gospel points one to humility, service and obedience. Interestingly, some notion of spirituality as a way to counter the less desirable attributes of the academy is found in higher education generally. Elizabeth Tisdell explored spirituality and culture in adult and higher education.[44] Arthur Chickering, Jon Dalton and Liesa Stamm described how authenticity and spirituality

---

[42]Dan Aleshire, *Evangelical Theological Education in 2000 Decade*, presented at the faculty workshop [audiocassette], Trinity Evangelical Divinity School, Deerfield, Ill., 2000.

[43]See also Dan Aleshire, *Earthen Vessels: Hopeful Reflections on the Work and Future of Theological Schools* (Grand Rapids: Eerdmans, 2008); Daniel Treier, "Theology as the Acquisition of Wisdom: Reorienting Theological Education," *Christian Education Journal* 3, no. 1 (1999): 127-39.

[44]Elizabeth Tisdell, *Exploring Spirituality and Culture in Adult and Higher Education* (San Francisco: Jossey-Bass, 2003).

could become part of the curriculum in higher education.[45] Surely, we can do no less in theological schools.[46] As we make decisions about ethos, we are forced to make decisions about mission and purpose. As we make decisions about mission and purpose, we are forced to make decisions about curriculum, faculty deployment, admissions criteria and even the way buildings are designed to accommodate "sacred space," learning and relationship.

Familiar organizational and curricular forms and patterns of relationship in theological schools resulted from decisions made across time. It is more than a suspicion that these forms are not serving us well in almost every area we would consider important. Church disenchantment and economic losses threaten the continued existence of conventional theological schools. What is it that will be lost to the Christian community if theological schools cease to exist? It is important how we answer that question, for the majority of Protestant churches today can do all they need to do without theological schools. But can they do without theological education? How will future leaders assess the decisions we make today about the nature, purpose and forms of theological education for the whole people of God?

---

[45]Arthur Chickering, Jon Dalton and Liesa Stamm, *Encouraging Authenticity and Spirituality in Higher Education* (San Francisco: Jossey-Bass, 2006).

[46]See Daniel Treier, *Virtue and the Voice of God: Toward Theology as Wisdom* (Grand Rapids: Eerdmans, 2006), for a discussion of implications for theological education related to theology as wisdom.

Name and Subject Index

Scripture Index